What People Are Saying About
Women of Influence . . .

"It's a definite benefit to hear of others' experiences, catalysts and beliefs. This book offers incredible wisdom to easily inspire an open mind."

Teresa Earnhardt

"This book holds priceless lessons from twenty remarkable women. Each lived according to her strongly felt beliefs and, in turn, affected positive changes that will last throughout time. Reading this book may change your life."

Marie Osmond
entertainer

"I have been so impressed and challenged by reading about these women of influence that Pat and Ruth Williams writes about. I can't wait to apply their life lessons to my coaching career."

Pat Summit
head women's basketball coach, University of Tennessee

"As my husband Larry King often says, 'This is a must-read.' Every page of *How to Be Like Women of Influence* is filled with motivational and inspirational material from the lives of twenty amazing women, and every page is guaranteed to impact your life. This is a book you will read more than once."

Shawn King
wife of CNN's Larry King

"There are many lessons to be learned from this book. The women profiled have great courage, conviction and heart. It's a perfect book to share with your daughters—and your sons, too!"

Tanya Tucker
entertainer

"I read this book and got excited with every page. All of these remarkable women set goals, pursued them with passion, and fought through the tough times. That's why they inspire all of us today. You'll love this book!"

Janet Evans
Olympic Swimming Gold medalist

"These extraordinary women you will read about have struck a high note with me. Their stories will inspire and encourage you to reach for a higher level of success in your own life as well—great tools for becoming a true woman of influence."

Maureen McGovern
entertainer/founder of the McGovern
Works of Heart project for music and healing

"*How to Be Like Women of Influence* is a terrific learning resource to engage your own spirit, soul and actions to reach your God-given potential. The inspirational stories are a tribute to what can be achieved by every woman, man and child in making the world a better and brighter place."

Andrea Jaeger
former #2-ranked tennis professional and
president of The Silver Lining Foundation

"Wow! This is a remarkable book of wisdom for women, filled with the hard lessons learned by women of historic achievement. They showed us how to overcome and what can be done with courage and determination."

Helen Thomas
Hearst Newspapers columnist

"Important? Readable? Important to read? Most definitely! You, woman or man, will never regret sitting down with *Women of Influence* and learning about and how to be like these incredible women! Thank you, Pat, for sharing your valuable insights."

Lee Meriwether
wife, mother and actress

"It seems that mentors for our youth are all but 'missing in action' these days. Therefore, kudos to Pat and Ruth Williams and

Michael Mink for standing in the gap with their inspired compilation of stories from heroic women throughout history who spark fading glimmers of hope into bonfires of enlightenment. *How to Be Like Women of Influence* shares recipes for greatness by exposing mediocrity as the thief of every generation."

Jennifer O'Neill
actress, author and speaker

"These twenty women are *Chicken Soup for the Soul* at its best! Each one of these inspiring stories has touched my heart, and I guarantee they will do the same for you."

Marci Shimoff
coauthor, *Chicken Soup for the Woman's Soul*

"I greatly admire women endowed with the gifts of courage, wisdom, compassion, strength and above all, strong faith. It is my earnest hope that every young woman will have the opportunity to read this outstanding book and learn life values from these incredible women. It's a powerful road map for a successful and fruitful life. I look forward to giving it to my grandchildren."

Rhonda Fleming
movie actress

"All of my favorite books are dog-eared with pencil markings cover to cover. You should see what I've done to this one. Mothers should keep this book readily available like a great cookbook. These are recipes for living we must pass on to our daughters."

Debby Boone
singer

"As an executive in a predominantly women's business, I am reminded daily how one woman can influence so many. Within these pages are examples of women who have used their influence to improve the minds and hearts of thousands."

Jenny Craig
founder, Jenny Craig International

"Every now and then a book comes along that really grabs me. This is just such a book. It's a book that celebrates the contributions of women. The twenty women in this book paved the way for us today to truly influence the world around us."

Joumana Kidd
mother, broadcaster and NBA wife

"These succinct, vivid biographies and the lessons learned from these remarkable women offer practical inspiration. A valuable history."

Janet Guthrie
first woman to compete in the
Indianapolis 500 and the Daytona 500

"This book is truly inspiring and showed me that when you think you should give up, that is the time you should fight more for what you believe in. *How to Be Like Women of Influence* will not only be an inspiration to young girls but those of us who may feel, 'What else can I possibly do with my life?' These women never stopped."

Vikki Carr
entertainer

"Here are twenty women who have had a tremendous impact on the world. Their lives will challenge you to live your life at the highest level possible."

Nancy Sinatra Sr.

How to Be Like
Women of
Influence

LIFE LESSONS FROM 20 OF THE GREATEST

Pat Williams
Ruth Williams
with Michael Mink

Health Communications, Inc.
Deerfield Beach, Florida

www.hcibooks.com

Library of Congress Cataloging-in-Publication Data

Williams, Pat, 1940–
    How to be like women of influence : life lessons from 20 of the
greatest / Pat and Ruth Williams with Michael Mink.
        p. cm.
    Includes bibliographical references.
    ISBN-13: 978-7573-0054-7 (trade pbk.)
    ISBN-10: 0-7573-0054-5 (trade pbk.)
    1. Women—Life skills guides.   2. Women—Anecdotes.
3. Women—Biography.   I. Mink, Michael, 1958–   II. Title.

HQ1221.W67 2003
305.4—dc22
                                                                              2003056679

© 2003 Pat Williams, Ruth Williams and Michael Mink

HCI, its Logos and Marks are trademarks of Health Communications, Inc.

Publisher: Health Communications, Inc.
            3201 S.W. 15th Street
            Deerfield Beach, FL 33442-8190

R-08-05

Cover design by Larissa Hise Henoch
Inside book design by Lawna Patterson Oldfield

To my sisters Carol and Ruth—
two women who have impacted my life

PW

To my eight daughters
who I hope will be inspired
to influence their world.

RW

For Lyle, Gerry, Natalie,
Sheldon, Deborah and in the
memory of Mom and Dad

MM

CONTENTS

Acknowledgments xi

Foreword xiii

Introduction xv

Eleanor Roosevelt: Compassion 1

Mother Teresa: Love 25

Anne Frank: Courage..43

Margaret Thatcher: Resolve..61

Sandra Day O'Connor: Values 73

Oprah Winfrey: Sincerity..85

Golda Meir: Wisdom 107

Rosa Parks: Strength..125

Helen Keller: Vision..145

Marie Curie: Persistence...167

Babe Didrikson Zaharias: Competitiveness 183

Amelia Earhart: Daring 199

Florence Nightingale: Steadfastness...........................213

Harriet Beecher Stowe: Empathy.................................235

Harriet Tubman: Righteousness 255

Sojourner Truth: Faith 271

Clara Barton: Determination 285

Susan B. Anthony: Relentlessness...............................297

Elizabeth Cady Stanton: Focus....................................315

Mary Kay Ash: Integrity 331

Epilogue...345

Book Club Questions for Discussion 348

Bibliography...351

About the Authors 357

ACKNOWLEDGMENTS

We would like to acknowledge the support, guidance and patience of the following people who helped make this book possible:

We extend special thanks to Bob Vander Weide and John Weisbrod of the Orlando Magic family for allowing us the time to write this book. We are so grateful.

We owe deep gratitude to my former assistant, Melinda Ethington, for all she contributed, and a heartfelt thanks to Diana Basch.

We would like to give a huge hats off to seven dependable associates—proofreaders Ken Hussar, Peg Matthews-Rose, Carol Williams and Ruth Cornelison; Hank Martens of the Orlando Magic mail/copy room; ace typist Fran Thomas; and intern Doug Grassian.

Hearty thanks are also due to Peter Vegso and his wonderful staff at Health Communications, Inc. Thank you all for believing that we had something important to say and for providing the support and the forum to say it.

To our cohort in writing this book, Michael Mink—thanks for your time, dedication and perseverance. We finally got it done. Great job!

Special thanks and appreciation go to our family. They are

truly the backbone of our lives and give us the inspiration to live each day to the fullest.

Pat and Ruth Williams

I would like to thank my friends who helped me so much: Michael Klein, Corena Buxbaum, Harold, Becky and Bailey Mintz, Keith Rayve, Sue and Savannah, Joe Burns, Lauren Humphrey, Tom Holquin, William Leventhal, Kinou Treiser Weiselman, and my writing mentor and friend, Joanne von Alroth.

I would like to acknowledge the historians, biographers and experts who were so kind to help me: Doulgas Brinkley, Louise Selanders, Joan D. Hedrick, Susan E. Cayleff, Dorothy Herrmann, Nell Irvin Painter, Anne Newbury, Yvonne Pendleton, Louise Foudray, The Clara Barton National Historic Site, and Supreme Court Justice Sandra Day O'Connor who graciously consented to an interview for our chapter on her.

Thanks to Pat and Ruth Williams for taking an interest in me and for their guidance and encouragement on this book and to the Health Communications Inc. staff and publisher Peter Vegso for making this opportunity possible.

Michael Mink

FOREWORD

Inherent within women is the desire to nurture. As nurturers, women can have a strong influence on their families, communities and churches.

Our choices are unlimited in how we can make a difference in this present time and in the world around us. Pressing the boundaries of race, religion, culture and socio-economic status, women who have a sense of purpose and are determined can make a significant impact on society.

Every woman should be challenged to live and experience life as deeply and fully as she can. Every woman should dare to be as expressive and definitive about what it is she desires to accomplish in life. Every woman should be challenged to be the beautiful image and reflection of her Creator as she allows life's trials and tribulations, joys and inspirations to shape her into the divine masterpiece God has created for such a time as this.

In chapter 12 of 1 Corinthians in the Bible, God tells us that he has given each of us certain gifts to minister to those around us on a daily basis. Some have the gift of wisdom to help advise others to make good decisions. Some have the gift of knowledge to share with others. Some are strong in their faith to set an example for the rest of us to follow. Some have the gift of encouragement. Some are strong prayer warriors.

Some are good administrators. Some have the gift of discernment to help others see things around them. Others are teachers or counselors or soothers. All of us are born with some special gift to illuminate and make the world a better place.

How to Be Like Women of Influence shares the portraits of women who have brought their gifts to the highest level. After reading about Oprah Winfrey, Eleanor Roosevelt, Golda Meir, Amelia Earhart, Rosa Parks and the other fifteen women of influence in this book, you'll discover that they possess common traits that can motivate each of us to strive for higher levels of success. These are women of extraordinarily strong character who took responsibility for their own lives. They pursued their passions in life, set specific goals, and never gave up. They worked very hard and refused to let anyone or anything limit them in their pursuit of their dreams. They were courageous and learned to overcome any obstacles that might hinder them in their quest. These women not only served others in some way along their journey, but also practiced their religious faith, giving homage to someone greater than themselves. These women, without exception, were lifelong learners and contributors to their world and made life more colorful for many along the way.

Their contributions were so noble that they transcended their own time and have impacted our world today. They held fast to their individual gifts and used them to make the world a better place for all of us.

I salute Pat and Ruth Williams and Michael Mink for the tremendous job they have done in writing this book. Each woman's story inspired and motivated me to live my life on a higher plateau. As you read the book, I'm confident your life will be impacted as deeply as mine has been.

—**Deloris Jordan**
Mother of Michael Jordan
Chicago, Illinois
August 2003

INTRODUCTION

Women of Influence

When my husband told me he and his collaborator, Michael Mink, were going to write a book about women of influence, I was elated. Then when Pat invited me to share my insights by participating in writing the book, I got even more excited. Pat has written over thirty books, all motivational and inspirational, about leadership, teamwork, sports legends, biblical heroes and world figures. These books have included stories about strong women, but he has never devoted a book entirely to women—until now. And it's about time.

In his 1998 book, *The 100: A Ranking of the Most Influential Persons in History,* by Michael H. Hart, not a single woman made the list. Why? Because the roles of women during the first one hundred years of our country were very limited. They were either mothering or teaching. There were no real alternatives unless one was a ballerina or opera singer or an actress. However, because of the Industrial Revolution, two world wars, the Civil Rights Act and the women's movement of the 1960s, women gradually moved into the spotlight and began blazing their own trails. Enrollment of women in law school and medical school has jumped substantially as well as in architecture and engineering. There are more and more

women with MBAs who are scaling the heights of the corporate ladder successfully. The choices women have today are
unlimited. The unique women you will meet in this book
were the catalysts who made it possible.

If you're a woman reading this book, and chances are you
are—according to statistics, many more women buy books
than men—you will be delighted, and you will probably identify with many of these women. You see, we all have influence, particularly if we're women. For example, you have a
great deal of influence in your home with your children. It
started in the cradle and has continued to the present. In fact,
I think one of the things that prompted Pat and me to write
this book was a book Pat read called *First Mothers*. It was
about the mothers of our presidents and the impact these
women had on the leaders of our nation.

One of my favorite stories about a woman's influence is
about a woman who is not famous. Her name was Annie
Johnson. In 1903, she found herself alone with two toddling
sons. Her husband had left with all the money and ran away
to marry another woman. Annie was six feet tall, big-boned
and had no education—and she was black. Her only choice
was to work as a domestic or starve. Neither option appealed
to her and she had to take care of her babies. So she decided
to focus on what she was good at—cooking. She wasn't a
gourmet, but she could "mix groceries well enough to scare
hungry away from a starving man."

She set up a meat pie stand on the dirt road between the
cotton gin and the lumber mill in her little town. Each day
right before lunchtime, she cooked fresh meat pies, and the
rich aroma brought men from the mills flocking to her little
stand. She was dependable, dedicated and hardworking. She
never disappointed her customers. Over the years, her little
stall became a grocery store where customers could buy all
kinds of goods. This woman of influence changed not only
her life and the lives of her children, but also changed the

economy of her town and the world of literature.

Who was Annie Johnson? The great-grandmother of Maya Angelou, the author and playwright. Mrs. Johnson's perseverance, tenacity and focus have certainly impacted our modern literary world. And she started by influencing those closest to her—her children.

We all affect the lives of others. The women profiled here have greatly influenced the world. They have led the way. They have left legacies that benefit all of us. Their achievements leave a blueprint that is open for anyone to follow.

This is not a book of biographies, although you will get glimpses of their history. The book's main focus is centered on the achievements of twenty extraordinary women and the life lessons they learned—principles you can apply in your own life. These are women like you and me who made their lives count for something.

As a consultant and executive coach, I work with many women. They all want to know how to be successful. Here's what I say: "The successful woman is the average woman— focused." The successful women in this book focused their lives on some kind of contribution to society. They were, and are, fearless, dedicated, hardworking, committed and courageous. They come from all walks of life: business, science, medicine, education, entertainment, sports and government. They had a mission and they followed through. They made a mark on the world. All of us can do the same.

I am excited about this book because of the role models it provides for my own daughters. Pat and I have nineteen children. No, that wasn't a misprint. We have nineteen: fourteen adopted from various countries around the world and five birth children between us. Eight of our children are women or girls becoming women. This is a great collection of success stories, which can inspire and challenge young women to live their dreams.

Eleanor Roosevelt said: "Example is the best lesson there is." That is, in a sentence, what this book is about. Enjoy!

—**Ruth Williams**
(Mrs. Pat Williams)
Winter Park, Florida
August 2003

ELEANOR ROOSEVELT
1884–1962

COMPASSION

I was not a gifted person but I was always
deeply interested in every manifestation
of life, good or bad. I never let slip an
opportunity to increase my knowledge
of people and conditions.

—*Eleanor Roosevelt*

leanor Roosevelt changed the traditional role of First Lady. Rather than limiting herself to strictly ceremonial duties, she immersed herself in the great issues of the day. Although she was born into privilege, she spent her life trying to improve the quality of people's lives around the world.

Eleanor's social conscience was developed and nurtured during a childhood that was filled with sadness. When she was eight, her mother, Anna, only twenty-nine, died of diphtheria on December 7, 1892. (Another December 7, forty-nine years later, would again test her—as it would the rest of the nation.) Roosevelt wasn't particularly close to her mother, and, sadly, was made to feel that she was a disappointment to her.

"My mother was troubled by my lack of beauty, and I knew it as a child senses these things," Roosevelt wrote in *The Autobiography of Eleanor Roosevelt*. "She tried hard to bring me up well so that my manners would compensate for my looks, but her efforts only made me more keenly conscious of my shortcomings." Photographs of Roosevelt as a child and teenager don't support her feelings, but her perception of herself was her reality, and it blocked out everything else. "I was deeply ashamed. . . . I felt, as only a young girl can feel it, all the pain of being an ugly duckling."

But there was a shining light in Eleanor's life—her father, Elliot. Elliot Roosevelt was the younger brother of future president Theodore Roosevelt. Elliot was a chronic alcoholic who embodied the tragedy of addiction. He did love Eleanor with all his heart, however, and in his arms she felt safe, loved and beautiful.

"My father would pick me up and hold me high in the air," Roosevelt wrote later in life. "He dominated my life as long as he lived, and was the love of my life for many years after he died. With my father I was perfectly happy."

Elliot was banished from his house by his brother, Theodore, while he underwent treatment for his addiction. Because he wasn't capable of taking care of Eleanor, her maternal grandmother raised her. Roosevelt would later remember that as a child she hoped that "Someday I would make a home for him again, we would travel together and do many things which he painted as interesting and pleasant, to be looked forward to in the future."

How Elliot must have wanted to take care of his little daughter. However, the all-consuming addiction that is alcoholism overcame him. Elliot Roosevelt, while drunk, fell and eventually died of a head injury. He was only thirty-four years old. Eleanor Roosevelt was not even ten.

Anna and Elliot Roosevelt also had very different views of the world, which strongly affected Eleanor. Anna was a proud part of a New York City "society" that, Eleanor contemptuously wrote, "thought itself all-important." Elliot Roosevelt and his family, while well-to-do, weren't as concerned about New York "society" as they were about the society where everyday people lived. In the short time that Elliot spent with his daughter, he taught her his social values and made an impact that helped shape her life.

"Very early I became conscious of the fact that there were people around me who suffered in one way or another," Roosevelt wrote. "I was five or six when my father took me to help serve Thanksgiving dinner in one of the newsboys' clubhouses. My father explained that many of these ragged little boys had no homes and lived in little wooden shanties in empty lots, or slept in vestibules of houses or public buildings or any place where they could be moderately warm."

From then on, Roosevelt's course of helping the disadvantaged was set. "Caring comes from being able to put yourself in the position of the other person," Roosevelt later said. "If you cannot imagine 'This might happen to me,' you are able to say to yourself with indifference, 'Who cares?'"

> *Eleanor could not pass a starving person without feeling hunger.*
> —Adlai Stevenson

As a member of society, the teenaged Eleanor Roosevelt was a debutante. Debutantes were expected to dabble in charity work as part of their coming out into society. Eleanor, however, didn't just do it for show as some did—she embraced it. The debutante work she chose was teaching in the slums of New York, an activity picked by very few young women. She also sought to improve the working conditions of people who labored in garment factories and department stores by joining an advocacy group called the Consumers League. Later, during World War I, Roosevelt—the mother of five—worked two to three shifts a week in a Red Cross canteen, and from 1927 until her husband Franklin's election to the presidency in 1932, she taught school in Manhattan.

Roosevelt despised people who were callously judgmental and thought themselves better than the less fortunate. She said one type of snob was the person "who has had a good many opportunities and looks down on those who lack them."

While Eleanor had always been involved in causes to help the disadvantaged, it was her marriage to Franklin Roosevelt in 1905 that set the course for her public life. When Franklin was later elected to New York's state senate in 1911, the Roosevelt family moved to the state capital of Albany, and Eleanor Roosevelt naturally took an interest in politics. "I began to discover," she said, "that interest leads to interest, knowledge leads to more knowledge, the capacity for understanding grows with the effort to understand."

Franklin went on to be appointed Assistant Secretary of the Navy by President Woodrow Wilson in 1913. In 1920, he was the Democratic candidate for vice president on a ticket that was crushed by Republican Warren Harding. Despite the loss, the thirty-nine-year-old Franklin was to have an exceptionally bright future.

When Franklin contracted polio in 1922, it looked as though his political career was over. His legs were paralyzed, and he would never be able to walk again. Franklin's domineering mother, Sara Delano Roosevelt, viewed her son as an invalid for the rest of his life. She wanted him to retire quietly to the family estate in Hyde Park, New York, and live out his years. "Her anxiety over his general health was so great that she dreaded his making any effort whatever," Eleanor Roosevelt recalled.

Eleanor Roosevelt, however, was a person who had not allowed the death of her two parents before she was ten to break her. She was too strong to feel sorry for herself, and she certainly wasn't going to let her husband give up.

"We never treated my husband as an invalid," Roosevelt wrote. And fortunately, Franklin Roosevelt didn't want to be treated like one. He was a fighter, a man who never complained about his physical condition and worked incredibly hard to make the best of it. He diligently exercised the muscles that he could, and even learned to give the appearance that he could walk. This was essential for the continuation of his political career. Voters in the 1920s and 1930s weren't going to elect a candidate who appeared to be physically helpless.

With his paralyzed legs strapped into heavy braces, Franklin grasped the arm of an aide with one hand and grasped his cane in the other. He first balanced himself, then swiveled his hip and placed a braced leg forward, then braced himself and did the same with his other hip. This had the effect of making him appear to be walking a few steps. To accomplish this caused him tremendous physical pain.

Eleanor was supportive of Franklin not only in his recuperation, but also in his political career. While he was recuperating and learning what adjustments he would need to make to continue his public appearances, Eleanor kept Franklin in the public eye by substituting for him and giving speeches to different groups. The work by both Roosevelts paid off. Franklin was elected governor of New York in 1928. Four years later, when he was elected president of the United States, he set an example for the country by "walking" roughly forty paces to the inaugural platform to take his oath of office on March 4, 1933.

After her husband's election to the presidency, Eleanor Roosevelt blazed a new path as First Lady, one of social activism rather than strictly ceremonial duties. As First Lady, she learned about the plight of the poor not by reading or hearing about it, but by actually going out and meeting people who were struggling. She wanted to understand their problems firsthand, and with America in the grip of the Great Depression, there was plenty to absorb.

Thirteen million citizens were unemployed. Industrial production had dropped to around 56 percent of what it had been just four years earlier. The Great Depression gave rise to the shantytowns, the Hoovervilles and the Dust Bowl. It was a time of hobos riding the railways and the enduring plea of "Brother, can you spare a dime?" Today, we may see the depression only in grainy black-and-white films, but then, real people were suffering. Families with children were living in terrible rural poverty or urban decay.

"I have always seen life personally," Roosevelt said. "That is, my interest or sympathy or indignation is not aroused by an abstract cause but by the plight of a single person whom I have seen with my own eyes. It was the sight of a child dying of hunger that made the tragedy of hunger become of such overriding importance to me." Her motto was: "Go out and see for yourself. Make others see what you've seen."

One of those "others" was her husband. Because his ability to travel was hampered by his desire not to be seen or photographed in a wheelchair, Eleanor took it upon herself to travel extensively around the country and report back to him on what she was seeing. It has been said many times since that she was his eyes and ears. People may have had a photograph of Franklin Roosevelt on a wall in their home, but they had Eleanor Roosevelt sitting in their living rooms trying to understand their problems.

"These trips gave me a wonderful opportunity to visit all kinds of places and to see and get to know a good cross section of people," Roosevelt said. In *Grandmere: A Personal*

History of Eleanor Roosevelt, her grandson David B. Roosevelt wrote: "One of the most remarkable qualities I remember was her ability to listen, to draw others out and extend an invitation for them to talk about things that really mattered to them. She did this with everyone, from heads of state, to friends, family members and most certainly her grand-children. We were all made to feel important—no concern was too trivial; no point of view too childish or insignificant."

President Roosevelt had initiated sweeping governmental relief efforts during his first one hundred days in office to alleviate the suffering that many Americans felt. Eleanor wanted to know if these New Deal agencies were actually making a difference in the lives of real people, or if they were just well meaning but cosmetic programs that generated good press but little more. "I visited as many government projects as possible," she said, "often managing to arrive without advance notice so that they could not be polished up for my inspection."

In time, critics claimed the New Deal was a failure by pointing to faceless economic reports. President Roosevelt reminded them that people are not "mere units in statistics." The New Deal gave real people in need jobs, loans to save farms and a better quality of life than they had since the depression began.

The lesson of the Depression, Eleanor believed, was that people throughout the world were "interdependent" on each other. "One part of the country or group of countrymen cannot prosper while the others go down hill," she said. "And that one country cannot go on gaily when the rest of the world is suffering. . . . If we can get back to the feeling that we are responsible for each other, the years of Depression would have been worthwhile."

Concerned about becoming a "captive" of the White House and Washington, D.C., Roosevelt traveled extensively so that she wouldn't develop blinders about what was going on in the world. She said she feared that, "if I remained in the White House all the time I would lose touch with the rest of the world. . . . I would begin to think that my life in Washington was representative of the rest of the country, and that is a dangerous point of view."

In fact, as Joseph Lash, a close friend of Roosevelt, wrote in *Eleanor and Franklin,* "Eleanor had demonstrated to herself and to an astonished country that the White House, far from being a prison, was a springboard for greater usefulness."

She didn't confine her concerns for people only to Americans either. Eleanor Roosevelt went to Puerto Rico in 1934, on the suggestion of President Roosevelt, to investigate labor conditions. There was a wealthy American colony in San Juan, but Eleanor wanted to get to the truth and see the real Puerto Rico, so she visited the poorer sections of the city. "I discovered that when I really wanted to know something I had to dig in," she said.

Doris Kearns Goodwin writes in her book *No Ordinary Time* that Roosevelt took journalists on a sight-seeing trip of the real Puerto Rico, the one where exploited laborers lived in "muddy alleys and swamps, to hundreds of foul-smelling hovels with no plumbing and no electricity, where women sat in the midst of filth embroidering cloth for minimal wages."

After helping to publicize the investigation's findings, Roosevelt urged American women to boycott Puerto Rico's embroidered goods, Kearns Goodwin writes. In addition, her investigations led to an effort to clean up the slums of Puerto Rico. The island's first housing project was named after her.

Housing the poor in decent living conditions remains one of Roosevelt's legacies.

"Eleanor Roosevelt moved with ease and grace among royalty, heads of state, and the social elite; she moved with awareness and empathy among the hungry, the injured, and the homeless. Then she took steps to alleviate their situations. Without regard for race, color, nationality, sex, religion, economic status, or creed, she fulfilled her lifetime purpose: to improve the lot of humankind," wrote Eileen Morey in her book *Eleanor Roosevelt*.

Roosevelt helped to alleviate suffering by reporting on conditions to her husband, but she also added her own strong opinions and feelings. "[Franklin] might have been happier with a wife who was completely uncritical," she wrote. "That I was never able to be . . . I think I sometimes acted as a spur, even though the spurring was not always wanted or welcomed." It was, however, a big hit with the American people. A poll showed that Roosevelt's popularity was equal to that of her husband's after his first year in office.

"I'm the agitator, [my husband's] the politician," she liked to say.

On December 7, 1941, America changed forever when the Japanese bombed Pearl Harbor in Hawaii. In their hour of need, Americans looked to the Roosevelts for strength. Franklin's gift as a leader, Eleanor said, whether in war or peace, was his inherent optimism. "I have never known a man who gave one a greater sense of security," she said. "I never heard Franklin say there was a problem that he thought it was impossible for human beings to solve. He recognized the difficulties and often said that, while he did not know the answer, he was completely confident that there was an answer and that one had to try until one either found it for himself or got it from someone else."

With World War II raging, Roosevelt answered her husband's call to go to London in October 1942. It was a dangerous time there because the Germans were still conducting deadly air raids over the city. Her mission was to observe the work that women were doing in place of men in previously male-dominated venues such as factories. She wanted to learn how such programs could best be implemented in the United States. With so many men in uniform, women in both countries had to take over jobs that were usually held by men to maintain production for the Allied war effort.

Roosevelt wasn't on a sight-seeing tour or going to have tea with the king and queen. "The trip to Great Britain seemed to offer me a chance to do something that might be useful," she said. In addition, she delivered a message of hope from President Roosevelt to the American servicemen stationed there who were preparing for the invasion of North Africa.

Roosevelt, on her own initiative, went to the South Pacific theater of war in 1942 and 1943. She traveled to Bora Bora, Samoa and Guadalcanal, visiting the troops at U.S. military bases and the wounded in their hospitals. Admiral William F. Halsey wasn't happy about having to divert his attention from fighting the Japanese to what he perceived as entertaining Eleanor Roosevelt. He said he "dreaded" her arrival. When she expressed her desire to visit Guadalcanal, Halsey said, "Guadalcanal is no place for you, Ma'am!" Roosevelt responded, "I'm perfectly willing to take my chances," which she did.

Watching her go about her business, Admiral Halsey realized that she wasn't a dignitary looking for a photo opportunity, but rather a caring American who just happened to be the president's wife. Halsey wrote that, among other things, in twelve hours she inspected two navy hospitals and an army hospital. "When I say that she inspected those hospitals, I don't mean that she shook hands with the chief medical officer, glanced into a sun parlor, and left. I mean that she went to every ward, stopped at every bed, and spoke to every patient: What was his name? How did he feel? Was there anything he needed? Could she take a message home for him?

"I marveled at her hardihood, both physical and mental; she walked for miles, and she saw patients who were grievously and gruesomely wounded. But I marveled most at their expressions as she leaned over them. It was a sight I will never forget."

Roosevelt struck a chord with Americans that is still felt today because she was truly one of the people. She rejected all the trappings of presidential power while in the public service of her country. When she moved into the White House, she rejected Secret Service protection and chauffeurs. "I never did consent to having a Secret Service agent," she remarked. She even preferred running the White House elevator herself. When she traveled to the South Pacific, she got up in the morning with the soldiers and ate breakfast with them. At the time, she was fifty-nine years old.

In order to help Americans understand what she and the president were doing to make the lives of people better, Roosevelt wrote a daily, nationally syndicated newspaper column called "My Day." In addition, she held regular press conferences just for women reporters (with the intent of forcing newspapers to hire more women). When she traveled to the South Pacific, she lugged along her typewriter and wrote her column every night, describing the courage and sacrifices of America's men in uniform.

Through her daily column, which she wrote for twenty-six years beginning in 1936, Roosevelt helped shape the national debate in America by getting out in front on such issues as civil rights, women's rights and world peace. In the 1950s, she spoke out forcefully against Senator Joseph McCarthy and his trampling of people's civil liberties during his witch-hunts for suspected communists.

Roosevelt fought for civil rights for black Americans not only in print and principle, but in the Oval Office. Her constant prodding led her husband to issue executive orders that barred discrimination in New Deal projects.

In 1939, an organization that she belonged to, the Daughters of the American Revolution, refused to allow contralto Marian Anderson to sing in Constitution Hall (which they owned) because she was black. Roosevelt, who'd invited Anderson to sing at the White House in 1936, was outraged and took action that caught the attention of the nation. In February 1939, in her "My Day" column, she wrote: "The question is, if you belong to an organization and disapprove of an action which is typical of a policy, should you resign or is it better to work for a changed point of view within the organization? To remain as a member implies approval of that action, and therefore I am resigning."

Roosevelt was no stranger to taking principled stands. She lived in public and in private by one simple formula: "In the long run there is no more liberating, no more exhilarating experience than to determine one's position, state it bravely and then act boldly."

In addition to resigning, she arranged for Anderson to give

a public concert in front of the very symbol of racial equality in Washington, D.C.—the Lincoln Memorial. Seventy-five thousand people turned out to hear the great Anderson sing. "Things were either right or wrong to me," Roosevelt said.

Joseph Lash wrote that Franklin's political career was "dependent on [Eleanor's] resolution, her encouragement, her readiness to serve as his proxy in politics. He had always needed her, more than he was ever able to recognize or that he could usually bring himself to say."

When Franklin, who was still president, died on April 12, 1945, Eleanor cabled her four sons, all of whom were serving their country in the military, to stay strong. "Father slept away. He would expect you to carry on and finish your jobs."

Franklin was relatively young, sixty-three, when he died. What gave Eleanor comfort was that he had lived a full and productive life, which to her was a measurement of success. She said: "If at the end one can say, 'This man used to the limit the powers that God granted him; he was worthy of love and respect and of the sacrifices of many people, made in order that he might achieve what he deemed to be his task,' then that life has been lived well and there are no regrets."

Their life as husband and wife wasn't always easy, especially after Franklin's well-chronicled infidelity with Eleanor Roosevelt's secretary, Lucy Mercer, in 1918. Still, she later remarked: "My husband and I had come through the years with an acceptance of each other's faults and foibles, a deep understanding, warm affection, and agreement on essential values."

Roosevelt's experiences with the deaths of her father and her brother Hal (in 1941), both from chronic alcoholism, surely shaped her outlook on not wasting the precious gift of life.

"Sorrow in itself and the loss of someone whom you love is hard to bear," she wrote. "But when sorrow is mixed with regret and consciousness of waste, there is added a touch of bitterness which is even more difficult to carry, day in and day out."

The Later Years

At the time of Franklin's death, Eleanor was sixty-one years old and arguably the most famous and admired woman in the world. If she had retired then and never done anything else, her place in history would have been secure. But she was far from finished in terms of her contributions to society. "I did not want to cease trying to be useful in some way," she wrote. "I did not want to feel old—and I seldom have."

For the last seventeen years of her life, Roosevelt dedicated herself to preventing future wars. Her trip to the South Pacific during the war had had a profound effect on her. There she saw firsthand the cemeteries of dead soldiers. In hospitals she saw the wounded and maimed. Roosevelt had learned the cost of war was far too high. "My rebellion has always been over the deaths of young people;

> *I was certainly influenced by Eleanor Roosevelt after she was a widow and became a woman on her own and went to the UN and had such an influence. There weren't many role models for my generation, and she was certainly one of mine. My generation had never seen a woman, a widow, strike out on her own and became so clearly a person in her own right.*
> —Joan Ganz Cooney,
> CREATOR OF *SESAME STREET*

and that is why I think so many of us feel particularly frustrated by war, where youth so largely pays the price," Roosevelt wrote in her "My Day" column of May 7, 1945.

When President Harry S. Truman appointed her to the first United Nations General Assembly in 1945, Roosevelt had the opportunity to affect world affairs, but she also had doubts about herself. *Oh, no! It would be impossible!* was her first reaction, she wrote. *How could I be a delegate to help organize the United Nations when I have no background or experience in international meetings?*

> *Being in a sense part of the Truman administration didn't dissuade Roosevelt from criticizing the president harshly when she believed it was necessary. "I would not have a quiet conscience.... unless I wrote you what I feel in these difficult times," she wrote in a letter to President Truman.*

Roosevelt made up for her lack of formal experience by learning what she didn't know and by just being herself. She exercised her own personal power of diplomacy by getting to know the women from other countries' delegations. She even invited all of them to a get-acquainted tea party to help foster better communication.

By 1946 Roosevelt had become chairwoman of the UN Commission for Human Rights. After two years of hard work, her commission presented the Universal Declaration of Human Rights, which was approved by the UN General Assembly on December 10, 1948. The Declaration defined the rights of all human beings. "I wanted, with all my heart, a peaceful world," Roosevelt later wrote in 1962. "And I knew it could never be achieved on a lasting basis without greater understanding between peoples. It is to these ends that I have, in the main, devoted the past years."

During the two years of drafting the Declaration, Roosevelt and the other members worked fifteen-hour days. At the same time she lectured regularly, continued to write "My Day" and wrote two autobiographies. She always made use of all the hours in her day, getting up around 7:30 and going to sleep after midnight. "I have never been bored, never found the days long enough for the range of activities with which I wanted to fill them," she said.

Roosevelt viewed her travel time as an opportunity to catch up on her reading. She considered reading essential if people were to reach

> *If I feel depressed, I go to work. Work is always an antidote to depression.*
> —Eleanor Roosevelt

greater "intellectual attainments." Only through a book, Roosevelt said, is it possible to explore "the most fascinating thing in the world—another person's mind." She never stopped trying to learn, wrote her grandson David Roosevelt in *Grandmere*. "Ever inquisitive and always curious, she never stopped learning from others: about people, events, and life itself. In public as in private, my grandmother was forever a student of life."

"I had really only three assets," Roosevelt remarked. "I was keenly interested, I accepted every challenge and every opportunity to learn more, and I had great energy and self-discipline."

On August 8, 1945, when the United States dropped the world's first atomic bomb on the Japanese city of Hiroshima, Roosevelt wrote in her "My Day" column of the new and dangerous world that man had entered: the nuclear age. "We have only two alternative choices: destruction and death or construction and life." When she traveled to Hiroshima some years after the bomb had been dropped, Roosevelt expressed compassion and empathy for the victims.

"To arrive in Hiroshima is an emotional experience," she wrote. "Here is where the first atom bomb ever to be dropped on human beings was actually used. The people of the United States believed that our leaders thought long and carefully before they used this dread weapon. We know that they thought first of the welfare of our own people, that they believed the bomb might end the war quickly with less loss of life everywhere than if it had not been dropped.

"In spite of this conviction, one cannot see a city and be shown the area that was destroyed by blast and fire and be told of the people who died or were injured without deep sadness.... contemplating the fate of Hiroshima, one can only say: 'God grant to men greater wisdom in the future.'"

Roosevelt continued to work at an age when many people retire. On her seventieth birthday she said, "Life has got to be lived." Her sage advice to the young and everyone alike was to live life boldly. "Perhaps the older generation is often to blame with its cautious warning: 'Take a job that will give you security, not adventure.' But I say to the young: 'Do not stop thinking of life as an adventure. You have no security unless you can live bravely, excitingly, imaginatively; unless you can choose a challenge instead of a competence.'"

Roosevelt kept working up to her death in 1962 at age seventy-eight. Her legacy is one of compassion and the highest ideals of integrity, which helped shape America and the world.

She also picked up her share of political enemies along the way. Secretary of State John Foster Dulles once called her "more subversive than Moscow."

Of her detractors, Roosevelt said, "While I weigh as honestly as I can their grounds for disapproval, when I feel that I am right in what I do, it seems to me that I cannot afford, as a self-respecting individual, to refuse to do a thing merely because it will make me disliked or bring down a storm of criticism on my head. I often feel that too many Americans today tend to reject [a thing], however right they believe it to be, that they want to do because they fear they will be unpopular or will find themselves standing alone instead of in the comfortable anonymity of the herd."

A friend and supporter of Roosevelt's, Congresswoman Helen Gahagan Douglas said that Roosevelt got even with her enemies "in a way that was almost cruel. She forgave them."

In a U.S. Gallup poll conducted in 1958, Roosevelt was chosen the most admired American. Many international polls showed that Roosevelt was the most admired woman in the world.

"I told her she was the first lady of the world," said former president Harry Truman. Truman was one of many dignitaries who campaigned

> *What I have learned from my own experience is that the most important ingredients in a child's education are curiosity, interest, imagination, and a sense of the adventure of life.*
> —Eleanor Roosevelt

unsuccessfully for her to receive the Nobel Peace Prize after her death. "If she didn't earn it, then no one else has," he wrote.

While she never considered herself to be gifted in any way, Roosevelt said of her life, "What basic objective I had, for many years, was to grasp every opportunity to live and experience life as deeply, as fully, and as widely as I possibly could. It seemed to me stupid to have the gift of life and not use it to the utmost of one's ability."

How to Be Like
Eleanor Roosevelt

1. **Strive to keep your social conscience awake and vibrant at all times.**

   "Caring comes from being able to put yourself in the position of the other person," Roosevelt said. "If you cannot imagine, 'This might happen to me,' you are able to say to yourself with indifference, 'Who cares?'"

2. **Blaze new paths and don't allow yourself to be restricted by outdated traditions.**

   When her husband was elected president, Roosevelt blazed a new path as First Lady: one of social activism rather than strictly ceremonial duties.

3. **See things for yourself, wherever you have to go to do so.**

   As President Roosevelt's eyes and ears, Roosevelt's motto was "Go out and see for yourself. Make others see what you've seen." A world traveler, she wasn't interested in getting her information solely from reports or other sources. She said: "If I remained in the White House all the time I would lose touch with the rest of the world."

4. **Don't shy away from making your opinions known.**

   Roosevelt expressed her opinions to her husband, to those who criticized her and to the American public. She is remembered for her outspoken courage.

5. **Pay attention to the details.**

   Admiral Halsey wrote that when Roosevelt visited

hospitals during her trip to the South Pacific, she stopped to speak with every wounded man to find out if he was getting what he needed. She even inspected the hospital kitchens.

6. **Communicate with everyone you need to.**

For twenty-six busy years, from 1936 to 1962, Roosevelt wrote her daily syndicated newspaper column "My Day." Through her column, lectures and press conferences, Roosevelt helped to shape the debate on issues such as civil rights, women's rights, Senator Joe McCarthy's communist witch-hunts, and world peace.

7. **When you feel something is wrong, take a stand.**

How many momentous events in history began with people who had the courage to stand up? In 1939, an organization that Roosevelt belonged to, the Daughters of the American Revolution, refused to allow contralto Marian Anderson to sing in Constitution Hall (which they owned) because she was black. Roosevelt was outraged and resigned from the organization. She made her feelings known in her "My Day" column. No stranger to taking many principled stands, Roosevelt lived her public and private life by a simple formula: "In the long run there is no more liberating, no more exhilarating experience than to determine one's position, state it bravely and then act boldly."

8. **Stay mentally strong.**

Roosevelt lost both her parents before she was ten years old. She lost her brother Hal to alcoholism. Yet she never felt sorry for herself or retreated to crutches such as alcohol abuse. She made sure Franklin wasn't treated like an invalid when he lost the use of his legs, and helped him to continue his political career.

9. **Realize you're never too old to contribute to society.**
Roosevelt was sixty-one years old when Franklin died in 1945. Yet she was in a sense just getting started. In 1958, thirteen years after she'd been first lady, Roosevelt was chosen the most admired American in a Gallup poll. "I did not want to cease trying to be useful in some way," she wrote. "I did not want to feel old—and I seldom have."

10. **Make use of all the hours in the day.**
Roosevelt got up early and worked late, even when she was well past seventy.

11. **Live your life with passion and boldness.**
Roosevelt said: "Perhaps the older generation is often to blame with its cautious warning: 'Take a job that will give you security, not adventure.' But I say to the young: 'Do not stop thinking of life as an adventure. You have no security unless you can live bravely, excitingly, imaginatively; unless you can choose a challenge instead of a competence.'"

12. **Do what your heart tells you and don't ever worry about what the critics say.**
"It seems to me that I cannot afford, as a self-respecting individual, to refuse to do a thing merely because it will make me disliked or bring down a storm of criticism on my head," Roosevelt once remarked.

13. **Make the most of every day of your life.**
"What basic objective I had, for many years, was to grasp every opportunity to live and experience life as

deeply, as fully, and as widely as I possibly could," Roosevelt said.

14. **Know your strengths.**

Roosevelt wrote, "I had really only three assets: I was keenly interested, I accepted every challenge and every opportunity to learn more, and I had great energy and self-discipline."

How to Be a Mother Like Eleanor Roosevelt

In a 1927 article, Roosevelt, the mother of four boys and one girl, offered her views on parenting:

- Furnish an example in living.
- Stop preaching ethics and morals. (In 1960 Roosevelt wrote, "Children cannot just be told. They must see the values you preach put into practice if they are to become real.")
- Have a knowledge of life's problems and an imagination.
- Stop shielding your children and clipping their wings.
- Allow your children to develop along their own lines.
- Don't prevent self-reliance and initiative.
- Have a vision yourself and bigness of soul. The next generation will take care of itself.

MOTHER TERESA
1910–1997

LOVE

Life is not worth living unless it is lived
for others.

—*Mother Teresa*

other Teresa was the living embodiment of compassion and love. She recognized no limitations—not even church policy—in her devotion to the world's poor and her desire to serve them.

She was born Agnes Gonxha Bojaxhiu on August 26, 1910, in Skopje, Macedonia. She took her religious name, Sister Teresa, in honor of the patron saint of missions when she took her first vows in 1931. Agnes said she was following God's will regarding her decision to become a nun. She felt his will for the first time when she was only twelve. It was a defining moment in her life and came while she was praying at the feet of the statue of Our Lady of Cernagore in Letnice, a small mountain town not far from Skopje.

"I first heard the divine call, convincing me to serve God and to devote myself to his service . . . and to the service of my neighbors," Mother Teresa wrote in *My Life for the Poor.* "It was then that I realized that my vocation was towards the poor."

Her deeply religious mother taught Agnes by example that she could serve God by serving the poor but was initially opposed to the idea of her daughter becoming a nun. She eventually supported the idea and offered this sage advice: "When you accept a task, do it willingly. If not, don't accept it."

After hearing God's call, Agnes decided to ask during confession how she could truly know if God was calling her to the sisterhood. The answer she received would guide her decisions then and

> *Be a living expression of God's kindness: kindness in your face, kindness in your eyes, kindness in your smile, kindness in your warm greeting.*
> —Mother Teresa

for the rest of her life. "You will know by your happiness," Mother Teresa recalled being told. "If you are happy with the idea that God calls you to serve him and your neighbor, this will be the proof of your vocation. Profound joy of the heart is like a magnet that indicates the path of life. One has to follow it, even though one enters into a way full of difficulties."

Agnes traveled to Ireland and began her formal religious training with the order of the Sisters of Loreto in 1928, but it was in India that she wished to practice and do God's work as a nun. She had been interested in the work that the Catholic missionaries were doing in India since she was in her early teens. Agnes loved to read, and through her studies she learned of the terrible poverty that India's poor were subjected to. People were starving, homeless and dying of diseases such as the dreaded leprosy.

When Sister Teresa arrived in Calcutta, India, in 1929 for her two-year training as a novitiate (after which she would take her first vows as a nun), she saw the face of poverty first-hand: hundreds of thousands of people were living on the streets. They lived in the midst of garbage and human waste. Their water was filthy and was a breeding ground for diseases such as smallpox, dysentery and tuberculosis.

"We were shocked to the depths of our beings by their indescribable poverty," Sister Teresa wrote. "Many families live in the streets, along the city walls, even in places thronged with people. Day and night they live in the open on mats they have made from large palm leaves—or, often, on the bare ground."

While working in a small hospital, Sister Teresa wrote of the toll that living in such horrible conditions had taken on some patients: "Their ears and feet are covered in sores. On their backs are lumps and lesions among the numerous ulcers."

From the time she arrived in India, Sister Teresa had helped the poor within the parameters of the Catholic Church, and within convent walls, according to the rule of enclosure. She was trained as a teacher and taught history and geography at convent schools. In 1935, however, Sister Teresa was given an exemption to teach the poor outside the convent at St. Teresa's school. On her daily walks to the school, she was brought into direct contact with the poverty-stricken people who lived on India's streets. Eventually, her church superiors revoked this exemption. Sister Teresa was again confined to teaching only inside the convent, but she wouldn't allow the faces and suffering of the poor to leave her mind.

Although she had taken her vows of poverty, chastity and obedience, Sister Teresa was searching for a way to best serve the poor regardless of church rules. On September 10, 1946, a date that would be remembered by her future religious order as "Inspiration Day," Sister Teresa realized what she had to do: "I again experienced a call to renounce everything and to follow Christ into the slums. . . . I understood that God wanted something from me. . . . the message was quite clear: I was to leave the convent and help the poor whilst living among them. It was an order. I knew where I belonged. I felt intensely that Jesus wanted me to serve him among the poorest of the poor, the uncared for, the slum dwellers, the abandoned, the homeless."

Leaving the convent would mean breaking her sacred vow to live her life in the Loreto order. Sister Teresa was advised to petition the church for the "privilege of exclaustration," meaning living and working as a nun outside the convent walls. Her request required the approval of church officials, including Pope Pius XII. She pursued the petition even without the support of Archbishop Ferdinand Perier, the head of the Catholic Church in Calcutta, who was against the idea. After two years, the Catholic Church granted Sister Teresa's request on a probationary one-year basis. A final decision would be rendered on the matter after that.

Sister Teresa left the convent at Darjeeling, a beautiful mountain town at the foot of India's breathtaking Himalayan mountains, for the wretched poverty of India's cities. Now she was a lone crusader for the poor. The uniform she chose was a peasant's white sari with blue trim. She stood barely five feet tall, but had an unforgettable smile that conveyed her love, and a purposeful walk that conveyed her determination. She was armed, she liked to say, with her prayer books.

To care for the poor, Sister Teresa first thought about their needs. They lacked proper medical care and education, so she first spent four months in the city of Patna learning basic first aid and nursing skills. She then opened a school for the poor in the city of Motijhil, near Calcutta. Since there was no money for an actual classroom, Sister Teresa taught the

> *I would rather make mistakes in kindness and compassion than work miracles in unkindness and hardness.*
> —Mother Teresa

students outside, using the dirt as her blackboard and sticks as her chalk.

Sister Teresa also became a persistent fundraiser, sometimes patiently waiting hours until she received what she came for. She asked people and organizations for money, and pharmacies for medical supplies. Financial donations allowed her to rent two rooms in a building, which she used for a classroom and medical facility.

During Sister Teresa's first year on her own, her reputation and selfless example brought many young women who wished to be trained as sisters and serve the poor as she did. Some of them were former students. After her one-year probationary period ended, and with Archbishop Perier now in her corner, Sister Teresa proposed the founding of her own religious order. She drafted a constitution in which she said God told her to name the order the Missionaries of Charity. She submitted the papers to the Church and ultimately to the Pope for approval, which was granted in October, 1950.

She was now Mother Teresa and had a flock of novice sisters training under her. To give clear direction to her new order, Mother added a fourth vow to be taken by all Missionaries of Charity (in addition to poverty, chastity and obedience), which said they were "to give wholehearted and free service to the poorest of the poor." Mother Teresa especially believed that their vow of poverty could not be compromised. Many of her novice sisters came from middle-class or upper middle-class families. She set an example by shunning comforts such as air conditioning and stoves, saying "I do not want them; the poor we serve have none. . . . Jesus invited me to serve him and follow him in actual poverty, to practice a kind of life that would make me similar to the needy in whom he was present, suffered and loved."

By living a life of self-denial, devoid of material comforts, Mother Teresa felt that she and her nuns would be better able to understand what the poor go through on a daily basis. "If we really want to know the poor, we must know what poverty is. It is why in our society, poverty is our freedom and our strength," Mother Teresa said. Her only compromise was on the amount of food they ate—which she had to be talked into. She realized that it was practical to eat well, for she and her nuns had to have the strength to do their daily work for the poor.

One of Mother Teresa's conditions in accepting a prospective sister into her order was that she had to have a "cheerful disposition." She said: "A cheerful giver is a great giver." Mother Teresa herself was known for her warm greeting and powerful smile, and she said to her sisters, "Let us always greet each other with a smile, for a smile is the beginning of love." Mother Teresa also expected her girls to "joyfully accept to spend 24 hours with . . . the poorest of the poor, covered with dirt. . . . They are the lepers, the abandoned destitute, the homeless, the sick, the dying."

Mother Teresa wrote: "The Missionaries of Charity do firmly believe that they are touching the body of Christ in his distressing disguise whenever they are helping and touching the poor. We cannot do this with a long face."

Mother Teresa explained to her nuns the clear, uncompromising principles of unconditional love and compassion. She expected them never to shy away from washing the sores of the diseased (while using commonsense precautions such as wearing gloves), changing bedpans and cleaning up after those who were ill. "If you don't have the zeal to help the poor, to take good care of the lepers," Mother Teresa would say to prospective sisters, "then [you] should pack up and go home . . . no need to stay."

The Missionaries of Charity grew because of Mother's ability to touch the hearts of people and raise money. At the same time, she believed people could give something more important that would make a greater difference to the poor: love. "Let us not be satisfied with just giving money," Mother Teresa said. "Money is not enough, for money one can get. I would like more people to give their hands to serve and their hearts to love—to recognize the poor in their own homes, towns and countries and to reach out to them in love and compassion, giving where it is most needed, and share the joy of loving with everyone."

In time, Mother Teresa and the Missionaries of Charity were able to open homes of hope such as Shishu Bhavan, which cared for orphans and disabled children, and the Home for the Dying in Kalighat, also known as Nirmal Hriday, meaning Home of the Pure Heart.

During an Indian monsoon, in 1952, Mother Teresa found an old woman dying in a pool of water. Mother Teresa picked her up and took her to a nearby hospital. The woman was near death, her life so neglected that her toes had been gnawed to the bone by rats. The hospital turned the woman and Mother Teresa away and said they could not help her. As Mother Teresa carried her to another hospital, the old lady died in her arms. The next day Mother went to see a city official and didn't mince any words: "It's a disgrace that people in this city are forced to die in the street," she said. "Give me a house where we can help the dying to appear before God in dignity and love." The city gave her a house and thus Nirmal Hriday was born.

"Nobody in the Home for the Dying in Kalighat has died depressed, in despair, unwanted, unfed, or unloved," Mother Teresa wrote. "We try to give them whatever they want—according to what is written in the book, be it Hindu, or Muslim, or Buddhist or Catholic or Protestant, or any other Society."

By the 1940s, medicines had been developed to cure the dreaded disease of leprosy. But even in 1955, India still had three million lepers. While others ran from the contagious and sometimes disfigured victims, Mother Teresa ran to them with open arms and a smile on her face. She established the Leprosy Fund and Leprosy Day, asking people to "touch the sufferer of leprosy with your kindness," rather than banish them to ill-equipped leper colonies as though they had brought the dreaded disease on themselves.

With the help of a large donation and an ambulance, she started a mobile leprosy clinic. Medical supplies were gathered and delivered to government leprosy centers where many patients received treatment. When Pope Paul VI gave Mother Teresa his white Lincoln Continental in 1964, she raffled it off for five times its value and raised $100,000. With that money, she started a humane and dignified leprosy colony where victims lived and worked while receiving proper medical care. The colony provided what the lepers needed most: love and compassion.

"The biggest disease today is not leprosy or cancer or tuberculosis," Mother Teresa said, "but rather the feeling of being unwanted, uncared for, deserted by everybody. The greatest evil is the lack of love and charity, the terrible indifference towards one's neighbor who lives at the roadside, the victim of exploitation, corruption, poverty, and disease."

Mother Teresa, who started in 1948 as a single warrior against poverty, without money or influence, became recognized internationally by the early 1960s. Among the awards she was given were the American Good Samaritan award and the Pope John XXIII peace prize. When an award came with cash, she immediately donated it to her order.

> *If you can't feed a hundred people, then feed just one.*
> —Mother Teresa

In 1965 Pope Paul VI gave the Missionaries of Charity permission to open outside of India, and by 1970 they were serving the poor in over 100 countries. Mother Teresa didn't want the Missionaries of Charity's work and the poor of India to be held up as unique to that country. If people wanted to help the poor, she said, they didn't have to look any farther than their own backyard. "You will find Calcutta all over the world if you have eyes to see," she wrote. "The streets of Calcutta lead to every man's door. I know that you may want to make a trip to Calcutta, but it is easy to love people far away. . . . very easy to think of the hungry people in India. You must see first that there is love at home and at your next-door neighbour's and in the street you live in, in the town you live in and only then outside."

Her example inspired thousands of people to join her cause. These "lay people" were made up of different races and religions and became known as the International Association of the Coworkers of Mother Teresa. In 1969, Pope Paul VI officially recognized them as part of the Missionaries of Charity.

"To my helpers and volunteers," Mother Teresa said, "discover ... through direct contact. Go to Kalighat, the Home for the Dying, and learn your lessons, not out of a book, but in the rough and tumble of life, among real people, in a setting you will never forget."

The Missionaries of Charity eventually grew to more than 4,500 nuns and 120,000 coworkers. There are over 600 houses in over 130 countries for the orphans, dying and needy. The order's assets, primarily donated buildings, make it a billion-dollar organization dedicated to helping the poor.

"Mother Teresa exhibited boldness when asking on behalf of the poor," wrote Father Edward Le Joly in *The Joy in Living,* a compilation of statements she had said or written. "During an interview with a Japanese editor of a leading newspaper," Le Joly wrote, "[Mother Teresa] said, 'Mr. Kato, you write so well, please write in your newspaper: Mother Teresa needs a house, a nice house. The Japanese are rich. A person owning two houses can give one.' Who but Mother Teresa could have said that!"

"As God gives good things freely, so we should give freely to needy people," Mother Teresa also said.

Mother Teresa's boundless energy stayed with her all her life. She would rise early (4:30 A.M.) and work late, often using the late-night hours to write letters to those who could help her cause. By the time she was eighty-five, Mother Teresa had suffered three serious heart attacks and had a pacemaker, but she refused to slow down. "I've never said no to Jesus," Mother Teresa said, "and I'm not going to begin now. Every day you have to say yes." Even in her advancing years, she still traveled to many different countries for speaking engagements.

She also traveled to every continent, many times, and into the most dangerous of places, but she wasn't afraid because of her faith. "When I was crossing into Gaza [in the Middle East]," Mother Teresa said, "I was asked at the checkpost whether I was carrying any weapons. I replied: 'Oh yes, my prayer books.'"

When she spoke to an audience, it was from the heart. "How do you speak, Mother?" Le Joly once asked her. "Father, I make a little cross on my lips with my thumb; then I look straight forward [and] deliver my message." Her talks, always easy to follow, [were] enlivened by moving stories of her experiences, Le Joly wrote.

Mother Teresa walked with presidents, prime ministers, kings and queens in order to bring attention to the needs of the poor. At the 40th anniversary of the United Nations, General Secretary Javier Perez de Cuellar said of Mother Teresa, who was in attendance, "I introduce to you the most powerful woman in the world."

Mother Teresa was featured on the cover of almost every important newsmagazine in the world. *Time* magazine called her "a living saint." In 1979 Mother Teresa was honored for her work when she was awarded the Nobel Peace Prize. "I accept the prize in the name of the poor," she said, and used the prize money to build homes for the poor. At the awards ceremony she told the audience: "We need to tell the poor that they are somebody to us, that they, too, have been created by the same loving hand of God, to love and be loved."

She put her Nobel Peace Prize in context when she stated, "Once a beggar came to me and said: 'Everybody is giving you something. I also want to give you something.' And he offered me a ten-paisa coin. If I accepted the money, he would go hungry, but if I didn't, he would be unhappy. I accepted it. And I felt within me that his gift was greater than the Nobel Prize because he gave me all that he had. I could see in his face the joy of giving."

Mother Teresa received many honors and became a celebrity, but she never let her fame go to her head. She credited God and Jesus for what she and the Missionaries of Charity accomplished and saw herself only as an instrument in their hands. "I am surer of this than of my own life," she said.

The ministry of Mother Teresa can be summarized by a story she told. "Sometime ago a woman came with her child to me and said: 'Mother, I went to two or three places to beg for food, for we have not eaten for three days, but they told me that I was young and I should work and earn my living. No one gave me anything.'" Mother Teresa went to get her some food, but "by the time I returned, the baby in her arms had died of hunger," Mother Teresa said.

"Charity begins today. Today somebody is suffering, today somebody is in the street, today somebody is hungry. . . . Do not wait for tomorrow."

She never did.

How to Be Like Mother Teresa

1. Do what you love.

Agnes felt that God was calling her to the sisterhood to serve the poor. She consulted experts and the priests at her church to help understand her feelings. "If you are happy with the idea that God calls you to serve him and your neighbor," Agnes recalled being told by a priest, "this will be the proof of your vocation. Profound joy of the heart is like a magnet that indicates the path of life."

2. Read constantly.

Reading helped Agnes understand the plight of India's poor. Her constant efforts to learn gave her greater depth and wisdom.

3. Accept no limitations for your life.

Sister Teresa had a desire to serve the poor more fully than the Catholic Church would permit. It seems certain she would have left the Church had she not been granted the privilege of exclaustration and permission to form a new order. "I again experienced a call to renounce everything and to follow Christ into the slums, to serve the poorest of the poor," she wrote. "I understood that God wanted something from me. . . . the message was quite clear: I was to leave the convent and help the poor whilst living among them. It was an order. I knew where I belonged."

4. Don't be afraid to ask for what you need.

Starting alone, Mother Teresa built the Missionaries of Charity into a worldwide organization through persistent fund-raising efforts. She boldly asked for money and medical supplies to help the poor.

5. **Clearly define what you want to accomplish.**

Mother Teresa added a fourth vow to be taken by the Missionaries of Charity: "To give wholehearted and free service to the poorest of the poor. . . . If you don't have the zeal to help the poor, to take good care of the lepers, then [you] should pack up and go home. . . . no need to stay."

6. **Set an example.**

The most effective way to lead is by example. Mother Teresa asked her sisters to take their vow of poverty farther than those in the convent to help them understand the "poorest of the poor." She said: "If we really want to know the poor, we must know what poverty is. . . . It is why in our society, poverty is our freedom and our strength."

7. **Be cheerful even if you don't feel like it.**

Even if you have problems in your life that make you unhappy, present a cheerful demeanor to the outside world. That doesn't mean you are ignoring your problems. Rather, you are putting yourself in the best possible frame of mind to solve them. One of Mother Teresa's conditions in accepting a prospective sister into her order was that she have a "cheerful disposition." Mother Teresa said, "A cheerful giver is a great giver." Mother Teresa was known for her warm greeting and powerful smile that conveyed her great love and caring. "Let us always greet each other with a smile, for a smile is the beginning of love," she said.

8. **Care about those in need.**

Mother Teresa became, in the words of United Nations General Secretary Javier Perez de Cuellar, "the most powerful woman in the world," because she cared for those in need. "The biggest disease today is not leprosy or cancer or tuberculosis," Mother Teresa said, "but rather the feeling of being unwanted, uncared for, deserted by everybody. The greatest evil is the lack of love and charity, the terrible indifference towards one's neighbor. . . ."

9. **Learn by experience.**

Mother Teresa said to her helpers and volunteers: "Discover . . . through direct contact. Go to Kalighat, the Home for the Dying, and learn your lessons, not out of a book, but in the rough and tumble of life, among real people. . . ."

10. **Write letters.**

Written communications, especially thank-you notes, are a powerful way to make a lasting impression. Florence Nightingale, Clara Barton, Eleanor Roosevelt and Margaret Thatcher were all great letter writers. Prime Minister Margaret Thatcher said: "I have always believed in the impact of a personal handwritten letter—even from someone you barely know."

11. **Don't let age slow you down.**

Mother Teresa had suffered three serious heart attacks by the time she was eighty-five and had a pacemaker, but she refused to slow down. "I've never said no to Jesus," she said, "and I'm not going to begin now. Every day you have to say yes."

12. **Speak from your heart.**

"I make a little cross on my lips with my thumb; then I look straight forward above the audience and deliver my message," Mother Teresa told Father Le Joly about her speaking style.

13. **Stay humble.**

A world figure and the recipient of a Nobel Peace Prize, Mother Teresa didn't get carried away with herself. She credited God and Jesus for what she and the Missionaries of Charity accomplished, and saw herself as God's vessel. "I am surer of this than of my own life," she said.

ANNE FRANK
1929–1945

COURAGE

We must be brave and strong, bear
discomfort without complaint, do whatever
is in our power and trust in God.
One day this terrible war will be over.

—Anne Frank, April 11, 1944

nne Frank wrote *The Diary of Anne Frank,* one of the most powerful and widely read books ever written. Much of the diary reads like what it was meant to be—the typical reflections of a normal teenaged girl growing up. The most important entries reflect why it is still cherished today—the brilliant, thoughtful work of the woman Frank never grew up to be. She died in a Nazi concentration camp just a few weeks before its liberation by Allied forces.

The diary—red and green in color, checkered in pattern—was one of many presents Anne received for her thirteenth birthday on June 12, 1942. A few weeks later, her father, Otto Frank, took Anne, her sixteen-year-old sister, Margot, and their mother, Edith, into hiding. The Franks were a Jewish family living in Holland, which had been occupied by Nazi Germany since 1940. It was a regime that targeted Jewish people for death.

During World War II, the Nazis murdered six million Jewish people and millions of non-Jews. Approximately 120,000 Jewish people lived in Holland when the German occupation began. By the end of the war, 106,000 of them had been murdered by the Nazis.

The Frank's hiding place at 263 Prinsengracht Street in Amsterdam, Holland, was a secret three-story annex connected to the back of the office/warehouse where Otto Frank made his living as a manufacturer of food ingredients. The Franks were joined a few days later by another Jewish family, Hermann and Auguste van Pels and their sixteen-year-old son, Peter. Hermann was one of Otto's employees.

Otto, along with five of his brave non-Jewish friends, who were also business associates, had been preparing the annex for months. When Margot Frank received a notice ordering her to report for transportation to a forced labor camp in Germany, Otto moved up his timetable and immediately took his family into hiding. Unable to escape from Holland, Otto hoped that the family could wait out World War II, until, hopefully, the Allies achieved victory.

"Writing in a diary is a really strange experience for someone like me," Anne wrote on June 20, 1942. "Not only because I've never written anything before, but also because it seems to me that later on neither I nor anyone else will be interested in the musings of a thirteen-year-old schoolgirl. Oh well, it doesn't matter. I feel like writing."

While Frank could not imagine the importance of her writing in terms of its impact and historical context, she was as wrong about interest in her work as Abraham Lincoln had been about his Gettysburg address, when he said that "the world will little note nor long remember what we say here."

Anne's diary, which she kept from June 12, 1942 to August 1, 1944, has been translated into more than fifty-five languages and has sold more than twenty million copies. In many schools around the world it is required reading. For many children, Frank is their first guide into the battle between the good and the dark side of humanity, but she tempers the journey with a message of hope and words of courage. Her writing is rich and expresses clear, powerful emotions. Frank's social and philosophical commentaries go far beyond her years.

"[Frank] showed an insight into the failings of human nature—her own not excepted—so infallible that it would have astonished one in an adult, let alone a child," wrote Dr. Jan Romein, a Dutch historian, in 1946.

While Frank was, of course, constantly worried about the fate of her family and herself, she never lost sight of the mass murder of Jewish and non-Jewish people alike that she knew was going on outside the confines of her hiding place. Frank's writings reveal a deep concern for other people. "I get frightened myself," Frank wrote on November 19, 1942, "when I think of close friends who are now at the mercy of the cruelest monsters ever to stalk the earth. And all because they're Jews." Earlier that year, on January 13, 1942, Frank had written: "Terrible things are happening outside. At any time of night and day, poor helpless people are being dragged out of their homes . . . families are torn apart; men, women and children are separated."

The more Frank wrote in her diary, the more she realized writing was what she loved to do. Despite her circumstances of living in hiding from the Nazis stalking her—"each and every day is filled with tension," she wrote—Frank refused to allow herself to be paralyzed by fear and its companion, inaction. "I can shake off everything if I write," Frank wrote. "[M]y sorrows disappear, my courage is reborn."

"The Nazi regime, which crushed human dignity under its boots . . . stole Frank's youth and forced her to grow up quickly," wrote Melissa Muller in *Anne Frank: The Biography*. "But instead of yielding to defeat, she lived a life of singular intensity."

READER/CUSTOMER CARE SURVEY

HEFG

We care about your opinions! Please take a moment to fill out our online Reader Survey at **http://survey.hcibooks.com**.
As a **"THANK YOU"** you will receive a **VALUABLE INSTANT COUPON** towards future book purchases as well as a **SPECIAL GIFT** available only online! Or, you may mail this card back to us and we will send you a copy of our exciting catalog with your valuable coupon inside.

(PLEASE PRINT IN ALL CAPS)

First Name		MI.	Last Name

Address			

State	Zip	Email	City

1. Gender
- ☐ Female ☐ Male

2. Age
- ☐ 8 or younger
- ☐ 9-12   ☐ 13-16
- ☐ 17-20   ☐ 21-30
- ☐ 31+

3. Did you receive this book as a gift?
- ☐ Yes   ☐ No

4. Annual Household Income
- ☐ under $25,000
- ☐ $25,000 - $34,999
- ☐ $35,000 - $49,999
- ☐ $50,000 - $74,999
- ☐ over $75,000

5. What are the ages of the children living in your house?
- ☐ 0 - 14   ☐ 15+

6. Marital Status
- ☐ Single
- ☐ Married
- ☐ Divorced
- ☐ Widowed

7. How did you find out about the book?
(please choose one)
- ☐ Recommendation
- ☐ Store Display
- ☐ Online
- ☐ Catalog/Mailing
- ☐ Interview/Review

8. Where do you usually buy books?
(please choose one)
- ☐ Bookstore
- ☐ Online
- ☐ Book Club/Mail Order
- ☐ Price Club (Sam's Club, Costco's, etc.)
- ☐ Retail Store (Target, Wal-Mart, etc.)

9. What subject do you enjoy reading about the most?
(please choose one)
- ☐ Parenting/Family
- ☐ Relationships
- ☐ Recovery/Addictions
- ☐ Health/Nutrition
- ☐ Christianity
- ☐ Spirituality/Inspiration
- ☐ Business Self-help
- ☐ Women's Issues
- ☐ Sports

10. What attracts you most to a book?
(please choose one)
- ☐ Title
- ☐ Cover Design
- ☐ Author
- ☐ Content

TAPE IN MIDDLE; DO NOT STAPLE

BUSINESS REPLY MAIL
FIRST-CLASS MAIL PERMIT NO 45 DEERFIELD BEACH, FL

POSTAGE WILL BE PAID BY ADDRESSEE

Health Communications, Inc.
3201 SW 15th Street
Deerfield Beach FL 33442-9875

FOLD HERE

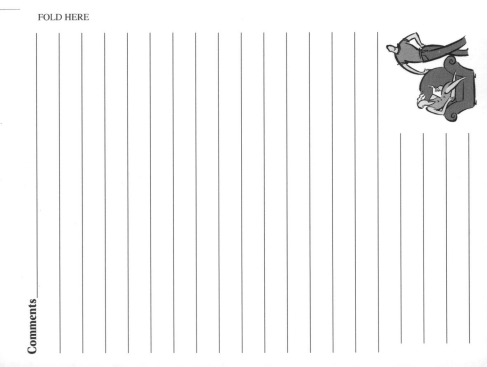

Comments

The constant discipline of daily writing taught Frank an important lesson about self-fulfillment, as she recounts in her July 6, 1944 entry: "Happiness . . . that's something you can't achieve by taking the easy way out. Earning happiness means doing good and working, not speculating and being lazy. Laziness may look inviting, but only work [gives] you true satisfaction."

Through her writing, Frank realized she wanted to become a writer and a journalist. "I know that I can write . . . whether I have real talent remains to be seen. . . . But, and that is the great question, will I ever be able to write anything great?" Frank wrote in April 1944.

She was motivated by the contributions she felt she could make to society in the future as a writer. "I shall not remain insignificant, I shall work in the world for mankind," Frank wrote on April 1, 1944. A few days later she added: "I don't want to have lived in vain like most people. I want to be useful or bring enjoyment to all people, even those I've never met. I want to go on living, even after my death!"

Little could Frank have imagined that she would realize her goal not for what she thought she could do in the future, but for what she was doing at the moment she penned those words. "Through her diary Anne really does live on," wrote Miep Gies in Melissa Muller's book. "She stands for the triumph of the spirit over evil and death." Miep was a friend and employee of Otto Frank, who, along with her husband, Jan, Victor Kugler, Johannes Kleiman and Bep Voskuijl, courageously took responsibility for hiding and caring for the group. Those who hid Jews, or who helped them in any way, were risking their own lives.

All through her two years and roughly two months in hiding, Frank was keenly aware of the chance her protectors were taking for the group and deeply appreciated it. "The Germans are generous enough when it comes to punishment," Frank wrote on October 9, 1942.

Frank had pledged to herself that she was going to continue to write whether she could make a profession out of it or not. "If I don't have the talent to write books or newspaper articles, I can always write for myself. But I want to achieve more than that," the ambitious Frank wrote on April 5, 1944. It was pursuing that desire—simply doing something for the love of it— that gave Frank worldwide success after her death. Yet she always treated writing itself as something important. "I don't really think of [writing] as a hobby," she wrote on April 6, 1944.

Frank's father, Otto, the biggest influence in her life, nurtured her persevering spirit in the face of adversity. Otto Frank was, Muller wrote, a man of "calm, courteous, and modest ways," with a "keen sense of justice." His manner earned him the loyalty of his employees. It was Victor Kugler and Jan Gies who helped Otto maintain ownership of his business while making it appear on paper to the occupying Nazi forces that it was solely an Aryan enterprise. (Before Jewish people were shipped off to the death camps, the Nazis first stripped them of any kind of ownership.)

Despite their circumstances, Otto taught his daughters to respect everyone and avoid looking for the things that divide people. "Whether you are a Jew or a Christian, there is only one God. Only the paths to him are a little different," he told his daughters.

During their years in hiding, Otto also made sure that Anne, Margot and Peter van Pels continued with their education. He created a semblance of normality for them. The teenagers kept a regular schedule of study that included, among other subjects, language, math and history. Muller wrote that Otto "regarded education as the most valuable thing parents could give their children."

Frank loved books, especially those about history. She'd been intellectually curious as a child, and she didn't lose the desire to expand her mind as a teenager. "I've been taking down notes from all the biographies and history books that I read; I even copy out many passages of history," Frank wrote, adding that reading was "surely the road to success."

When she wasn't immersing herself in her writing, Frank dealt with adversity and fear by finding things to be optimistic about. Although she certainly wasn't immune to fear about her family's situation, she would not be broken emotionally by the Nazis. "Beauty remains, even in misfortune," Frank wrote on March 7, 1944. "If you just look for it, you discover more and more happiness and regain your balance. A person who's happy will make others happy; a person who has courage and faith will never die in misery."

Frank's courage and optimism came from her faith in God. "Without God I should long ago have collapsed," she recorded in her diary on March 12, 1944. "I know I am not safe, I am afraid of prison cells and concentration camps, but I feel I've grown more courageous and that I am in God's hands!"

Frank's writings reveal the depth of her thoughts about religion and faith, and the profound wisdom she developed about them. "You don't even have to live in fear of eternal punishment," she wrote. "[T]he concepts of purgatory, Heaven and Hell are difficult for many people to accept, yet religion itself, any religion, keeps a person on the right path.

> *How noble and good everyone could be if, at the end of each day, they were to review their own behavior and weigh up the rights and wrongs.... Everyone is welcome to this prescription; it costs nothing and is definitely useful. Those who don't know will have to find out by experience that 'a quiet conscience gives you strength!'*
> —Anne Frank,
> JULY 6, 1944

Not the fear of God, but upholding your own sense of honor and obeying your own conscience."

On April 9, 1944, burglars entered the warehouse where the secret annex was located and rummaged through the building. A watchman summoned the police to investigate after the burglars left. The group was extremely shaken; they could easily have been discovered. Fear was rampant among them. Frank was scared also, but practiced what she preached in her diary. "We must behave like soldiers," she told Mrs. van Pels. "If our time has come, well then, it'll be for Queen and Country, for freedom, truth and justice, as they're always telling us on the radio. The only bad thing is that we'll drag the others down with us!"

Frank had a great deal of selflessness and empathy. "We're so selfish that we talk about 'after the war' and look forward to new clothes and shoes, when actually we should be saving every penny to help others when the war is over, to salvage whatever we can." A small everyday example of Frank's empathy, and her father's influence, was seen when Friedrich Pfeffer joined the group. Frank had to adjust and share living space with him, as did the others. "I'm not exactly delighted at having a stranger use my things," she wrote on November 19, 1942." [B]ut you have to make sacrifices for a good cause, and I'm glad I can make this small one. 'If we can save even one of our friends, the rest doesn't matter,' said Father, and he's absolutely right."

While living in hiding in the secret annex required sacrifices, Frank was aware enough of the situation in Holland to be grateful for the hiding place. "If I just think of how we live here, I usually come to the conclusion that it is a paradise compared with how other Jews who are not in hiding must be living," Frank wrote on May 2, 1943.

The growth of Frank as a young adult is seen in her ability to be honest about herself. She called that her "one outstanding character trait." She wrote about this ability in her diary on July 15, 1944: "I can watch myself as if I were a stranger. I can stand across from the everyday Frank and, without being biased or making excuses, watch what she's doing, both the good and the bad. This self-awareness never leaves me. I'm beginning to realize the truth of Father's adage: 'Every child has to raise itself.' Parents can only advise their children or point them in the right direction. Ultimately, people shape their own characters."

Once a person had taken an honest self-inventory, Frank believed it was then imperative to correct the deficiencies. "I know my various faults and shortcomings better than anyone else," she wrote. "[B]ut there's one difference: I also know that I want to change, will change and already have changed greatly! I can't imagine how anyone could say 'I'm weak' and then stay that way," she also wrote. "If you know that about yourself, why not fight it, why not develop your character?"

The theme of taking responsibility for one's actions and admitting one's mistakes, taught to her by Otto, permeates Frank's diary. She displayed this trait early in her life. While attending public school in 1941, Frank allowed a friend to copy from her test during a French exam. When the teacher caught them red-handed, Frank's friend, Hannah, upset at being caught, told the teacher all the students in the class were cheating. Frank took it upon herself to write a letter of apology to her classmates: "Anne Frank and Hannah Pick-Goslar herewith offer the pupils of Class 16 II their sincere apologies for the cowardly betrayal. . . . It was an unpremeditated, thoughtless act, and we admit without hesitation that we are the only ones who should have been punished."

Frank lived during one of the darkest times in history, and she tried to understand what drove the dark side of humanity. The young teenager again articulated the heart of the matter. "There's a destructive urge in people, the urge to rage, murder and kill," she wrote on May 3, 1944. "And until all of humanity, without exception, undergoes a metamorphosis, wars will continue to be waged, and everything that has been carefully built up, cultivated and grown will be cut down and destroyed, only to start again!"

She put the responsibility for evil not only on oppressive regimes, but also on everyday people. "Oh no, the common man is every bit as guilty; otherwise, people and nations would have rebelled long ago!"

It was Frank's desire to see her diary published as a book. She was further inspired by a radio speech she heard on March 28, 1944. Gerrit Bolkestein, the Dutch Minister of Education and Culture, who was in exile in London, called for handwritten accounts from his countrymen to document the cruelty of the Nazis occupying their country. "History cannot be written on the basis of official decisions and documents alone," Bolkestein said. "What we really need are ordinary documents—a diary, letters from a worker in Germany, a collection of sermons given by a parson or a priest. Not until we succeed in bringing together vast quantities of this simple, everyday material will the picture of our struggle for freedom be painted in its full depth and glory."

Frank immediately answered Bolkestein's call. She started to rewrite passages of her diary on loose-leaf paper while continuing to write new entries. On May 25, 1944, she wrote, "The world's been turned upside down. The most decent people are being sent to concentration camps, prisons and lonely cells, while the lowest of the low rule."

On August 4, 1944, the "lowest of the low" came to the hiding place of Frank and the group. The Nazi police—the Gestapo—acting on a tip, arrested the Frank and van Pels families, along with Friedrich Pfeffer, for the "crime" of being Jewish. They were taken away to the Nazi death camps.

"You traitor, aren't you ashamed to have helped this Jewish trash?" the Gestapo officer in charge, Karl Silberbauer, yelled at Miep Gies. Some two years before, Otto Frank cautioned Miep of the danger that she would be facing in helping to care for the group. When he asked her if she was willing to do it, despite the risks, her answer was "Of course." Miep Gies and Bep Voskuijl weren't arrested, but Victor Kugler and Johannes Kleiman were. When Otto offered an apology for the fate they now faced for helping the group, Kleiman answered "Don't give it another thought. It was up to me, and I wouldn't have done it differently."

It was Miep and Bep who collected Frank's diary, which lay scattered about in a pile of books and newspapers after the Gestapo had ransacked the secret annex. Frank's writings had outgrown the actual diary to include other notebooks and 327 loose sheets of paper. "Everything was in utter confusion,"

Miep recalled in 1959. "I came across Anne Frank's diary on the floor [along] with notes by Anne and a number of loose sheets of copy paper, which were also covered with Anne's handwriting. . . . I locked all of these writings of Anne's in my office desk." It was her hope to one day give the diary back to Frank personally.

In a great irony, the Nazis, who would go to any lengths to deny their crimes after the war, had left behind one of the most powerful documents of testimony to their cruelty and inhumanity ever written.

It was the Nazis—who cowardly hid behind their uniforms and depraved ideology at the Nuremberg War Crimes Tribunal—who offered the world a pathetic cry of "we were just following orders" as their excuse for murdering millions of men, women, teenagers, children and babies.

It was Frank—armed only with her pen—who "has become a universal symbol of the oppressed in a world of violence and tyranny," Melissa Muller wrote. Muller calls Frank, "probably Hitler's most famous victim."

After being discovered by the Gestapo in their hiding place, Anne, Margot and their mother, Edith, were sent to the Auschwitz death camp. "I can still see [Anne] standing at the door and looking down the camp street as a herd of naked Gypsy girls was driven by to the crematory, and Anne watched them go and cried," a woman recalled who was with Frank in Auschwitz (and who was quoted in *The Importance of Anne Frank* by John F. Wukovits). "And she cried also when we marched past the Hungarian children [waiting]) in front of the gas chambers. . . . Anne nudged me and said, 'Look, look. Their eyes.'"

Edith bravely tried to look after her daughters, but would

see them no more after October 1944, when Anne and Margot were transferred to the Bergen-Belsen concentration camp in Germany. It was there that Frank was reunited with her school friend, Hanneli Pick-Goslar. It was also at Bergen-Belsen, in March 1945, that a malnourished Anne Frank died of typhus. Her sister, Margot, had died of the same illness a few weeks earlier. Frank was just a few weeks short of her sixteenth birthday, and just a few weeks short of liberation by the Allies and the end of the war.

After the war, Miep gave Frank's diary to Otto. The heartbroken father of the Frank family was the sole survivor of the group. His family and the rest of the group had died in the Nazi concentration camps. "To my great and abiding sorrow," Miep Gies would later recall in Muller's book, "I was not able to save Anne's life. But I was able to help her live two years longer. In those two years she wrote the diary that gives hope to people all over the world and calls for understanding and tolerance."

Frank's diary came to the attention of Dr. Jan Romein after Otto Frank had shown it to Romein's wife, Annie, who was also an educator. In an April 1946 article, Romein wrote: "By chance a diary written during the war years has come into my possession. The Netherlands State Institute for War Documentation already holds some two hundred similar diaries, but I should be very much surprised if there were another as lucid, as intelligent, and at the same time as natural."

Dr. Kurt Baschwitz was a professor of journalism and mass psychology in Amsterdam. After being shown the diary by Otto, he encouraged him to publish it, calling it "the most moving document about that time I know, and a literary masterpiece as well." Otto decided it would be in accordance with Frank's wishes to publish the diary. Three versions were released. Version A is Frank's unedited diary. Version B includes the rewrites. Version C is a smaller combination of both, edited by Otto Frank and released in 1952 as *The Diary of a Young Girl: The Definitive Edition*.

Eleanor Roosevelt wrote in the introduction to the 1952 edition that Frank's diary was "one of the wisest and most moving commentaries on war and its impact on human beings" that she had ever read. Muller wrote that the impact of Frank's diary has been that her name alone invokes "humanity, tolerance, human rights, and democracy . . . her image is the epitome of optimism and the will to live."

In Utrecht, Holland, a beautiful statue of Frank can be found. A school in Amsterdam that she attended is now called the Anne Frank School. In the city where she died, Bergen, there is an elementary school named in her memory. In Israel, a forest of ten thousand trees is named in her honor. Johanna Hurwitz writes in her book *Anne Frank: Life in Hiding,* that, "Today, the house at 263 Prinsengracht does not need to hide anyone. Instead, it has become a museum where visitors of all faiths and from every country come to view the rooms where Anne and the others hid from the Nazis. There, one can still see the fading photographs of Anne's favorite movie stars. One cannot help but realize with irony that not one of those stars has a face or name that is as well known today as Anne's."

On July 15, 1944, just a couple of weeks before their discovery by the Gestapo, Frank wrote an entry that concludes with one of the most quoted lines from her diary. The belief about people that she expresses here is what gave her the strength to endure her two-plus years in hiding and to write a diary that will last for eternity:

"It's difficult in times like these: ideals, dreams, and cherished hopes rise within us, only to be crushed by grim reality. It's a wonder I haven't abandoned all my ideals, they seem so absurd and impractical. Yet I cling to them because I still believe, in spite of everything, that people are truly good at heart."

How to Be Like Anne Frank

1. **Follow your heart.**

   Frank wrote in one of her early diary entries: "It seems to me that later on neither I nor anyone else will be interested in the musings of a thirteen-year-old schoolgirl. Oh well, it doesn't matter. I feel like writing."

2. **Develop your social conscience to its fullest.**

   Frank was just a teenager hiding in the small confines of the secret annex, but she knew of the cruelty exploding in the world outside. She cared about other people, and never lost sight of the fact that there were millions of people, Jews and non-Jews alike, who were suffering at the hands of the Nazis. This made her a better person, and a better writer. Having a social conscience makes all of us better at what we do. "I get frightened myself when I think of close friends who are now at the mercy of the cruelest monsters ever to stalk the earth," Frank wrote. "And all because they're Jews."

3. **Don't let fear paralyze you into inaction.**

   Frank lived under the constant fear of discovery and death. She wasn't immune to it, but writing in her diary gave her strength. "I can shake off everything if I write," she wrote. "[M]y sorrows disappear, my courage is reborn."

4. **Don't be fooled by the easy way out.**

   Frank wrote: "Earning happiness means doing good and working, not speculating and being lazy.

Laziness may look inviting, but only work gives you true satisfaction."

5. **Know what you want from life.**

Once Frank started writing in her diary, she knew her destiny was set. She was motivated by the contributions she felt she could make to society as a writer. "I shall not remain insignificant, I shall work in the world for mankind," she wrote on April 1, 1944. A few days later she added: "I don't want to have lived in vain like most people. I want to be useful or bring enjoyment to all people, even those I've never met. I want to go on living, even after my death!"

6. **Be serious about what's important to you.**

"I don't really think of [writing] as a hobby," Frank wrote on April 6, 1944. Her work reflects that.

7. **Read.**

Frank loved books, especially books about history. She wrote that reading was "surely the road to success." Historian Stephen E. Ambrose said: "I guarantee you the No. 1 asset that you're going to bring to whatever it is that you're going to do is reading. We, the human race, have not ever invented anything that can surpass reading as a way of learning."

8. **Search for the silver lining.**

Thankfully, most of us have never had to deal with anything on the order that Frank and the other victims of the Holocaust did. Frank was only human and wasn't immune to the fear she was facing, but she would not be broken emotionally by the Nazis. "Beauty remains, even in misfortune," she wrote in March 1944. "If you just look for it, you discover more and more happiness and regain your balance. A person who's happy will make others happy; a person who has courage and faith will never die in misery."

9. **Never lose your faith.**

Frank wrote: "Without God I should long ago have collapsed. I know I am not safe, I am afraid of prison cells and concentration camps, but I feel I've grown more courageous and that I am in God's hands!"

10. **Be honest with yourself.**

Frank called her self-honesty her "one outstanding character trait." She wrote: "I know my various faults and shortcomings better than anyone else, but there's one difference: I also know that I want to change, will change and already have changed greatly!"

11. **Once you have identified areas where you need to improve—act.**

Frank wrote: "I can't imagine how anyone could say 'I'm weak' and then stay that way. If you know that about yourself, why not fight it, why not develop your character?"

12. **Be brave and courageous.**

Frank left her readers a recipe for courage. She showed us by her belief in God, by never losing her humanity and by refusing to live her life paralyzed in fear, that a person can triumph in the end. "We must behave like soldiers," she told Mrs. van Pels. "If our time has come, well then, it'll be for Queen and Country, for freedom, truth and justice."

MARGARET THATCHER
b. 1926

RESOLVE

Any leader has to have a certain amount of steel in them, so I am not that put out about being called the Iron Lady.

—*Margaret Thatcher*

argaret Thatcher was England's first female prime minister and served the second longest tenure in England's history. She came to power by staying true to her convictions—and never compromised them to stay there.

In May 1979, fifty-four-year-old Thatcher became the first woman ever elected prime minister in England, when she led her Conservative Tory Party to a victory. By October 1980, however, she appeared to be on the road to failure. Great Britain was in its worst economic struggle since the 1930s. Almost 2.5 million people were out of work, interest rates were around 22 percent and a record number of businesses were going bankrupt. The British public pointed their finger solely at Thatcher's economic program, which called for income tax reductions and reductions in government spending.

Thatcher lost the confidence of many moderates in her own Conservative Party because of her devotion to her policies. When her own cabinet rebelled, she replaced them with people who believed as she did. At the Conservative Party Conference in October 1980, Thatcher signaled her resolve when she stated "To those waiting with bated breath for that favourite media catchphrase, the 'U-turn,' I have only one thing to say. You turn if you want to. The lady's not for turning. I say that not only to you, but to our friends overseas—and also to those who are not our friends." (Bernard Garfinkel, author of *Margaret Thatcher* wrote that Thatcher was referring to a well-known English play called *The Lady's Not for Burning*.)

"I was utterly convinced of one thing," wrote Thatcher in her book *Downing Street Years*. "There was no chance of achieving that fundamental change of attitudes which was required to wrench Britain out of decline if people believed that we were prepared to alter course under pressure."

The economic slide continued, and Thatcher's approval rating among the British public eventually fell to 28 percent. As she approached the Conservative Party Conference of October 1981, she was again under pressure to declare her policies a failure and attempt new ones. Thatcher would not be swayed. "I will not change just to court popularity," she said in a speech to her fellow Tory Party members.

Thatcher's father, Alfred Roberts, taught her to stand up for her beliefs. He had been a grocer, a city councilman and then a small-town mayor. Thatcher had great respect for her father and viewed him as a superb role model. "He taught me that you first sort out what you believe in," she wrote. "You then apply it. You don't compromise on things that matter."

The thing that mattered to Prime Minister Thatcher in the midst of Britain's economic problems was the Falkland Islands. The Falkland Islands lie off the coast of South America and had been a British territory since 1833. Argentina had always laid claim to them. In turn, the people of the Falkland Islands were permitted to break away from the British empire and switch their allegiance to Argentina anytime their citizens voted for such a move. In April 1982, however, Argentina took over the islands by military force, along with South Georgia Island and the South Sandwich Islands.

> *Always bear in mind that your own resolution to succeed is more important than any other one thing.*
> —Abraham Lincoln

The islands had no economic or military value. The population consisted of about 1,800 British citizens and the 650,000 sheep they herded. (Presumably, the island's largest majority, ten million penguins, didn't care who ruled the islands as long as the fish supply remained plentiful!) Nevertheless, Thatcher stood on her principles regarding Argentina's use of military force to take over the islands. She was a child of World War II. "My life . . . was transformed by the Second World War," she said. "I drew from the failure of appeasement the lesson that aggression must always be firmly resisted." Argentina wasn't Nazi Germany rolling through Europe, but she stated firmly that Argentina's military aggression "must be ended. It will be ended."

After failing to regain the islands through diplomatic channels, Prime Minister Thatcher decided a military response was necessary. Again, she drew on the lessons of World War II. She wrote in her memoirs: "The ultimate victory of the Allies persuaded me that nations must cooperate in defence of agreed international rules if they are either to resist great evils or to achieve great benefits. That is merely a platitude, however, if political leaders lack the courage and farsightedness.

"Civilisation could never be taken for granted and had constantly to be nurtured, which meant that good people had to stand up for the things they believed in."

United States Secretary of State Alexander Haig witnessed Prime Minister Thatcher's determination when he arrived in London for talks with her during the Falkland's crisis. "She rapped sharply on the tabletop," Haig recounted, "and recalled that this was the table at which Neville Chamberlain sat in 1938 and spoke of the Czechs as a faraway people about whom we know so little [and that led] to 'the deaths of over 45 million people.'" Thatcher was worried that an unopposed Argentina would "send a signal round the world with devastating consequences."

> No one can defeat us unless we first defeat ourselves.
> —Dwight Eisenhower

Thatcher sent a fleet of 98 ships and 8,000 soldiers to retake the Falklands. After conferring with her military experts, she declared she wanted victory with the minimal loss of soldiers. "Politicians must never make decisions in war without full consideration of what they mean to our forces on the ground," she said. In just over two months, British forces achieved victory, but 255 British soldiers died, and another 777 were wounded.

The victory restored Britain's national pride and Thatcher's popularity. The economy improved slightly and that helped her win reelection as prime minister in October 1982. She led her Tory Party to the largest victory in over thirty years, with 144 more seats than their opposition. Thatcher's resolve had carried the day. "If you have a sense of purpose and a sense of direction," she said, "I believe people will follow you. Democracy isn't just about deducing what the people want. Democracy is leading the people as well."

> You cannot lead from the crowd.
> —Margaret Thatcher

Leadership requires a sharp mind. Thatcher's father played a major role in cultivating her intellect. He went to the local library weekly and checked out nonfiction books for her to study. "As a result," she recalled, "I found myself reading books which girls of my age would not generally read. I soon knew what I liked—anything about politics and international affairs." She excelled in school and earned a scholarship to Oxford University. She wanted to participate in debate, but was prohibited because she was a woman.

When she graduated in 1947 with a degree in chemistry, Thatcher found employment as a research chemist, but her real interest was in politics. In 1950 she went back to Oxford to study law and was admitted to the bar in 1954. In 1951 she married Denis Thatcher and two years later gave birth to twins, Mark and Carol. Margaret and Denis forged a strong relationship.

"Being prime minister is a lonely job," Thatcher wrote. "[B]ut with Denis there I was never alone. What a man. What a husband. What a friend."

From the beginning of their marriage, Denis supported his young wife's political ambitions. "I was especially fortunate in being able to rely on Denis's income to hire a nanny to look after the children in my absences," Thatcher wrote. "I could combine being a good mother with being an effective professional woman, as long as I organized everything intelligently down to the last detail. It was not enough to have someone in to mind the children; I had to arrange my own time to ensure that I could spend a good deal of it with them."

Thatcher had been active in her local Conservative Party since the late 1940s. In 1950 she ran for a seat in the House of Commons when she was only 23. Thatcher was considered a long shot and was defeated, but gained valuable experience. By 1959, with years of experience as an attorney and in politics, she ran again for the House of Commons. This time she was the favorite, and she won.

Thatcher described herself as a "born worker" and moved up the Conservative Party hierarchy. She quickly introduced her first bill, which required local government councils to open their meetings to the public and press. She had the support of the Newspaper Editors' Guild, but left nothing to chance.

She wrote: "In the end, however, there is no substitute for one's own efforts. I wanted to get as many MPs (Members of Parliament) as possible to the House on a Friday (when most MPs have returned to their constituency) for the bill's second reading—this was the great hurdle. I have always believed in the impact of a personal handwritten letter—even from someone you barely know. So just before Second Reading I wrote 250 letters to Government backbenchers asking them to attend and vote on my measure."

Thatcher's bill was passed into law and a new star emerged on Britain's political stage.

To connect with the public, Thatcher believed that politicians should use "more honest language and simple illustrations to ensure that people understood their policies." She added, "There is no better way to clarify your own thinking than to try to explain it clearly to someone else."

Thatcher ran for leadership of the Conservative Party in 1975, when her candidate, Keith Joseph, was forced to withdraw from the race after making some insensitive remarks in a speech. Thatcher was opposed to the leading Conservative candidate, former Prime Minister Ted Heath, because he had abandoned his conservative principles and changed course in the face of opposition. Thatcher had served in his cabinet as Education Secretary.

"I heard that Keith Joseph was not going to run against Ted (Heath)," Thatcher recalled. "Someone had to. I said to Keith, 'If you are not, I shall.' There was no hesitation, there was no doubt, there has been no doubt since. It might have put me on the backbenches for life, or out. I did not know. But the one thing I seemed to have was the power to make a decision when a decision had to be made." Her chances of winning were considered a long shot. When Thatcher told Heath that she'd be opposing him, he said, without looking up from his desk, "You'll lose."

Thatcher won the election and at age 48 became the first woman to head one of England's major political parties. She came to the prime minister's office as a staunch anticommunist who believed in open markets and international law. She aligned herself with a fellow conservative, Ronald Reagan. Together, they formed a 1980s partnership that brought back memories of the one shared by Franklin Roosevelt and Winston Churchill.

Thatcher and Reagan first met in London in 1975 when he was governor of California. He recalled that first meeting, telling British journalist Hugo Young, author of *Iron Lady*, "[Thatcher] was extremely well-informed, but she was firm, decisive, and she had targets in mind of where [America and Britain] should be going. I was just greatly impressed."

The Soviet Union first gave Thatcher the nickname "The Iron Lady," while she was still leader of the Conservative Party. "In 1976," Hugo Young wrote, "The Russians designated her the Iron Lady after two speeches she made, announcing with a ferocity that long predated the presidency of Ronald Reagan her militant hostility to the communist empire and all its works. Yet she did not stereotype all Soviet leaders as robotic copies of each other programmed to Soviet communist dogma. When she first met Mikhail Gorbachev in 1984, she quickly got the attention of the free world when she said, "I like Mr. Gorbachev; we can do business together."

"I spotted him because I was searching for someone like him," Thatcher later said. "And I was confident that such a person could exist, even within that totalitarian structure."

As prime minister, Thatcher rose at 6:30 A.M. and usually retired at 1:00 A.M. When choosing people for her cabinet, Thatcher looked for more than just ability. "Goodness is not to be underrated as a qualification for those considered for powerful positions," she wrote. Thatcher was honest enough to see her own faults as well: "I am often impatient with people . . . in a broader sense, patience is required if a policy for long-term change is to work," she wrote in her book *Path to Power*.

She believed that with power comes trust from the people, which must be upheld. Thatcher could be honest about England's past failings. She visited Czechoslovakia in 1988 and addressed the Federal Assembly in Prague in her official capacity as prime minister: "We failed you in 1938 when a disastrous policy of appeasement allowed Hitler to extinguish your independence. Churchill was quick to repudiate the Munich Agreement, but we still remember it with shame."

She visited Czechoslovakia again in 1999, to celebrate the tenth anniversary of the fall of communism there, and to dedicate a statue of Winston Churchill. In a speech to several thousand people, she said: "I am very glad that you have found a place for this new statue. It will remind you here, as every generation has to be reminded—and amid all this beauty—that the price of freedom can be high, and that it may indeed require the sacrifice of 'blood, toil, tears and sweat.' This statue of Sir Winston Churchill will also remind you, as it reminds me, of something else—that liberty must never be allowed to perish from the earth; it must endure forever."

As the longest serving British prime minister in the twentieth century, and second longest in her nation's history, Thatcher relied on what she called, "Thatcher's law: No matter how well prepared you are, the unexpected happens. How you cope then remains, of course, the real test."

In 1999, *Time* magazine recognized Thatcher as one of the twenty most important political figures of the twentieth century. In the magazine *British*, historian Paul Johnson wrote of Thatcher: "The world enters the twenty-first century and the third millennium a wiser place, owing in no small part to the daughter of a small shopkeeper, who proved that nothing is more effective than willpower allied to a few clear, simple and workable ideas." Author Hugo Young wrote: "Margaret Thatcher is the most famous British leader since Winston Churchill."

In the end, Thatcher always had clear direction for herself because of her unwavering principles. "I am a conviction politician," she said. "The Old Testament prophets didn't merely say: 'Brothers, I want consensus.' They said: 'This is my faith and vision. This is what I passionately believe. If you believe it too, then come with me.'"

How to Be Like Margaret Thatcher

1. Know yourself and decide what you stand for.

Amid pressure to change her policies, Prime Minister Thatcher stayed true to herself. "I will not change just to court popularity," she once said in a speech to her fellow Tory Party members. Thatcher resisted pressure from her own Conservative Party and stuck to her values. "The lady's not for turning," she said.

2. Learn from the past.

Thatcher was a student of history, especially World War II. "My life . . . was transformed by the Second World War. . . . I drew from the failure of appeasement the lesson that aggression must always be firmly resisted," she said.

3. Follow your heart.

Thatcher was trained as a chemist, but went back to school to become a lawyer. Her law background led to her political career.

4. Combine your career and family life.

"I could combine being a good mother with being an effective professional woman, as long as I organized everything intelligently down to the last detail. It was not enough to have someone in to mind the children; I had to arrange my own time to ensure that I could spend a good deal of it with them," Thatcher said.

5. Be responsible.

Depend on yourself because you are the only person

you have control of. "In the end, however, there is no substitute for one's own efforts," Thatcher remarked.

6. **Write personal notes and letters.**

"I have always believed in the impact of a personal handwritten letter—even from someone you barely know," Thatcher wrote.

7. **Speak clearly.**

Thatcher said she used "more honest language and simple illustrations to ensure that people understood. . . . There is no better way to clarify your own thinking than to try to explain it clearly to someone else."

8. **Be open-minded.**

The staunch anticommunist Thatcher, whom the Soviets nicknamed the "Iron Lady," immediately recognized that Mikhail Gorbachev was a different type of Soviet leader. "I spotted [Gorbachev]," she said, "because I was searching for someone like him. And I was confident that such a person could exist, even within that totalitarian structure."

9. **Be patient.**

Thatcher was honest enough to see her own faults: "I am often impatient with people . . . in a broader sense, patience is required if a policy for long-term change is to work," she wrote.

SANDRA DAY O'CONNOR
b. 1930

VALUES

Each one of us will be a leader at some time in our lives. Whether we lead a family, a group of friends, a larger group, or a major segment of society, each of us will act in ways to influence others.

—*Sandra Day O'Connor*

andra Day O'Connor is the first woman Supreme Court justice of the United States, and one of the most influential justices in history. O'Connor graduated from Stanford Law School third in her class in 1952 and expected to practice as an attorney. But she soon discovered that her credentials, while impressive, were not going to be enough to land her the position she wanted.

She received just one job offer from a law firm, as a legal secretary, O'Connor recalled in an interview. "I discovered that none of the law firms in California, where I was living, would give me an interview. And I learned that none of them had hired a woman as a lawyer and they didn't plan to. That was a huge shock. . . . that was an obstacle."

She approached the problem logically. "It wasn't an emotional issue," O'Connor said. "[I]t was trying to get a job as a lawyer, which was a very practical issue. I had heard that the district attorney in San Mateo County, California, had once had a woman lawyer on his staff, so I went to see him and asked him if he would hire me. He said 'Well, I'd just be pleased to, except I don't have an office and I don't have a vacancy.' I spent a couple of months trying to persuade him that he needed me . . . and that I would sit in his secretary's office if she'd have me, and that I'd work for nothing if that's what it took. Finally, he hired me."

Persistence produced her first job. Merit would win O'Connor her last one. In July 1981, President Ronald Reagan nominated O'Connor, then a judge on the Arizona Court of Appeals, to fill the vacant seat on the United States Supreme Court. The U.S. Senate unanimously confirmed her by a vote of 99–0, and when she took her oath of office on September 25, 1981, O'Connor became the first woman Supreme Court justice in the history of the United States.

Months earlier, Reagan administration Attorney General William French Smith contacted O'Connor about her potential nomination. O'Connor recalled Smith's call with humor in her 2003 book, *The Majesty of the Law: Reflections of a Supreme Court Justice.* "In 1989 I had the pleasure of returning to the law firm that offered me a secretarial position on the occasion of its one hundredth birthday—and recounting that story to the assembled partners and guests. I also told them that, in 1981, one of their former partners, William French Smith, who was then attorney general of the United States, telephoned me in Arizona to ask whether I could go to Washington, D.C., to discuss a position there. Naturally, knowing of his long association with that law firm, I assumed it was a secretarial position. But was it secretary of commerce or secretary of labor?"

The road to the Supreme Court started with the many life lessons O'Connor learned growing up on her family's 198,000-acre cattle ranch, the Lazy B, on the Arizona–New Mexico border. At an early age, she learned how to ride horses and perform other ranch skills. O'Connor's parents, Harry and Ada Mae Day, were her mentors and role models. They gave her, she recalled, "A curiosity. A need to do your job, and do it well." But they also told her, "Don't expect praise, and don't mess it up."

> *For the world of work, it's do your best with every job you have, however small. It may be unimportant, it may be a nothing sort of a job, but do your best with it. And I think if you do that, people notice and it leads to something better.*
> —Sandra Day O'Connor

By age four, Ada Mae had taught O'Connor to read. "[My mother] was a patient and loving mother," wrote O'Connor in her bestselling book, *Lazy B*. "She read endlessly to all three of her children. [My father] never talked down to his children; he spoke to us as adults and wanted to know our thoughts and views. The value of hard work and honest, fair dealing were drilled into us constantly."

During her childhood, O'Connor learned, from a nursery rhyme, one of the most important life lessons she would rely on as an adult: "Good, better, best. Never rest until good be better, and better be best."

> *We pay a price when we deprive children of the exposure to the values, principles, and education they need to make them good citizens.*
> —Sandra Day O'Connor

She learned about sacrifice at age six. The Lazy B wasn't close enough to any adequate schools, so her parents were forced to send Sandra to live with her maternal grandmother in El Paso, Texas, for each school year until she graduated from high school. Ada Mae recalled, "We missed her terribly, and she missed us. . . . but there was no other way for her to get a good education."

In 1954, after serving as a county attorney in San Mateo, Sandra moved to West Germany with her husband, John O'Connor, then an army officer and lawyer, when he was transferred there. She found work as a civilian lawyer with the Quartermaster Corps. When they returned to Arizona two years later, they started a family and by 1962 had three sons—Scott, Brian and Jay. Her commitment to public service, inspired by a Stanford professor, led O'Connor to find a way to contribute to society, even as a full-time mother.

Between 1960 and 1965, O'Connor first served the Republican Party as a county precinct committee member, legislative district chair and as a member of the Maricopa County Republican Committee.

O'Connor raised her children to school age while putting her career on hold, and had no regrets about doing so. "In the long run, nothing was lost. . . . The joy of having our children is one that lasts a lifetime—far beyond one's professional career," O'Connor wrote. "[Many women] discover that they actually can reenter the profession and they can make up for lost ground."

From 1965 to 1969, O'Connor served as an Arizona assistant attorney general. In 1969, she was chosen to fill her district's vacant state senate seat. O'Connor was only thirty-nine and was paid only $6,000 a year, but she was doing the work she enjoyed and found fulfilling. "I have had an interest in helping to try to make my community, my faith, my nation, a better place," she said. "It is the individual who can and does make a difference even in this increasingly populous, complex world of ours. The individual can make things happen."

O'Connor threw herself into her new position with her customary zeal. "I devoted my whole life to it," she said. She was meticulous in drafting legislation and relentless in supporting her points with facts. "My approach as a legislator," she wrote, "was to try to develop as much background knowledge and expertise as possible in the subject areas of the legislation, and to develop community contacts that would provide the necessary public support for my positions. I also made efforts to entertain at my home all my colleagues at least once each legislative session, to try to keep our inevitable disagreements 'agreeable.'"

By 1973 O'Connor had won the respect of her Republican colleagues to such a degree that they elected her senate majority leader. However, her love was the law, so O'Connor ran for a judge seat, emphasizing her commitment to law and order. She was elected to the Maricopa County Superior Court of Arizona in 1974.

On the bench, O'Connor demonstrated her perseverance, attention to detail and no-nonsense attitude. Peter Huber, who worked at the U.S. Supreme Court as a law clerk for O'Connor, wrote in his book, *Sandra Day O'Connor*, of her days on the Superior Court bench: "Lawyers who appeared before O'Connor recall her as a 'formidable' judge. She expected the attorneys in her courtroom to be vigorous, well-prepared representatives of their clients; she also expected them to be as hard-working and knowledgeable about the law as she was. And that, said the lawyers, was asking a lot. 'She frequently knew more about a case from having reviewed the file than the lawyers did,' said one observer." Huber also quotes Alice Benheim, a Phoenix attorney who worked with O'Connor: "You didn't want to go in there if you weren't prepared, if you hadn't filed the papers when you were supposed to, if you hadn't researched your case properly, if you came in there on an

> *I have a certain curiosity about how things work.*
> —Sandra Day O'Connor

argument without any authority and tried to snow her."

In 1979 there was speculation that O'Connor was running for governor, but instead she was appointed to the Arizona Court of Appeals. After eighteen months, the Arizona State Bar Association rated O'Connor very highly for her detailed and thoughtful opinions. In 1980, candidate Ronald Reagan made a campaign promise to appoint a woman to the U.S. Supreme Court. When Justice Potter Stewart announced his retirement in June 1981, President Reagan had his opportunity.

"Without a doubt," Reagan said in announcing O'Connor's nomination, "the most awesome appointment a president can make is to the United States Supreme Court. . . . That is not to say I would appoint a woman merely to do so. That would not be fair to women, nor to future generations of all Americans whose lives are so deeply affected by decisions of the court. Rather, I pledged to appoint a woman who meets the very high standards I demand of all court appointees."

In her opening statement to the U.S. Senate before her confirmation hearings, O'Connor paid homage to those women whose hard work and struggles made her appointment possible. "As the first woman to be nominated as a Supreme Court justice," she said, "I am particularly honored, but I happily share the honor with millions of American women of yesterday and today whose abilities and conduct have given me this opportunity for service."

As the confirmation hearings progressed, O'Connor made it clear to the committee that as a Supreme Court justice she would make rulings based on the individual merits of each case. She would not be held hostage to a conservative ideology, in spite of her political leanings. "I do not believe that as a nominee I can tell you how I might vote on a particular issue which may come before the court," she said. "[T]o do so would mean that I have prejudged the matter or have morally committed myself to a certain position."

Republican Senator Jeremiah Denton tried repeatedly to get O'Connor to comment on how she'd vote on abortion issues that could come before the court, but she stuck to her stated principle. Chairman Joseph Biden informed Denton that his time was up, but he'd give him another fifteen minutes if that would help. "I do not know whether another month would do, Mr. Chairman," Denton said.

During her years on the Supreme Court, O'Connor, a conservative, has shown a judicial independence. She is particularly concerned with protecting the rights of the individual. "Society as a whole . . . benefits immeasurably from a climate in which all persons, regardless of race or gender, may have the opportunity to earn respect, responsibility, advancement and remuneration based on ability," she said.

O'Connor accepted the responsibility of being a role model to women because she was the first woman to sit on the Supreme Court. She received many letters from women who expressed their pride and who were inspired to believe that they, too, could attain any position for which they were qualified. "Part of my time is spent dealing with a mass of correspondence," O'Connor wrote. "Many letters are from schoolchildren who want information from me or about me. I do the best I can to process and answer these."

O'Connor understood the value of role models. She also wrote: "It mattered a great deal to me as a young woman lawyer that another Arizona woman was on my state's highest court, and that she showed an interest in the progress of other women in the legal profession."

Her boundless energy is a big part of her success, she has claimed. While that may be a natural gift, she keeps it ignited by staying intellectually curious. "I hope, and I think, I'm still learning things every day," she has said. O'Connor has always been physically active, playing golf and tennis, and skiing. When she joined the court, she organized early-morning aerobics classes for female court

> *The appointment of a woman to the Supreme Court of the United States opened many doors to young women all across the country.*
> —Sandra Day O'Connor

employees and continues with them today in her seventies. "I'm more productive with my work when I feel good physically."

When O'Connor was faced with a breast cancer diagnosis in 1988, she worked up to the day of her surgery. She returned to work ten days later and made a commitment not to miss any oral arguments during her recovery. O'Connor scheduled her debilitating chemotherapy treatments on Fridays, allowing her the weekend to recuperate, making it possible for her to be present during oral arguments. Peter Huber wrote that "Characteristically . . . she treated her illness not as a catastrophe but as a challenge."

O'Connor treats her staff with appreciation and generosity. She often buys them Mexican lunches and brings them on field trips to such places as the National Arboretum, the Folger Library and the Smithsonian Institute.

O'Connor has never viewed herself as a woman judge, but a judge who happens to be a woman. "This should be our aspiration," she wrote, "that, whatever our gender or background, we all may become wise—wise through our different struggles and different victories, wise through work and play, wise through profession and family."

She concluded an interview with her best advice for success: "Never stop learning. Never stop trying to help."

How to Be Like Sandra Day O'Connor

1. Never take no for an answer.

Upon graduating from Stanford Law School, O'Connor found that no law firms in California were interested in hiring a female attorney. O'Connor knew the district attorney in San Mateo County, California, had once hired a female lawyer, so she approached him. "I spent a couple of months trying to persuade him that he needed me," O'Connor said, "and that I would sit in his secretary's office if she'd have me, and that I'd work for nothing if that's what it took. Finally, he hired me."

2. Keep working to improve yourself.

O'Connor said a childhood nursery rhyme sums up one of her most important life lessons: "Good, better, best. Never rest until good be better, and better be best." Her most important life lessons have been to "Never stop learning. Never stop trying to help."

3. Look for ways to contribute to society.

"I have had an interest in helping to try to make my community, my faith, my nation, a better place," O'Connor has said.

4. Find the time to contribute to society, even if your time is limited.

While still a stay-at-home mother, O'Connor first served the Republican Party in different administrative and legislative positions. She was rewarded for her work when chosen to fill her district's vacant state senate seat. Her political and judicial career was thus set in motion.

5. Always be prepared.

As a legislator and judge, O'Connor has been recognized for being aware of all the details.

6. Be a role model.

O'Connor accepted the sphere of influence that came with being the first woman Supreme Court justice. She understood the pride women and girls felt, the message her appointment sent and her obligation to the legacy. "Part of my time is spent dealing with a mass of correspondence," she has said. "Many letters are from schoolchildren who want information from me or about me. I do the best I can to answer these."

7. Stay physically fit.

Today, in her seventies, O'Connor still stays physically active. She has always enjoyed golf, tennis and skiing. When she joined the court in 1981, she organized early-morning aerobics classes for female court employees that continue to this day. "I'm more productive with my work when I feel good physically," she has said.

OPRAH WINFREY
b. 1954

SINCERITY

Don't complain about what you don't have. Use what you've got. To do less than your best is a sin.

—*Oprah Winfrey*

**O**prah Winfrey has distinguished herself as the host of *The Oprah Winfrey Show* and as a prominent businesswoman and philanthropist. She has also been a strong voice for the rights and protection of children.

Life didn't start out easily for Oprah. She was born into rural poverty and into a South where many black people were so emotionally beaten down by the white racist status quo that they came to accept lack of opportunity as a way of life. "Nobody," Winfrey said, "had any clue that my life could be anything but working in some factory or a cotton field in Mississippi. Nobody." Except Winfrey. From a young age, she resolved that her life would be better than that.

Oprah was the daughter of an unwed sixteen-year-old, Vernita Lee, who wasn't ready to be a mother. For the first six years of her life, Oprah was raised by her grandmother, Hattie Mae Lee, and her grandfather, Earless, on their small farm in Kosciusko, Mississippi. Hattie Mae taught her discipline and to embrace God, and she became the first positive influence in Winfrey's life. "I am what I am because of my grandmother," Winfrey has said. "My strength. My sense of reasoning. Everything. All that was set by the time I was six."

When she was six, Oprah went to live with her mother, who was working as a maid and living in a poor section of

Milwaukee, Wisconsin. Vernita had two more children and little time to take care of Oprah. She had maintained contact with Winfrey's father, Vernon, and when Oprah was eight years old, Vernita called him to see if he would take care of her. Vernon had met Vernita when he was in the military. He was now settled in Nashville, Tennessee, where he had a job as a maintenance worker. He and his wife, Zelma, took Oprah into their home.

> *I feel strongly that my life is to be used as an example to show people what can be done.*
> —Oprah Winfrey

Because of his military background, perhaps, Vernon was a loving but strict father. He expected Oprah to get good grades in school. He and Zelma, who took the time to teach Oprah multiplication tables, were both very religious and further reinforced that value in her. She had a good and stable life, but in the summer of 1963, Vernita asked to have Oprah for the summer—and wound up not allowing her to return to Vernon.

The adversity that Oprah Winfrey would have to overcome began for her at the tender age of nine, when she was raped by a nineteen-year-old cousin. He warned her that she had better not tell anyone. Years later Winfrey said, "I was a child who did not tell, because I did not feel that I would have been validated." Tragically, that was only the beginning of the destruction of young Oprah's childhood. A boyfriend of Vernita also sexually abused her, and so did an uncle. This sexual abuse continued for five years.

Like many innocent victims, Oprah Winfrey blamed herself. Abuse of any kind robs a person of self-worth, and Winfrey came to believe that she must have done something to deserve the immoral treatment she endured. Years later, in

1991, Winfrey realized that of course she wasn't to blame. "The truth is the child is never to blame," she said. "It took me thirty-seven years to figure that out."

The abuse Winfrey experienced manifested itself outwardly. Her behavior became out of control, and she was promiscuous in her early teens. Winfrey felt frustrated and disappointed that nobody protected her: "There were people, certainly, around me who were aware of [the abuse] . . . but they did nothing." Vernita eventually reached the point where she felt she couldn't live with Oprah and attempted to put her in a home for wayward girls. As fate would have it, the home had no space for her. Vernita then called Vernon to ask him again to take their daughter. Vernon agreed.

At fourteen years of age, Oprah showed up on Vernon's doorstep. She was pregnant and eventually gave birth prematurely to a baby boy, who died shortly thereafter. Vernon again began the process of instilling discipline in Oprah. He told her she could live with him only if she obeyed his rules, which included a strictly enforced curfew. "When my father took me, it changed the course of my life," Winfrey said. "I was definitely headed for a career as a juvenile delinquent. He saved me. He knew what he wanted and expected, and he would take nothing less."

One of the things Vernon stressed again was education. Oprah herself had always loved to read, but she was only earning Cs in her classes. That wouldn't do, Vernon said, because she was capable of doing better work in school. Oprah rededicated herself to her studies and became an honor roll student. "No person has had a greater influence in extolling the importance and value of a good education than my father," she said in 1987. "It is because of him that I am where I am today."

While the importance of Vernon in his daughter's life cannot be minimized, neither can Winfrey's own emotional strength. Because of the abuse Winfrey suffered as a child, she certainly could have continued to rebel. As a victim of abuse, she had the background that has led countless others to drug and alcohol addictions. But Oprah Winfrey wasn't looking to check out from life; she was looking to lead a productive and fulfilling life. Her optimistic spirit never left her. Vernon's love and guidance, together with her strong religious convictions, helped her to grow into the person she is today. "There's only one way I've been able to survive being raped, molested . . . only one way to cope with fears of pregnancy, my mother on welfare . . . my faith in God got me through," Oprah Winfrey said.

> *I act as if everything depends upon me and pray as if everything depends on God.*
> —Oprah Winfrey

Winfrey also took responsibility for the outcome of her life. What was done to her by men in her life was immoral. "You lose your childhood when you've been abused," she said. But having been dealt adversity, Winfrey still felt it was up to her to overcome it and conquer it. "I think of myself as somebody who from an early age knew I was responsible for myself," she said, "and I had to make good."

> *Don't depend on forces outside of yourself to get ahead.*
> —Oprah Winfrey

Winfrey's career path took shape during her senior year in high school. She was working to raise money for the March of Dimes through a walkathon. She needed businesses to sponsor her, and she approached a local black television station in Nashville—WVOL. One of the disc jockeys, John Heidelberg, agreed to sponsor Winfrey. After she returned from the walkathon to collect the sponsorship money, Heidelberg, who was impressed by Winfrey's manner, asked her to tape an audition for the station. Winfrey had been active in public speaking in church and speech tournaments in school. WVOL's general manager, Clarence Kilcrease, needed part-time announcers, and after listening to Winfrey, he hired her.

Still only sixteen and in high school, Winfrey began earning $100 a week reading news on the air. She continued her work at WVOL while attending Tennessee State University. Her good work eventually helped her, in 1973, to become Nashville's first African-American and first woman anchor at WTVF-TV, a CBS affiliate.

By 1976, station WJZ-TV, an ABC affiliate in Baltimore, Maryland, wooed and hired Winfrey as an anchor while launching a major advertising campaign trumpeting her arrival. But within nine months she was demoted from anchor to reporter. However, the very problems she had in Baltimore as an anchor would prove to be her great strength in a talk show setting: Winfrey had a compassion she just couldn't, and maybe didn't want to, hide. "I really was not cut out for the news," Winfrey said. "I'd have to fight back the tears if a story was too sad. I just did not have the detachment."

She didn't have it in Nashville either, recalled WTVF-TV news director Chris Clark, as quoted in *Oprah Winfrey,* by Belinda Friedrich. "The problem with [Oprah] was that she was just too people-oriented to be a hard-nosed reporter. If she went out and covered somebody's house burning down, instead of coming back and writing the story like a good reporter would, she would be working the phone lines trying to get them clothes, or help, or worrying about it."

A fateful decision was made in April 1977, when WJZ decided to use Winfrey as cohost of their morning talk show, *People Are Talking*. Winfrey recognized immediately that this was the format that her personality and talent was best suited for. "The minute the first show was over, I thought 'Thank God, I've found what I was meant to do.' It's like breathing to me."

A touching story of Winfrey's compassion was told by Dick Maurice, entertainment editor of the *Las Vegas Sun,* in Friedrich's book. Before her show, Maurice was talking to Winfrey about his father, a World War II veteran who, due to battlefield injuries, had been left with disfiguring scars on his face. "I was telling [Oprah] how kids would call me the son of Frankenstein," he recalled, "and how my father used to drop me off two blocks from school, rather than bear the embarrassment. . . . I looked over and tears were coming down [Oprah's] face. . . . She had a special quality about her that made her unique. There was this way she had of looking at you, and you felt that, when you were talking to her, the only person she was thinking about was you. It was a look in her eyes. You could see a soul there."

> *I believe that you tend to create your own blessings. You have to prepare yourself so that when opportunity comes, you're ready.*
> —Oprah Winfrey

When Debra DiMaio, a former associate producer who worked with Winfrey at WJZ, moved to Chicago to work on a morning talk show, *A.M. Chicago* on WLS-TV, she suggested that Winfrey audition to be the new host of the show. Winfrey had now been cohosting *People Are Talking* for six years. Station manager Dennis Swanson thought her audition tape was "sensational," and far above those of the other candidates. While Swanson was ready to hire her, Winfrey had her doubts about whether she was right for the job or the job was right for her.

"I would be the first black host of this show in a city known at the time for racial volatility," Winfrey said, recalling her feelings. In addition, she was already a success in the Baltimore market. Oprah Winfrey's show was even beating the number-one rated national talk show at that time, *The Donahue Show*, hosted by Phil Donahue. Further intimidating her was the fact that Donahue filmed his show in Chicago.

She said to Swanson, "I'm black and that's not going to change. I'm overweight and that's probably not going to change either." Winfrey recalled his response, as quoted in *The Right Words at the Right Time*, by Marlo Thomas. "You have a gift, a way of connecting with people," Swanson said. "Donahue is killing us [ratings-wise] every day. . . . We don't expect you to beat him, of course. Just go on the air and be yourself."

"Those words freed me and set the trajectory for what unfolded to become *The Oprah Winfrey Show*," she said. "I felt completely uninhibited to speak with my own voice. To create my own path."

Winfrey's first *A.M. Chicago* show was broadcast on January 2, 1984. Its 9:00 A.M. time slot was the same as *The Donahue Show*. In just four weeks, Winfrey—the student who'd been studying Donahue for years—was now besting the teacher ratings-wise in the Chicago market. "I watched Phil every day to see what I could learn. I learned a lot. [For example]—how to listen and interrupt only when necessary."

Winfrey's genius lay in just being herself. Her honesty and compassion won over her audiences. "My head hurts when I have to be in any situation where people are being phony," she has said. "So if I can't be myself and take my shoes off when my feet hurt, then I'm not going to do very well." *Ebony* magazine has called Winfrey's interview style "effusive, off-the-cuff." Winfrey says, "I ask the questions that they [the audience] want to know, because I also want to know them."

> *Doing this show is my way of fulfilling myself ... It is a ministry, and it does what a ministry should do: uplift people, encourage them, and give them a sense of hope about themselves.*
> —Oprah Winfrey

Her audience also could see that Winfrey was engaged in something she loved when doing her show. "I'm a person who lives my life with great passion, and I think that comes across on camera," she said. "I believe you're here to live your life with passion. Otherwise, you're just traveling through the world blindly—and there's no point in that."

By 1986, the success of Winfrey and *A.M. Chicago* led to a syndication deal with King World Productions, Inc. to take Winfrey national. On September 8, 1986, Winfrey and her show, newly titled *The Oprah Winfrey Show,* made its national debut. Winfrey's contract with King World called for her to receive 24 percent of the show's earnings, which were projected at $125 million in the first year. Oprah Winfrey, who had been making the substantial salary of $200,000 annually, would make around $30 million in that first year. She quickly became one of the richest people in the United States. Today, Winfrey's net worth is estimated at around one billion dollars. But the pursuit of money was never her objective, only the pursuit of quality.

"Part of the reason why I am as successful as I have been [is] because success wasn't the goal. The process was. I wanted to do good work," Winfrey said.

In 1988, Winfrey was named Broadcaster of the Year by the International Television and Radio Society. She was the youngest person ever to win the award and joined the company of legends such as Walter Cronkite, David Brinkley, Barbara Walters and Ted Koppel.

"I'd like to set the record straight and let people know I really am not defined by dollars," Winfrey said in 1987. "I would do what I'm doing even if I weren't getting paid. And I was doing this when I was getting paid much, much less. At my first job in broadcasting, my salary was $100 a week. But I was just as excited about making that amount of money and doing what I love to do as I am now."

With her newfound wealth, Oprah Winfrey gave back generously to her family. She made it possible for her mother, Vernita, never to have to work again. Vernon, owner of a barbershop in Nashville, wanted to keep working and really didn't want anything from Winfrey, but she still showered him with some wonderful gifts. Oprah Winfrey's employees have enjoyed her extreme generosity too.

> *If money is your motivation, forget it.*
> —Oprah Winfrey

Giving back to society in a meaningful way has also distinguished Oprah Winfrey. To help fulfill her commitment to education, Winfrey set up ten scholarships worth $77,000 each at her old college, Tennessee State University. Winfrey put the scholarships in the name of Vernon Winfrey, in honor of him. She has also provided money to Morehouse College in Atlanta, the Chicago Academy of Arts and Chicago's public schools. "Education is freedom," Winfrey said, "and that is one way you can make a huge difference in someone's life." Additionally, in 1997 Winfrey started Oprah's Angel Network, which encourages viewers to make financial contributions and do volunteer work for those in need.

To Winfrey, reading goes hand in hand with education. As a little girl she could almost always be found with a book in her hand. "I was treated as though something was wrong with me because I wanted to read all the time," she said. Reading brought her comfort and perspective, especially when she was young and troubled. "Books showed me there were possibilities in life, that there were actually people like me living in a world I could not only aspire to but attain. Reading gave me hope. For me, it was the open door."

To share the value of reading and the worth of books with her audience, Winfrey started her own book club in 1996. It lasted six years and in that time, all of the forty-eight books that she said she felt "absolutely compelled" to recommend became instant bestsellers. It was another testament to the trust that she'd built with her audience. (In February 2003, Winfrey announced she was reviving the club, this time to focus on the classics of literature.)

To have more control over her product, Winfrey founded Harpo Productions in 1988 and bought her show and a production studio in Chicago. She was now producing *The Oprah Winfrey Show*, in addition to other projects. Winfrey became just the third woman—and the first African-American—to own a film studio.

As the chief executive officer of her company, Oprah Winfrey set out to be fair with her employees while still

> *Seek harmony and compassion in your business and personal life.*
> —Oprah Winfrey

insisting on excellence from them. "To me, one of the most important things about being a good manager is to rule with a heart," Oprah Winfrey said. "You have to know the business, but you also have to know what's at the heart of the business, and that's the people. People matter."

In keeping with her first priority to turn out a quality show, Winfrey set out at Harpo Productions to "create an environment so stimulating that people will love coming to work." From the start, she was called a perfectionist. Winfrey refused to allow complacency to set in even though she had the number-one rated talk show and had won numerous Daytime Emmy Awards. In 1994 she decided that her topics, which had helped bring her to the top, were for the most part too frivolous. She wanted to do shows with more substance that made a difference in people's lives. "I want to use television not only to entertain," she said, "but to help people lead better lives. I realize now, more than ever, that the show is the best way to accomplish these goals."

> *The only thing greater than Oprah's accomplishments . . . is the size of her heart.*
> —Barbara Walters

Oprah Winfrey's gift for connecting with the audience is rooted in her honesty, and she refuses to compromise on that virtue. For example, while interviewing a guest about drug use in 1995, Winfrey admitted her own experience with drugs right on the air. She called it her "great shame." Winfrey said that when she was in her early twenties and in a relationship with a man who used crack cocaine, she also used the drug as a way to stay close to him. Because of her honesty and remorse, the confession didn't hurt her with her fans or the public. "I would have felt like a hypocrite," Winfrey said, "not saying [I had smoked cocaine], talking to people about baring their souls and standing there like I didn't know what they were talking about. . . . My heart was beating fast. I could see the tabloids before me. But I would have felt like a fraud if I hadn't said it. What I learned that day is that the truth really will set you free."

In 1990, the secret of

> *One of my greatest assets is knowing I'm no different from the viewer.*
> —Oprah Winfrey

Winfrey's teenage pregnancy and the subsequent death of her premature baby were revealed by her younger [by seven years] half-sister, Patricia Lee, who sold the story to the tabloids. Winfrey felt betrayed that such a private and painful personal matter came out in that way, and for money. For two years, Winfrey didn't speak to Patricia. Then, Winfrey decided it was time to talk as a family. She invited her mother, Vernita, and several other relatives to her farm for a weekend of working to understand the pain that each had caused the other. "I didn't feel I could continue to go on the air speaking to people about forgiveness," she said, "if I couldn't do it myself. There was a lot of pain, a lot of stuff let out. But I did it so that we could go on and live with each other."

Winfrey has used her celebrity and public platform for the public good. In early 1991, Angelica Mena, a four-year-old girl, was molested and then murdered by a man who was a convicted child abuser. Winfrey was especially outraged when she learned of the man's past criminal record. He had been convicted twice before of kidnapping and raping children.

He'd been sentenced to fifteen years in jail and was released after serving only seven years. "I did not know the child, never heard her laughter," Winfrey said. "But I vowed that night to do something, to take a stand for the children of this country."

Winfrey hired former Illinois governor James Thompson, who was a practicing attorney, to draft a proposed law that would create a national registry of people convicted of child abuse. This would make it possible for anyone who was hiring a person to work around children to easily check their background to see if they had ever been convicted of any form of child abuse.

Winfrey lobbied hard for the bill, which was sponsored by Senator Joseph Biden of Delaware. She testified before the Senate Judiciary Committee about the need for it. As a victim of child abuse herself, she knew and explained how defenseless a child is at the hands of a predator. In December 1993, the National Child Protection Act, which was nicknamed the "Oprah Bill," became law.

Children have always been close to Winfrey's heart. "If I could change just one thing, I would stop people from beating their kids," she has said. "Not just beating, but molesting kids, verbally abusing kids, neglecting kids. The dishonor of children is the single worst problem in this country. If we ended it, there would be an incredible ripple effect on society. From the thousands of shows I have done over the past ten years, I see that the way people were treated as children causes them to grow up and behave certain

> *I think the ones who survive in life do it by hammering at it one day at a time. . . . that puts you in the best place tomorrow.*
> —Oprah Winfrey

ways as adults. I see it as the root of almost every problem in our society."

Sojourner Truth and Harriet Tubman are numbered among Winfrey's role models. Since childhood, she's been keenly aware and proud of her black heritage. She has acted in movies that deal with the subject, such as *The Color Purple* in 1986, for which she received an Oscar nomination for Best Supporting Actress. Winfrey has also produced movies dealing with the subject of black heritage, such as *Beloved*, in which she also starred in the lead role. In some ways, Winfrey has said, she feels her voice is an extension of and a bridge to what Sojourner and Harriet began.

Oprah Winfrey has said she overcame what others perceived as her negatives to succeed. "They said I was black, female, and overweight. They said Chicago is a racist city and the talk-show formula was on its way out." Still, Winfrey has succeeded in areas where a black woman hasn't ever been able to before. She has pointed to her battle with her weight as an example that she succeeded and reached the top of her field without meeting the unrealistic expectations of the entertainment industry when it comes to ideal female body type.

Winfrey has become the most important kind of model: a role model. "The greatest contribution you can make to women's rights, to civil rights, is to be the absolute . . . best at what you do," she has said.

How to Be Like
Oprah Winfrey

1. **Don't let others define you or tell you what you can't do.**

   Oprah Winfrey said: "Nobody had any clue that my life could be anything but working in some factory or a cotton field in Mississippi. Nobody." For her entire life, people have been telling Winfrey what she can't do—and why. But Winfrey hasn't listened to them. Rather, she says, she listens to her own instincts. "Gut [instinct] is what got me where I am today," she said in 1998.

2. **Take responsibility for your life.**

   That doesn't mean you have to absolve others of wrongdoing if you've experienced that in your life. It just means you still have to overcome it. As a victim of sexual abuse, Oprah Winfrey had the triggers that have led countless others to drug and alcohol addictions. But Winfrey wasn't looking to check out from life; she was looking to lead a productive and fulfilling life. She took responsibility for how her life would turn out. "I think of myself as somebody who from an early age knew I was responsible for myself, and I had to make good," she said.

3. **Embrace God.**

   Oprah Winfrey said: "There's only one way I've been able to survive being raped, molested . . . only one way to cope with fears of pregnancy, my mother on welfare . . . my faith in God got me through." Reading the Bible has been part of Winfrey's everyday routine. She has said: "I act as if everything depends upon me and pray as if everything depends on God."

4. **Have compassion for others.**

Winfrey had a compassion she just couldn't, and maybe didn't want to, hide. While this was considered a "negative" for a news anchor by her bosses, it proved to be one of her great strengths as a talk show host.

5. **Study the competition.**

When Winfrey was starting out, Phil Donahue was the king of the talk shows. "I watched Phil every day to see what I could learn," she said.

6. **Just be yourself.**

Winfrey's genius lay in just being herself. She said, "My head hurts when I have to be in any situation where people are being phony. So if I can't be myself and take my shoes off when my feet hurt, then I'm not going to do very well."

7. **Live your life with passion.**

Winfrey's audience could see that from the start she was engaged in something she loved when she was doing her show. "I'm a person who lives my life with great passion, and I think that comes across on camera. . . . I believe you're here to live your life with passion. Otherwise, you're just traveling through the world blindly—and there's no point in that."

8. **Pursue quality in your work first—money will follow.**

Pursue the work you love, which allows you to do it to the best of your ability. It is only then that money will follow. Today, Winfrey's net worth is estimated at around one billion dollars, making her one of the wealthiest women in the world. But the pursuit of money was never her objective, only the pursuit of quality. "Part of the reason why I am as successful as I have been [is] because success wasn't the goal. The process was. I wanted to do good work," she said.

9. **Have a generous heart.**

After the murder of four-year-old Angelica Mena at the hands of a convicted child abuser, Winfrey hired former Illinois governor James Thompson to draft a law that would create a national registry of people convicted of child abuse. Winfrey then lobbied hard for it. In December 1993, the National Child Protection Act, which was nicknamed the "Oprah Bill," became law. Winfrey has also used her wealth to give her family a better quality of life and to help needy and worthy students attend college on scholarships, in addition to other numerous charitable causes. "Education is freedom, and that is one way you can make a huge difference in someone's life," she said.

10. **Read.**

As a little girl, Winfrey could almost always be found with a book in her hand. Reading brought her comfort and perspective, especially when she was young and troubled. "Books showed me there were possibilities in life, that there were actually people like me living in a world I could not only aspire to but attain. Reading gave me hope. For me, it was the open door."

11. **Continue to grow—personally and professionally.**

By 1990 Winfrey decided that her topics, which had

helped bring her to the top, were for the most part too frivolous. She wanted to do shows of more substance that made a difference in people's lives. By growing as a host, Winfrey has stayed influential and relevant. "I want to use television not only to entertain, but to help people lead better lives. I realize now, more than ever, that the show is the best way to accomplish these goals," she said.

12. **Guard against hypocrisy.**

In January 1995, during a show that dealt with a guest talking about her drug use, Winfrey admitted her own drug use when she was in her early twenties. She called it her "great shame." She said: "I would have felt like a hypocrite, not saying [I had smoked cocaine], talking to people about baring their souls and standing there like I didn't know what they were talking about." Regarding her relationship with her half-sister, Patricia Lee, who sold the tabloids the story of Winfrey's teenage pregnancy and her premature baby's subsequent death, Winfrey said: "I didn't feel I could continue to go on the air speaking to people about forgiveness if I couldn't do it myself. There was a lot of pain, a lot of stuff let out. But I did it so that we could go on and live with each other."

13. **Strive to be the best.**

"The greatest contribution you can make to women's rights, to civil rights, is to be the absolute . . . best at what you do," Winfrey said.

In 1989, in a speech to the American Women's Economic Development Corporation, Oprah Winfrey listed her personal ten commandments. This list appears in *Oprah Winfrey Speaks: Insight from the World's Most Influential Voice*, by Janet Lowe.

Oprah Winfrey's Ten Commandments for Success

1. Don't live your life to please others.
2. Don't depend on forces outside of yourself to get ahead.
3. Seek harmony and compassion in your business and personal life.
4. Get rid of the backstabbers—surround yourself only with people who will lift you higher.
5. Be nice.
6. Rid yourself of your addictions—whether they are food, alcohol, drugs or behavior habits.
7. Surround yourself with people who are as smart or smarter than you.
8. If money is your motivation, forget it.
9. Never hand over your power to someone else.
10. Be persistent in pursuing your dreams.

On May 30, 1997, Oprah Winfrey gave the commencement address to Wellesley College, in Wellesley, Massachusetts. "She told the graduates that she'd learned five important lessons that made her life better," Janet Lowe wrote. Winfrey said:

- Life is a journey. Everyday experiences will teach you who you really are.

- When people show you who they are, believe them the first time. This is especially helpful with men. Don't force them to beat you over the head with the message.

- Turn your wounds into wisdom. Everyone makes mistakes. They are just God's way of telling you you're moving in the wrong direction.

- Be grateful. Keep a daily journal of the things you are thankful for. It will keep you focused on the abundance in your life.

- Create the highest, grandest vision possible for your life because you become what you believe.

GOLDA MEIR
1898–1978

WISDOM

Anybody who believes in something without reservation, believes that this thing is right and should be, has the stamina to meet obstacles and overcome them.

—*Golda Meir*

**G**olda Meir helped found the state of Israel. She later served as the first female prime minister of a Middle Eastern country. The roots of Golda Meir's commitment to a Jewish homeland were planted when she was just a child.

She was born Golda Mabovits in Kiev, Ukraine. Her childhood was filled with memories of vicious anti-Semitic pogroms (from the Russian word for "devastation") that she and her fellow Jews were subjected to. "I didn't know then, of course, what a pogrom was," Meir wrote in her autobiography, "but I knew it had something to do with being Jewish and with the rabble that used to surge through town, brandishing knives and huge sticks, screaming 'Christ killers' as they looked for the Jews, and who were now going to do terrible things to me and to my family.

"I can remember how I stood on the stairs that led to the second floor, where another Jewish family lived, holding hands with their little daughter and watching our fathers trying to barricade the entrance by nailing boards of wood. That pogrom never materialized, but to this day I remember how scared I was. . . . and, above all, I remember being aware that this was happening to me because I was Jewish."

Those types of childhood experiences led Meir to an inescapable conclusion as an adult: "If one wanted to survive, one had to take effective action about it personally," she said.

In search of a better life for his family, Meir's father, Moshe, immigrated to the United States in 1903. By 1906 he'd saved enough money to bring over his wife, Golda and her older sister, Sheyna. The Mabovits family settled in Milwaukee, Wisconsin, and it was there that little Golda displayed the compassion and initiative she would become known for as an adult. At her elementary school, in the fourth grade, Golda made her first attempt as a fund-raiser when she saw children in need. The school was free, but it charged for textbooks. Some of the children's families couldn't afford them. "Obviously, someone had to do something to solve the problem," Meir wrote, echoing a theme of her life. At a public meeting that she organized, Meir tried to reach the heart of those who could donate money to help her needy classmates.

"I spoke about the need for all children to have textbooks whether they had money or not," Meir wrote. The fundraiser was successful, and she even wound up with her picture in the paper, along with an article about her accomplishment.

> I thought—and still think today—that teaching is the noblest and the most satisfying profession of all. A good teacher opens up the whole world for children, makes it possible for them to learn to use their minds and in many ways equips them for life.
>
> —Golda Meir

Meir's commitment to Zionism, the name of the movement for a Jewish homeland, grew even stronger through her teenage years. When she moved to Denver, Colorado, she lived with her older activist sister, Sheyna, and met many of her friends in the Zionist movement. Meir believed with all her heart that the Jewish people had to become "masters of their own fate." Soon she began to entertain thoughts about moving to Palestine in the Middle East, where the ancient home of Israel once existed. Palestine was then under control of the British. "I knew that I was not going to be a parlor Zionist," Meir said, "advocating settlement in Palestine for others—and I refused to join the Labor Zionist Party until I could make a binding decision."

After World War I, Jewish people in the Ukraine and Poland were victims of anti-Semitic pogroms led by Simon Petlyura, commander of the Ukrainian army. Entire Jewish communities were destroyed. Meir helped organize what turned out to be a very successful protest march in Milwaukee against the pogroms. It was during the march that Meir realized where she belonged. "However hard it might be for those who were dearest to me," she wrote, "I could no longer put off making up my mind about where I was going to live. Palestine, I felt, not parades in Milwaukee, was the only real, meaningful answer to Petlyura's murderous mobs. The Jews must have a land of their own again—and I must help build it. . . . by living and working there."

Meir's decision to go to Palestine reflected her philosophy about living. "Nothing in life just happens. It isn't enough to believe in something," she said. "You have to have the stamina to meet obstacles and overcome them, to struggle."

Activism in Meir's family was a way of life. She recalled that her family was always involved in different causes to try to help people. And it was Sheyna, who at the time was only fourteen, who set an example for the younger Meir to follow. Sheyna risked her life to become a member of the Socialist-Zionist movement while the family was living in Russia. From Sheyna, Golda learned an important lesson about conducting her life. "There is only one way to do anything: the right way," she wrote. "Sheyna was already a perfectionist at fifteen, a girl who lived according to the highest principles, whatever the price."

In Palestine, Meir and her husband, Morris Meyerson, lived on a small agricultural cooperative called a kibbutz. Morris had married Meir in Milwaukee, then reluctantly agreed with her wishes to settle in Palestine. Eventually, however, Morris grew unhappy with kibbutz life, and he and Meir moved to the city of Jerusalem. Morris found work as a bookkeeper and Meir settled into life as a wife and mother. They didn't have much, but that didn't bother Meir at all. What did bother her was not working toward the purpose for which she came to Palestine in the first place. "Instead of actively helping build the Jewish national home and working hard and produc- tively for it," Meir wrote, "I found myself cooped up in a tiny apartment in Jerusalem."

When she received an offer to become the secretary of the Women's Labor Council, called the *Moetzet*

> *Meir had no material-istic desires. She only longed to be of service: "I had never been particularly interest-ed in my immediate sur-roundings," she wrote, "as long as they were clean, neat, and reasonably attractive."*

Hapoalot, she jumped at the opportunity. The *Moetzet Hapoalot* was a branch of the General Federation of Jewish Labor called the *Histadrut.* Meir had entered the world of politics and now had a chance for "the kind of purposeful, interesting life for which I so yearned."

At around the same time, her marriage to Morris ended in divorce, although they remained close until his death. Meir stayed a devoted mother and was never away from her children, Sarah and Menachem, "even an hour more than was strictly necessary," she wrote.

In her efforts to first secure, and then sustain the Jewish homeland of Israel, Meir was willing to travel anywhere and lobby any person, organization or country on behalf of the cause. "We must miss no opportunity to explain to influential people what we want and what we are," Meir wrote to her sister, Sheyna.

Jewish resolve toward a homeland was, of course, seen as an absolute must because of the murder of six million Jewish people by the Nazis during the Holocaust that took place during World War II. There was also the lesson of Britain's 1939 White Paper. The White Paper severely limited Jewish immigration to Palestine. Thus many European Jews were denied entrance to Palestine and subsequently wound up being murdered in the Nazi death camps. It was a tragedy made even worse because Britain's actions defied sane reason. Meir struggled to understand the great British contradiction of fighting the oppressor and the oppressed.

"I suppose I must have tried a thousand times since 1939 to explain to myself—let alone to others—just how and why it happened that during the very years that the British stood with so much courage and determination against the Nazis. They were also able . . . to find the time, energy and resources to fight so long and as bitter a war against the admittance of Jewish refugees from the Nazis to Palestine. But I have still not found any rational explanation—and perhaps there is none," Meir wrote, getting to the heart of the matter as she always did.

Out of the White Paper tragedy, a clear lesson, soaked in the blood of millions of innocent victims, emerged for the

Zionists. "It was then that we all knew what many of us had always suspected," Meir wrote. "No foreign government (even one standing for democracy) could or would ever feel our agonies as we felt them, and no foreign government would ever put the same value on Jewish lives that we did."

When the British government refused to allow ships filled with Jewish refugees to enter Palestine in 1946, the refugees staged a hunger strike, and Meir joined them in a show of support. A British officer said to her, "Mrs. Meyerson, do you think for a moment that His Majesty's government will change its policy because you are not going to eat?" Meir replied with her customary brilliance for clarifying a situation: "No, I have no such illusions. If the death of six million didn't change government policy, I don't expect that my not eating will do so. But it will at least be a mark of solidarity."

The six million Jewish men, women and children murdered by the Nazis were always in the heart of Meir and her fellow Zionists. "In our darkest hours," she said, "it was the memory of their spirit that gave us heart, inspired us to go on and, above all, lent validity to our own refusal to be wiped out to make life easier for the rest

> Meir said of Nazi war criminal and mass murderer Adolf Eichmann, who was captured by Israel, tried, found guilty and hanged, that his trial and punishment "was not, in any sense, a question of revenge. As the Hebrew poet Bialik once wrote, not even the devil himself could dream up an adequate revenge for the death of a single child, but those who remained alive—and generations still unborn—deserve, if nothing else, [to know] in all its dreadful detail what was done to the Jews of Europe and by whom."

of the world. In the final analysis, it was the Jews of Europe, trapped, doomed and destroyed, who taught us once and for all that we must become the masters of our own undertaking, and I think it can be said that we have kept faith with them."

After years of lobbying for their cause, the Zionists were successful. On November 29, 1947, the United Nations voted to partition Palestine into one Jewish state and one Arab state. The state of Israel was reborn. Meir and her fellow Zionists' dream had become a reality. "The State of Israel! My eyes filled with tears, and my hands shook," Meir wrote. "We had done it. We had brought the Jewish state into existence—and I, Golda Mabovits Meyerson, had lived to see the day. . . . the long exile was over."

But potential annihilation lay just around the corner after the celebration. The Arab nations rejected the UN partition plan, and their armies were preparing for war at the moment of partition implementation—May 14, 1948. Israel needed money to fight a war. Meir, who was then the head of the Political Department of the Jewish Agency, was off to America to try to raise the necessary funding.

In Chicago on January 21, 1948, Meir addressed the General Assembly of the council of Jewish Federations and Welfare Funds. These were not Zionist organizations. Meir made her passionate and eloquent appeal for Israel's survival as she did in all of her speeches, by speaking from her heart. She rarely used a prepared text. "The Jewish community in Palestine is going to fight to the very end," she said. "If we have arms to fight with, we will fight with them. If not, we will fight with stones in our hands. My friends, we are at war. You cannot decide whether we should fight or not. We will. . . . You can only decide one thing: whether we shall be victorious."

When she returned to Palestine in March 1948, Meir had raised $50 million. She made return trips to the United States in 1948, raising another $150 million. "The state of Israel, I told Jews all over America, could not survive on applause," Meir said. "The war would not be won by speeches or declarations or even tears of happiness."

Meir would go anywhere to raise money, but also to try to secure peace. The loss of lives—both Jewish and Arab soldiers and civilians—was something she detested. "We can forgive you for killing our children, but we can never forgive you for making us kill your children," Meir said to Israel's Arab neighbors.

In the six months between the UN resolution creating Israel and its formal implementation, Meir secretly met twice with King Abdullah of Jordan to try to avert the oncoming war. The second time she met with the king, she'd agreed to travel to Amman at great personal risk to her own safety. She was disguised as an Arab woman. "I was much too concerned with the outcome of our mission to think about what would happen if, God forbid, we were caught," Meir recalled.

The mission ultimately failed. King Abdullah couldn't turn back the tide of the other Arab nations. War came and with it a terrible price: 6,000 dead Israeli soldiers, which amounted to 1 percent of the entire population. But the money Meir raised helped Israel buy the weapons it needed to win the war and firmly establish their existence in 1948. "Someday when history will be written, it will be said that there was a Jewish woman who got the money which made the state [of Israel] possible," said David Ben-Gurion, Israel's first prime minister.

Meir kept trying to reach out, in the name of peace, to Israel's Arab neighbors her entire career. When she became

Israel's first female foreign minister, she consistently tried to arrange personal meetings with representatives of Arab countries, but was rebuffed by them. In 1969, when she became the first female prime minister in the Middle East at seventy years of age, she reached out again—this time as Israel's political leader.

> *In later years, Meir recalled how she felt right before the 1948 war for Israel's existence: "I was very frightened—and with good reason. Still, there is a great difference between being frightened and lacking faith."*

"All my attempts to establish direct contact with the Arab leaders had failed miserably—including the appeal I made on the first day I assumed office, when I had declared that 'we are prepared to discuss peace with our neighbors, any day and on all matters,'" Meir later wrote.

While she couldn't win over the Arab governments, her sincerity and clarity of purpose helped her win the admiration of such world leaders as Presidents John Kennedy, Lyndon Johnson and Richard Nixon; General Charles de Gaulle; and Secretary of State Henry Kissinger, to name a few. "I loved Golda Meir because of her strength, her warmth, her humanity, her sense of humor," said Henry Kissinger. "She was sort of the earth-mother of elemental strength."

Arab leaders King Abdullah and Egyptian President Anwar Sadat respected her. Both of them were eventually assassinated. In Abdullah's case, it was surely in some part due to his relatively moderate views on Israel. In the case of Sadat, his assassination was due directly to his historic peace agreement with Israel in 1979. "Golda Meir was a noble foe," Sadat would say before his death, "who always proved that she was a political leader of the first category, worthy of occupying her place in your history and worthy of the place she occupied in your leadership."

Meir didn't campaign for the prime minister's office. She was drafted by party members after Prime Minister Levi Eshkol died suddenly of a heart attack. "I had never planned to be prime minister," she wrote. "I had never planned any position in fact. I had planned to [go] to Palestine, to go to [a kibbutz], to be active in the labor movement."

Meir was always a good and loyal political soldier. Prime Minister David Ben-Gurion asked Meir to become Israel's first minister to Russia in 1948, but with war raging with the Arab states, she didn't want to go at first. She felt she could do more good at home. Then Meir realized she was thinking about her needs rather than her responsibilities. "Who was I to disobey or even demur at a time when each day brought news of fresh casualties?" Meir wrote. "One's duty was one's duty—and it had nothing to do with justice. So what if I longed to be in Israel? Other people longed for their children to be alive or whole again."

Meir typically worked sixteen-hour days, thirty days a month, even in her advancing years. It was a habit left over from her life during World War II that had stayed with her. "During those war years I learned a very important lesson: One can always push [one's] self a little bit beyond what only yesterday was thought to be the absolute limit of one's endurance," Meir said.

She continued her pace when she became prime minister in 1969. What most people didn't know about her was that she'd been diagnosed with cancer of the lymphatic system back in 1963. But she didn't let it stop her, and with treatment, Meir was able to live another highly productive fourteen years.

As prime minister, Meir wouldn't allow the contention of the Arab-Israeli conflict to change her values and that of the nation she now led. Even as Israel remained the target of Arab extremism and terrorism, Meir refused to respond in kind and go down the road of hatred and revenge. "The notion of attacking Arabs indiscriminately, regardless of whether or not they were the particular perpetrators of an outrage, was morally abhorrent to me," Meir said. "A specific attack had to be repelled, and a specific criminal had to be punished. Well and good. But we were not going to kill Arabs just because they were Arabs or engage in the kind of wanton violence that typified the Arab method of fighting us."

Meir believed that a necessary component in the formula for achieving peace was military strength. "I believe that we will have peace with our neighbors, but I am sure that no one will make peace with a weak Israel. If Israel is not strong, there will be no peace."

> *Golda Meir showed simultaneously the qualities of extreme toughness and warmth.*
> —President Richard Nixon

"Golda Meir lived under pressure that we in this country would find impossible to understand," said the great newsman Walter Cronkite. "She is the strongest woman to head a government in our time and for a very long time past."

Meir was also a powerful speaker who brilliantly shaped her arguments by quickly getting to the heart of a matter. In 1957, for example, speaking at the UN, Meir presented her position regarding Israel's Arab neighbors. "The Arab world with its ten sovereignties and 3,000,000 square miles (compared to 8,000 for Israel) can well afford to accommodate itself to peaceful cooperation with Israel," she said. "Does hate for Israel and the aspiration for its destruction make one child in your country happier? Does it convert one hovel into a house? Does culture thrive on the soil of hatred? We have not the slightest doubt that eventually there will be peace and cooperation between us. This is a historic necessity for both peoples. We are prepared; we are anxious to bring it about now."

During her government service, first to the Jews of Palestine and then to the citizens of Israel, Meir saw her people and cause tested many times—and learned an enduring lesson from them: "I suppose there are only two reasonable or even possible responses to national adversity. One is to collapse, to give in and to say, 'It just can't be done.' The other is to grit your teeth and to fight on as many fronts as necessary for as long as necessary—which is exactly what we did and, as it turns out, exactly what we are still doing now."

Meir's tenure as prime minister began during a war with Egypt, and she took responsibility for the lives of Israel's soldiers. Meir never allowed herself or her nation to look at the war's dead as routine or acceptable. The first instruction she gave as prime minister was that she be informed immediately when reports came in regarding military action—even if they came in the middle of the night. "I knew that I wouldn't be able to bear the idea of sleeping soundly through the night not even knowing if soldiers had been killed or wounded," Meir said.

Israel's military advantage over its enemies, Meir believed, lay not in military might but in something far more important. "Although we are a very small people and there is no comparison between the numbers in our army and those in any of the countries fighting us," she said, "and although we do not have the wealth of arms and ammunition they have, we do have two things that give us an advantage over them— our hatred for war and for death."

Meir left the world with a verbal treasure of wisdom, such as her words about terrorism. They are as relevant today in the wake of the September 11 attacks as they were in her time: "It is my most profound conviction—and consolation— that the seeds of the inevitable failure of . . . terrorism lie in the very concept of terrorism itself. No movement, regardless of the money available to it . . . can succeed for long . . . if its only commitments are to blackmail and bloodshed. . . . It is not by killing and maiming children, hijacking aircraft or murdering diplomats that real movements of national liberation accomplish their aims. They must also have content, goals that will serve them long after the immediate crisis has passed, and they must—to use an old-fashioned word—have some claim to intellectual and moral purity."

> *There can be no deals with terrorism.*
> —Golda Meir

As prime minister, Meir returned to her old elementary school in Milwaukee in 1971 to address the children there. She shared with them her values about character and the way she had conducted her life. "It isn't really important to decide when you are very young just exactly what you want to become when you grow up," Meir told the children. "It is much more important to decide on the way you want to live: If you are going to be honest with yourself and honest with your friends, if you are going to get involved with causes which are good for others."

How to Be Like Golda Meir

1. Determine exactly what you want out of life.

Meir's commitment to a Jewish homeland was far more than just a cause—it was truly her life. She believed that the Jewish people had to become "masters of their own fate," and worked to that end.

2. Take action.

Meir's childhood experiences of living in fear because she was Jewish shaped her outlook on life. "If one wanted to survive, one had to take effective action about it personally," she said. "Nothing in life just happens. It isn't enough to believe in something; you have to have the stamina to meet obstacles and overcome them, to struggle."

3. Get involved.

As a child in the fourth grade, Meir saw poor children who couldn't afford needed textbooks. She didn't just ignore it and say it wasn't her problem; she did something about it. She would conduct her entire life in this manner.

4. Don't expect others to do what you won't.

Meir said she wouldn't "be a parlor Zionist—advocating settlement in Palestine for others."

5. Be aware and be willing to learn.

Meir first learned from her older sister, Sheyna, that "there is only one way to do anything: the right way. Sheyna was already a perfectionist at fifteen, a girl who lived according to the highest principles, whatever the price."

6. **Don't get sidetracked.**

Meir realized it wasn't enough just to be in Palestine, she had to be active in bringing a Jewish state into existence.

7. **Talk to anyone—anywhere—who can help your cause.**

Meir traveled anywhere she had to, to any country, for the cause of Israel. "We must miss no opportunity to explain to influential people what we want and what we are," she wrote.

8. **Speak from your heart.**

Meir relied on speaking from her heart when she delivered her powerful speeches, whether she was trying to raise money for Israel or addressing the UN.

9. **Never give in to hatred and revenge.**

In spite of the terrorism directed toward Israel, Meir never allowed herself to go down the road of hatred and revenge. "The notion of attacking Arabs indiscriminately, regardless of whether or not they were the particular perpetrators of an outrage, was morally abhorrent to me," she said.

10. **Be a good soldier.**

You have to follow before you can lead. Meir didn't want to be minister to Russia, but she put her personal feelings aside to do what her government asked of her. "Who was I to disobey or even demur. . . . One's duty was one's duty."

11. **Never give up on peace.**

Working for peace is never a waste of time, even if you can't accomplish your aim. Meir never stopped trying to reach out to Arab leaders to find peace between Israel and her Arab neighbors.

12. **Work hard.**

Meir typically worked sixteen-hour days, thirty days a month, even in her advancing years. It was a habit left over from her life during World War II that stayed with her. "During those war years I learned a very important lesson: One can always push one's self a little bit beyond what only yesterday was thought to be the absolute limit of one's endurance."

13. **Never lose your compassion.**

Meir sent her soldiers off to battle, but never thought anyone was expendable. She agonized over the deaths and casualties of soldiers like they were her own children, even insisting that she be awakened at any hour of the night the moment military reports came in. She cared about Arab losses, too. And while she was thankful for Israel's military success when necessary, she didn't rejoice in victory over Israel's enemies.

14. **Never stop hating war, even when it's necessary.**

Meir said, "We do have two things that give us an advantage over [our enemies]—our hatred for war and for death."

15. **Live your life with character and decency.**

Prime Minister Golda Meir told the school-children at her old elementary school in Milwaukee: "Decide on the way you want to live: If you are going to be honest with yourself and honest with your friends, if you are going to get involved with causes which are good for others."

ROSA PARKS
b. 1913

STRENGTH

I would like to be known as a person who is concerned about freedom and equality and justice and prosperity for all people.

—*Rosa Parks*

**R**osa Parks helped ignite the civil rights movement and change the United States when she refused to give up her seat on a segregated bus in Montgomery, Alabama, in 1955. Her name was brought to national prominence, but standing up for herself was nothing new to Rosa Parks.

She was born Rosa McCauley in the segregated South of 1913 in Tuskegee, Alabama. The Civil War had ended only forty-eight years earlier, and what the South lost in war it tried to regain by other brutal means. While the constitution protected black Americans and their rights, the Ku Klux Klan and Jim Crow laws (the name given to the system of racial segregation) tried to take them away. The weapons of choice were a favorite of oppressive tyrants throughout the ages: fear and violence.

Rosa Parks would take her place in history on a bus, but as a child, she watched as white children rode to school on one while she and her friends walked. There were no school buses for the black children. The white children acknowledged the black children, as Parks remembers, by hurling their trash at them as their bus passed by.

As an adult, Parks wasn't bitter over that and even worse treatment. Hate, she said, is taught. "It wasn't that the white children meant to be as cruel as they were, but they had been indoctrinated with that type of attitude by the adults around them," Parks wrote in *Rosa Parks: My Story,* with Jim Haskins. "Segregation itself is vicious," she said.

When Parks was about ten years old, a white boy of the same age threatened her with his fist. Parks picked up a brick to defend herself. The boy backed off and so did Parks. When she told her grandmother about the incident, she received a warning and a lesson in the ways of the South in the early twentieth century. "[My grandmother] scolded me very severely about how I had to learn that white folks were white folks and that you just didn't talk to white folks or act that way around white people," Parks wrote. "You didn't retaliate if they did something to you. I got very upset about that. I felt that I was very much in my rights to try to defend myself if I could.

"My grandmother remarked that I was too high-strung and that if I wasn't careful, I would probably be lynched before I was twenty years old. Much later I came to understand that my grandmother was scolding me because she was afraid for me. . . . In the South in those days black people could get beaten or killed for having that attitude."

The lesson was noted, if not always acted on. For example, when a white child on roller skates tried to push Parks off the sidewalk, she responded by pushing him. The boy's mother witnessed the incident and warned her she could have her put in jail for pushing her son. "I just couldn't accept being pushed, even at the cost of my life," Parks later reflected.

The adult Parks, while still committed to fighting segregation, was a proponent of nonviolence and an admirer of Mahatma Gandhi and Dr. Martin Luther King, Jr. "The teachings of Jesus Christ had convinced her instead, as they had

Martin Luther King, Jr., that a heart filled with love could conquer anything, even bigotry," wrote historian Douglas Brinkley in his book *Rosa Parks*. Her childhood incidents serve to illustrate what gave her the strength to fight injustice as an adult: "I was a regular person, just as good as anybody else," Parks wrote. "I was raised to be proud."

> *I remember finding such comfort and peace while reading the Bible. . . . Its teaching became a way of life and helped me in dealing with my day-to-day problems.*
> —Rosa Parks, excerpted from *Rosa Parks* by Douglas Brinkley

Nonviolence was a pillar of the civil rights movement because, paradoxically, the civil rights black Americans sought could only be granted by the white majority that had been denying them. "Somehow we had to change the [segregation] laws. And we had to get enough white people on our side to be able to succeed," Parks said.

Parks didn't view all white people as hostile to blacks. She had some good experiences with whites. One of her mentors was a white teacher named Alice L. White. Parks attended her school for the seventh and eighth grade before the elderly Miss White had to give up teaching. The school was officially called the Montgomery Industrial School, but became known unofficially as simply Miss White's school. Alice White was from Melrose, Massachusetts. She'd gone south to Montgomery, Alabama, specifically to teach black girls. The entire faculty of her school was white. They experienced hostility from the white community, but that didn't stop them from their commitment to black students. Through her kindness and wisdom, Miss White made a difference in the lives of these young women.

"What I learned best at Miss White's school was that I was a person with dignity and self-respect," Parks wrote, "and I should not set my sights lower than anybody else just because I was black. We were taught to be ambitious and to believe that we could do what we wanted in life. This was not something I learned just at Miss White's school. I had learned it from my grandparents and my mother too. But what I had learned at home was reinforced by the teachers I had at Miss White's school."

Rosa entered adulthood with pride and values. Her social consciousness was further nurtured when she married Raymond Parks in 1932. Raymond Parks was an activist and a member of the National Association for the Advancement of Colored People (NAACP). At the time Rosa met him, he was working on behalf of the Scottsboro Boys—nine black males, ranging in age from fourteen to nineteen, who had been railroaded into a death sentence on a trumped-up rape case. Eventually the United State Supreme Court ruled that none of the defendants had received a fair trial and overturned their convictions. Raymond Parks led the legal defense fund that helped free the Scottsboro Boys, but only after some had spent many years falsely incarcerated.

"I thought it was awful that they were condemned to die for a crime they did not commit," Parks later wrote. "It demonstrated how little regard segregationists had for the lives of black people and the lengths they would go to keep us in fear."

Raymond Parks risked his life in his work for the Scottsboro Boys. The racists of the time were greatly offended when blacks showed the temerity to question guilty verdicts and death sentences imposed by all white juries and judges, even though there was often no real evidence. Raymond and Rosa Parks shared the same values about justice. As Parks later said, "I was proud of Raymond for working on behalf of the Scottsboro Boys. I also admired his courage. He could have been beaten or killed for what he was doing. Later I came to understand that he was always interested in and willing to work for things that would improve life for his race, his family, and himself."

As was Rosa Parks in the years leading up to December 1, 1955. "Rosa Parks was in rebellion against Jim Crow laws from her teenaged years onward," said historian Douglas Brinkley in an interview. "This is a woman who was about to sue the state of Alabama (in 1945) for not allowing her the right to vote (which she wound up receiving). This is a woman who led a group of kids to march, on her own and without NAACP help, and brought them to the steps of the main library in Montgomery, Alabama, demanding that the black children were able to get equal access to books. This is a woman who went around the state and interviewed black women who had been raped by white men. She interviewed all these women and kept files on them. She corresponded with African-Americans in jail who she thought should not be in prison."

In 1943, Parks, who made her living as a seamstress, began to donate her free time as secretary to the local NAACP office in Montgomery, Alabama. That same year she had a disturbing incident on a bus. The bus drivers in Montgomery were a law unto themselves. Like urban stagecoach drivers, they administrated their own brand of justice—Old West style—and were authorized to carry guns. The rules on buses were simple and draconian: The first ten seats in the bus were reserved exclusively for whites. Blacks were expected to sit in the ten seats in "the back of the bus." A sign at the back of some buses further dehumanized black riders: "This part of the bus for the colored race."

The bus driver decided who sat in the middle sixteen seats of the bus, but naturally, they were used first for the overflow of any white passengers. If the back ten seats were filled, the bus driver might allow blacks to fill some of those seats. To add to the humiliation, blacks were expected to enter the bus at the front, pay their fare, then walk back outside the bus and reenter through the back door.

One day in 1943, Rosa Parks got on a bus and walked straight back to take her seat. The bus driver—"tall and thick set with an intimidating posture," she recalled—ordered Parks to get up, exit at the back door and then get back on. "I told him I was already on the bus and didn't see the need of getting off and getting back on when people were standing in the stepwell," Parks said.

The bus driver came back and grabbed Parks's coat sleeve. She then walked up to the front of the bus to exit it. Along the way she dropped her purse. Defiantly, rather than bending down to pick it up, she sat in a seat reserved for whites and reached for it. The bus driver was infuriated. "He was standing over me and he said, 'Get off my bus' . . . He looked like he was ready to hit me," Parks remembered. She said to him, "I know one thing. You better not hit me." With that she got off the bus and didn't get back on. After that incident, every time she took a bus, Parks looked to see if it was that bus driver, whom she dubbed "that mean one." She never wanted to be on his bus again.

Parks wrote that no segregation law upset black people in Montgomery more than bus segregation. Over 60 percent of bus customers were black. They formed the majority of passengers and kept the bus line in business. But rather than being welcomed as preferred customers, they were treated as second-class citizens.

Parks's chapter of the NAACP was looking for a test case to challenge the constitutionality of the law concerning segregation on buses. At least two young black women in 1955 had refused to give up their bus seats to white people and were arrested. The NAACP deemed that neither met the criteria they were looking for to carry a test case. One of the women was an unmarried, pregnant teenager; another pled guilty and paid her fine.

What the NAACP in Montgomery needed was someone akin to what Brooklyn Dodgers' general manager Branch Rickey needed to break baseball's color line: a Jackie Robinson. The Montgomery NAACP needed someone like Robinson who was above reproach and could be presented in a favorable light to the scrutinizing white public. Rickey found Jackie Robinson and made him Major League Baseball's first modern black player. Fate would find Rosa Parks.

On December 1, 1955, Parks got off work from her seamstress job at a department store and went, as usual, to catch the Cleveland Avenue bus to go home. Parks was then going to a youth group meeting at her local NAACP that evening. She paid her fare and took her seat on the bus. Then she realized something: She hadn't been paying attention and had boarded the bus driven by the driver she had been avoiding for twelve years—"that mean one." Parks sat in one of the sixteen seats in the middle section of the bus. At one of the stops, white people filled up the white seats, with one white man left standing.

"Let me have those front seats," Parks remembered the bus driver saying. "Y'all better make it light on yourselves and let me have those seats."

Parks moved over to a window seat. The bus driver persisted. He wanted to know if Parks was going to give up her seat. "No," she said. The driver, whose name was James Blake,

> *Parks [embraced] Gandhi's maxim. "Action is my domain. It's not what I say but what I do that matters."*
> —Douglas Brinkley in *Rosa Parks*

told Parks he was going to have her arrested. "You may do that," Parks responded. Blake got out of the bus and waited for the police. Parks stayed anchored in her seat on the bus. "As I sat there," Parks wrote, "I tried not to think about what might happen. I knew that anything was possible. I could be manhandled or beaten. I could be arrested."

Parks said that being a test case and the NAACP's candidate wasn't a factor in her stand. "I knew the NAACP needed a plaintiff who was beyond reproach, because I was in on the discussions about the possible court cases. But that is not why I refused to give up my bus seat to a white man on Thursday, December 1, 1955. I did not intend to get arrested. If I had been paying attention, I wouldn't even have gotten on that bus.

"People always say that I didn't give up my seat because I was tired, but that isn't true. I was not tired physically, or no more tired than I usually was at the end of a working day. I was not old, although some people have an image of me as being old then. I was forty-two. No, the only tired I was, was tired of giving in," Parks wrote.

At the police station Parks was denied the courtesy of having even a sip of water. She was told to wait until she was in her jail cell. She was then fingerprinted and had her mug shot taken. She was treated like a true criminal, despite the injustice being done to her. Her husband, Raymond, raised the $100 bail and was joined at the police station by an NAACP official, E. D. Nixon, and two of Parks's white friends, attorney Clifford Durr and his wife, Virginia.

> *From my upbringing and the Bible I learned people should stand up for rights . . . just as the children of Israel stood up to the Pharaoh.*
>
> —Rosa Parks

After about two hours in jail, Parks arrived home around 9:30 P.M. "I knew that I would never, never ride another segregated bus, even if I had to walk to work. But it still had not occurred to me that mine could be a test case against the segregated buses," Parks said. E. D. Nixon first suggested the idea to her that night. Her husband and her mother thought she should do it. "I had worked on enough cases to know that a ruling could not be made without a plaintiff. So I agreed to be the plaintiff," Parks recalled.

Nixon had what he said was the perfect plaintiff, and she was right under his nose all the time. He told the reporters later, "Rosa Parks worked with me for twelve years prior to this. . . . she was secretary of everything I had going. . . . she was honest, she was clean, she had integrity. The press couldn't go out and dig up something she did last year, or last month, or five years ago. They couldn't hang nothing like that on Rosa Parks."

Parks's trial was set for the following Monday, December 5. The NAACP sent out flyers asking all black passengers to "stay off the buses Monday in protest of the arrest and trial. Don't ride the buses to work, to town, to school, or anywhere on Monday. You can afford to stay out of school for one day. If you work, take a cab or walk. But please, children and grown-ups, don't ride the bus at all on Monday. Please stay off all buses Monday."

The boycott gained steam. Eighteen cab companies owned by blacks arranged to make stops at all the bus stops and charged black passengers only ten cents—the same amount as the bus fare.

As Parks entered the courthouse for her trial, the street was lined with overflowing crowds of supporters. One girl yelled out, "They've messed with the wrong one now."

"The reason the city of Montgomery's black community, 50,000 strong, galvanized around Rosa Parks was they knew she'd been fighting segregation and racism all these years," Brinkley said. "She was an honored, church-going woman. A leader in the African Methodist Episcopal (AME) Church, somebody who gave a lot of her time to different causes. Everything about her kind of spoke of a holiness and good-ness. Her arrest, and the visceral response to it, wasn't just because she was a random woman that day on the bus. It was because she was in Montgomery that they arrested Rosa Parks."

"Everybody knew in the black community that she'd worked for E. D. Nixon, and that she'd worked for the NAACP. She probably logged more grass roots hours for the Civil Rights movement before December 1, 1955, than anyone else in the state of Alabama."

Parks's lawyers, Charles Langford and Fred Gray, entered a "not guilty" plea for her. They had no intention of putting on a defense. The point was to have Parks found guilty so they could appeal the conviction to a higher court—where they had the best chance of striking down the segregation law.

Parks was found guilty, given a suspended sentence, fined ten dollars and ordered to pay four dollars in court costs.

Parks and the case galvanized Montgomery's black community. "There was a strange religious glow about Rosa—a kind of humming Christian light, which gave her a unique majesty," said James Farmer, founder of the Congress of Racial Equality (CORE), and quoted in historian Douglas Brinkley's book, *Rosa Parks.*

On the evening of December 5, black leaders held a meeting at the Holt Street Baptist Church. The topic of discussion was whether to extend the bus boycott, because to continue it would guarantee violence by whites. E. D. Nixon spoke to the crowd: "You who are afraid, you better get your hat and coat and go home. This is going to be a long, drawn out affair. I want to tell you something: For years and years I've been talking about how I didn't want the children who came along behind me to have to suffer the indignities that I've suffered all these years. Well, I've changed my mind—I want to enjoy some of that freedom myself."

Then another speaker rose to address the crowd: a twenty-six-year-old minister named Dr. Martin Luther King, Jr. "There comes a time that people get tired," King said. "We are here this evening to say to those who have mistreated us so long that we are tired—tired of being segregated and humiliated, tired of being kicked about by the brutal feet of oppression. One of the great glories of democracy is the right to protest."

He continued: "[If] you will protest courageously and yet with dignity and Christian love, when the history books are written in future generations the historians will pause and say, 'There lived a great people—a black people—who injected new meaning and dignity into the veins of civilization.' That is our challenge and our overwhelming responsibility."

The demands of the bus boycott, officially called a "protest" by black leaders, were spelled out by another future leader of the civil rights movement, the Rev. Ralph Abernathy: First, blacks wanted courteous treatment on buses. Second, they wanted seating on a first-come, first-served basis (while

> *In the spring of 1989, when a lone Chinese student stood defiantly before an army tank in Beijing's Tiananmen Square as hundreds of millions of people watched around the world, it was, as South African president Nelson Mandela put it, 'A Rosa Parks moment.'*
> —Douglas Brinkley
> in *Rosa Parks*

making the gracious concession of whites in front and blacks in back). Third, they wanted the hiring of black drivers for black bus routes. The audience was asked to vote if they wanted to continue the boycott. Every person in church stood, and the crowd outside roared its approval with a resounding "Yes!"

Parks became a member of the executive board of the newly created Montgomery Improvement Association (MIA), which was running the bus boycott. She'd been discharged from her job at the Montgomery Fair department store, but Parks was told the reason had nothing to do with the boycott. The reason given was that since the store had lost its tailor, it didn't need a seamstress. Parks, who was given two weeks pay and bonus money, generously took the store officials at their highly suspect word. "I do not like to form in my mind an idea that I don't have any proof of," she later wrote.

Raymond left his job as a barber when an order came down from the shop's owner that there was to be no discussion or mention of the bus boycott or Rosa Parks. "Raymond said he would not work anywhere where his wife's name could not be mentioned," Parks said. In addition, Brinkley wrote, Parks "was labeled a 'nigger traitor' by half of the southern democrats in the U.S. Senate."

Law enforcement officials did whatever they wanted in order to break the boycott. Police arrested cab drivers and managed to cite them for not charging full fares, as if the owners of companies weren't free to set their own fares. Parks worked as a dispatcher for the MIA. She took calls from people who needed rides and then arranged them through private people or churches. Parks estimated that the MIA managed to transport around 30,000 people per day.

The MIA's peaceful protest was soon met by white violence. The homes of Dr. King and E. D. Nixon were bombed. Parks received threatening, anonymous phone calls saying "You're the cause of all this. You should be killed," but she wasn't scared off.

The boycott was proving to be effective. Without black passengers, many black bus routes were stopped. The residual effect was on businesses, which felt the boycott in their pocketbooks. In the old South there were laws to cover every situation to keep blacks oppressed. There was actually an old law on the books that prohibited boycotts. Amazingly, a grand jury indicted Dr. King on eighty-nine direct and related counts. Other black leaders were indicted, including Parks, although nothing really resulted from the legal action.

In June 1956, a federal district court ruled in favor of the MIA suit against the segregation law on buses. The Montgomery city commissioners appealed the decision to the U.S. Supreme Court.

Finally, on November 13, 1956, the Supreme Court ruled that segregation on the Montgomery buses was unconstitutional. What Rosa Parks had started concluded with a change in the law from the highest court in the land. The boycott was ended after 381 days. The battle was won, but the trouble was far from over. Snipers shot at the now integrated buses, and the city, ever relentless in harassing its black citizens, imposed a five o'clock curfew on buses. This meant that many black people had no bus to catch once they got off work.

> *My lifetime mission has been simple ... that all men and women are created equal under the eyes of our Lord.*
> —Rosa Parks in a letter to Pope John Paul II

"Eventually most of the violence died down," Parks wrote. "Black people were not going to be scared off the buses any more than they were going to be scared onto them when they refused to ride."

Because of what happened in Montgomery, African-Americans in other southern cities started their own boycotts of segregated buses. Parks's actions and the boycott of the city's buses "is now considered the beginning of the American civil rights movement," Douglas Brinkley wrote in *Rosa Parks*.

Over time, Parks's celebrity made her a very visible figure in the civil rights movement. Presidents and statesmen sought her company. Nelson Mandela asked to meet her in 1990, on his first trip to the United States after twenty-seven years in a South African prison. When Pope John Paul II visited the United States in 1999, he met Rosa Parks and blessed her "in recognition of her Christian contribution to humanity." In 1999, she received a congressional medal for lifetime achievement from President Bill Clinton. *Time Magazine* named Parks one of the one hundred most significant people of the twentieth century, for, Brinkley wrote, "her 'modesty' and 'serenely human' bravery."

The bus where Parks made her stand was located on Cleveland Avenue. The street eventually was renamed Rosa L. Parks Avenue. In 1991, a bust of Parks was unveiled at the Smithsonian Institute in Washington, D.C.

In 1987, Parks co-founded the Rosa and Raymond Parks Institute for Self-Development, in Detroit, Michigan, where they relocated from Montgomery in 1957. (The Parks had been the targets of death threats and couldn't find employment after being ostracized by white business leaders for daring to stand up to segregation.) The Rosa and Raymond Parks Institute helps young people pursue their education and life skills through the researching of American history. Parks devoted time and energy raising money to launch and sustain the organization.

Despite all the accolades, Parks always viewed herself as a regular person who took a principled stand. "As time has gone by," she wrote in 1992, "people have made my place in the history of the civil rights movement bigger and bigger. They call me the Mother of the Civil Rights Movement and the Patron Saint of the Civil Rights Movement. I have more honorary degrees and awards than I can count, and I appreciate and cherish every single one of them.

"Interviewers still only want to talk about that one evening in 1955 when I refused to give up my seat on the bus. Organizations still want to give me awards for that one act more than thirty years ago. I am happy to go wherever I am invited and to accept whatever honors are given me. I understand that I am a symbol."

She was much more than that, as Brinkley points out. Parks's entire life before and after the moment she came to national prominence, has been spent fighting racism in her own dignified manner.

"This is a woman who spent her summer before the bus boycott at the Highlander Folk School, which was the [progressive] civil disobedience school near Chattanooga, Tennessee.... That's who Rosa Parks was. And so her big act of defiance on December 1, 1955, was a culmination of a lifetime fighting against Jim Crow, against inequality."

How to Be Like Rosa Parks

1. **Stand up for what you believe in.**

   Parks believed that as a black American she was not inferior to anyone. The foundation of her strength was simple: "I was a regular person, just as good as anybody else," she wrote. "I was raised to be proud."

2. **Surround yourself with people who bring out your best.**

   Parks shared the same values as her husband, Raymond Parks. "I was proud of Raymond for working on behalf of the Scottsboro Boys," Parks said. "I also admired his courage. He could have been beaten or killed for what he was doing."

3. **Be part of the solution.**

   Parks didn't just talk about equal rights for black Americans. In addition to working as a seamstress, Parks gave her time to the NAACP as a secretary for twelve years before refusing to give up her seat on the bus in 1955.

4. **Be a person of integrity.**

   Parks would not have been approached to serve as the face of the NAACP's legal challenge to the segregation laws had her reputation not been exemplary.

5. **Accept responsibility.**

   "I had worked on enough cases to know that a ruling could not be made without a plaintiff. So I agreed to be the plaintiff," Parks said of the Montgomery bus boycott.

6. Be fair.

When Parks was discharged from her job at the Montgomery Fair department store, it was probably due to her high visibility. She refused, however, to speculate or level false accusations.

7. Be humble.

Parks was the bus boycott's human face, but she never forgot that the boycott was a team effort. She said: "As time has gone by, people have made my place in the history of the civil rights movement bigger and bigger.... Organizations still want to give me awards for that one act more than thirty years ago. I am happy to go wherever I am invited and to accept whatever honors are given me. I understand that I am a symbol."

8. Have faith in God.

Parks has always had a deep faith in God. "She was part of the African Methodist Episcopalian Church since her childhood and that was a constant in her life to the point that even now she still goes to [church] at age ninety. Her belief in God is what Rosa Parks is all about. She's a spiritual, religious woman. She's a devout Christian. God is her light," Brinkley said.

HELEN KELLER
1880–1968

VISION

Self-pity is our worst enemy and if we yield to it, we can never do anything wise in the world.

—*Helen Keller*

elen Keller became the most famous disabled person of her time—and in history. Her life serves as an inspiration, and the wisdom she left behind remains a treasure to all people. Helen Keller saw what many people didn't: infinite possibilities for her life and for all those with disabilities.

Although Keller had been blind and deaf since she was nineteen months old, she eventually learned how to communicate with the world. She was first taught the manual finger alphabet by the woman she called "Teacher," Anne Sullivan, who helped bring Helen out of her dark and silent world when she was seven years old.

Helen was born healthy, with sight and hearing, in 1880. When she was nineteen months old, she developed a fever one winter night. When the fever left, her parents discovered she was blind and deaf. Helen may have had either scarlet fever or spinal meningitis. "When I awoke and found that all was dark and still," Keller later wrote, "I suppose I thought it was night and I must have wondered why day was so long in coming. Gradually, I got used to the silence and darkness that surrounded me and forgot that it had ever been different."

Through her sense of touch and smell, Helen was able to distinguish between her mother (Kate), father (Arthur), baby sister (Mildred) and other relatives. She had developed her own simple sign language to indicate who and what she wanted, and became sensitive to vibrations. Helen knew, for example, when someone was approaching her or when someone was at the front door. It was her inability to fully communicate, however, and the subsequent frustration it caused, that made her, by her own definition, an "incorrigible" child. "The few signs I used became less and less adequate," Keller later wrote, "and my failures to make myself understood were invariably followed by outbursts of passion."

She began to throw violent temper tantrums when she didn't get her way. Her parents, of course, felt tremendous sympathy for her and allowed her to do just about anything she wanted. When food was served, for example, Helen was allowed to wander from person to person and simply take whatever she wanted right off someone's plate.

"I do not remember when I first realized that I was different from other people; but I knew it before my teacher came to me," she wrote. "I had noticed that my mother and my friends did not use signs as I did when they wanted anything done, but talked with their mouths. Sometimes I stood between two persons who were conversing and touched their lips. I could not understand, and was vexed. I moved my lips and gesticulated frantically without result. This made me so angry at times that I kicked and screamed until I was exhausted.

"I think I knew when I was naughty, for I knew that it hurt Ella, my nurse, to kick her, and when my fit of temper was over I had a feeling akin to regret. But I cannot remember any instance in which this feeling prevented me from repeating the naughtiness when I failed to get what I wanted."

One time, in a fit of jealousy, she overturned her baby sister

Mildred's cradle. "The baby might have been killed had my mother not caught her as she fell," Keller wrote.

Family members urged Helen's parents to place her in a mental institution. They believed that blindness and deafness had affected Helen's mind and advised giving up on her as a human being. Her mother's brother conveniently said, "You really ought to put that child away, Kate. She is mentally defective, and it is not pleasant to see her about."

Helen's mother and father wouldn't hear of putting her in an institution. They knew the answer was not in giving up on her, but in finding a way to help her. They had a strong supporter in Arthur's sister, Eveline, who said of Helen: "This child has more sense than all the Kellers. . . . if there is any way to reach her mind."

Kate Keller had been searching for an answer, and in 1887 she read about Laura Bridgman. Laura had lost her sight and hearing at the age of two, but learned how to communicate through the manual alphabet. She'd been taught at the Perkins Institution for the Blind, located in Boston, and had lived almost her entire life there. Unfortunately, Kate learned that Laura's teacher, Dr. Samuel Gridley Howe (husband of Julia Ward Howe, who wrote "The Battle Hymn of the Republic"), had died some ten years earlier. Kate was in despair, wondering if there was anybody who could teach Keller as he had taught Laura.

Kate and Arthur had visited eye doctors (oculists) many times, hoping that someone could find a way to restore Helen's sight. When Helen was six, they heard of a man in Baltimore, a Dr. Chisholm, who'd achieved success with seemingly hopeless cases. They took Helen to him, and he told the Kellers what they'd heard before: Nothing could be done for

Helen medically. What Dr. Chishom did have to offer was the opinion that Helen could be taught, and he had just the man to advise them: Alexander Graham Bell. Bell, the inventor of the telephone, was also a teacher of the deaf, and helping deaf people was dear to his heart. Bell's mother and wife were deaf, and his father had been involved for many years in developing ways to help the deaf communicate.

From the moment Keller met Bell, there was a wonderful, instant connection between the two. They would become lifelong friends. "He held me on his knee while I examined his watch. . . . he understood my signs, and I knew it and loved him at once. But I did not dream that the interview would be the door through which I should pass from darkness into light, from isolation to friendship, companionship, knowledge, love," Keller wrote.

Bell suggested to her parents that they contact Michael Anagnos, the director of the Perkins Institution in Boston, to see if they had a teacher there who could do

> *Science may have found a cure for most evils; but it has found no remedy for the worst of them all—the apathy of human beings.*
> —Helen Keller

for Helen what Dr. Howe had done for Laura Bridgman. Anagnos replied in a letter that he did have a twenty-year-old woman named Anne Sullivan. She had just graduated from Perkins, and he felt she could help Helen Keller.

Anne Sullivan's life had been tragic. Born into wretched poverty, Anne watched her mother die from tuberculosis when she was only eight. She was raised by her alcoholic father, who beat her viciously with a whip. In addition to all this, Anne suffered the then dreaded eye disease trachoma (curable since 1937), a chronic bacterial infection which left her half-blind. When Anne Sullivan was ten, her father abandoned her and her five-year-old brother, Jimmie.

At first, the two lived with their father's relatives, who had the means to take care of them but lacked the humanity to do so. Both children had handicaps (Jimmy had a tubercular hip), and their father's family felt they would be too much of a burden. Anne and Jimmie were banished to the poorhouse at the State Infirmary in Tewksbury, Massachusetts, in 1876.

Anne's new "home" at Tewksbury was filthy and overcrowded. She and Jimmie were thrown in with mental patients and those who had highly contagious diseases. (An abundance of rats and cockroaches also called Tewksbury home.) Their sleeping quarters were in a part of the building where only a partition separated them from the corpses of recently deceased residents.

Three months later, Jimmie died, and Anne was devastated. She wrote, years later, about seeing her little brother's body: "The light from the half-window fell upon the bed, and Jimmie's little white face, framed in dark curls, seemed to lift from the pillow," Sullivan said. "Before they could stop me, I jumped up and put my arms around him and kissed and kissed and kissed his face—the dearest thing in the world—the only thing I have ever loved. . . . I sat down beside my bed and wished to die with an intensity that I have never wished for anything else" (in *Helen Keller: A Life,* by Dorothy Herrmann).

Sullivan stayed strong, however, and endured the agony of Tewksbury for four years. When she found out that a state committee was investigating the atrocious conditions there and was going to inspect it, Sullivan took action. She followed the group and literally threw herself into the arms of the chairman of the committee, Frank B. Sanborn. Sullivan pleaded with him that she wanted to go to a school for the blind. Sanborn happened to be on the Perkins Institution's board of trustees, and something about Sullivan moved him. He arranged for the half-blind fourteen-year-old Sullivan to be transferred there; the horror of Tewksbury came to an end and her new life began.

At Perkins, Sullivan met Laura Bridgman and learned the manual alphabet. In time, Sullivan received operations that helped her vision improve. When she graduated from Perkins, she had risen to class valedictorian and gave the commencement address: "And now we are going out into the busy world to take our share of life's burdens," she said, "and do our share of life's burdens, and do our little to make the world better, wiser and happier."

Sullivan was armed with an idealism that needed an outlet. It came when Michael Anagnos received Arthur Keller's letter asking for a teacher for Helen. Anagnos, who wrote that Sullivan was "strictly honest, industrious," and that "her moral character is all that can be desired," suggested her for the job even though she'd never taught before. She was familiar with "the methods of teaching deaf, mute and blind children," Anagnos added. When she was offered the job she needed (for twenty-five dollars a month plus room and board), doing the work she wanted to do, the destiny of Sullivan and Keller was forged.

To prepare herself for teaching Helen, Sullivan studied Dr. Howe's reports regarding Laura Bridgman and many relevant books. And she had learned firsthand from Laura, who was still there when Sullivan left for the Kellers.

Sullivan arrived at the Keller home, in Tuscumbia, Alabama, on March 3, 1887. Helen sensed there was an impending visitor because her mother was scurrying around the house, getting it ready for company. Keller remembered the first time she met Sullivan: "I felt approaching footsteps. I stretched out my hand. . . . Someone took it, and I was caught up and held close in the arms of her who had come to reveal all things to me, and, more than all things else, to love me."

Sullivan gave Helen a doll, which was a gift from the blind children at Perkins. "Miss Sullivan slowly spelled into my hand the word 'd-o-l-l,' " Keller remembered. She imitated the finger symbols Sullivan made, but made no connection about their relevance. "I was simply making my fingers go in monkey-like imitation," she wrote.

While Helen was by nature a sweet, loving little girl, her disability had manifested itself in wild, sometimes violent temper tantrums. Sullivan was the recipient of one upon their first meeting. Sullivan realized before she could really make progress teaching Helen, she would have to have obedience from her. "I saw clearly," Sullivan wrote, "that it was useless to try to teach [Keller] language or anything else until she learned to obey me. . . . The more I think, the more certain I am that obedience is the gateway through which knowledge, yes, and love, too, enter the mind of a child."

Sullivan proposed to the Kellers that she and Helen be permitted to live alone for a couple of weeks in the Kellers' small guesthouse. To make Helen feel that she was alone with Sullivan and thus couldn't cry out for her parents, she was taken on a long drive to create the illusion of being taken somewhere far away. In addition, the furniture of the guesthouse was rearranged to ensure that Helen wouldn't figure out the plan.

Sullivan had earlier put an end to Helen's buffet-style eating habits, but not before Helen threw one of her wild tantrums. Sullivan let her go through her tantrums without trying to pacify her. Whereas Helen's parents naturally felt sorry for her (as did Sullivan), there was a difference: Sullivan was there to teach Helen rather than baby-sit her. When Helen pinched Sullivan out of anger, she received a slap back. But the most painful way Sullivan disciplined Helen was to deny her communication. Over time Helen learned a lesson: If she wanted to be communicated with, she would have to behave herself and respect others.

Although Helen learned to mimic the finger motions that Sullivan taught her for objects like a pin, hat and cup, she still didn't make the connection that the finger movements were words consisting of letters. She didn't understand, for example, that the finger symbols for her "d-o-l-l" applied to any doll, not just that one in particular. She couldn't comprehend that a "m-u-g" holds water, but "w-a-t-e-r" is not a "m-u-g."

On April 5, 1887, Helen had what she would later call "my soul's awakening." Sullivan and Helen were walking "down the path to the well house," Keller wrote. "Someone was drawing water and my teacher placed my hand under the spout. As the cool stream gushed over one hand, she spelled into the other the word water, first slowly, then rapidly. I stood still, my whole attention fixed upon the motions of her fingers. Suddenly I felt a misty consciousness as of something forgotten—a thrill of returning thought; and somehow the mystery of language was revealed to me. I knew then that 'w-a-t-e-r' meant the wonderful cool something that was flowing over my hand. That living word awakened my soul, gave it light, hope, joy, set it free! ... I left the well house eager to learn. Everything had a name, and each name gave birth to a new thought. As we returned to the house every object which I touched seemed to quiver with life."

With her intellect awakened and now a means to use it, Helen's progress from that point on was rapid. Within a year, she could read braille and write. Michael Anagnos titled the Perkins Institution's 1888 annual report, "Helen Keller: A Second Laura Bridgman." He wrote: "It is no hyperbole to say she is a phenomenon. History presents no case like hers ... in quickness of perception, grasp of ideas, breadth of comprehension, insatiate thirst for solid knowledge, self-reliance and sweetness of disposition she clearly excels [Laura Bridgman]."

Anagnos continued: "As if impelled by a resistless instinctive force [Keller] snatched the key of the treasury of the English language from the fingers of her teacher, unlocked its doors with vehemence, and began to feast on its contents with inexpressible delight."

> *Helen once eagerly asked a friend who had just taken a long walk through the woods what she had seen, and was amazed by the friend's reply: "Nothing in particular."*
> —*The Three Lives of Helen Keller,* BY RICHARD HARRITY AND RALPH G. MARTIN

Keller's achievements, which gained publicity initially from Anagnos's report and from Alexander Graham Bell, led to her becoming world-famous by the age of ten. She was now the one being sought out. She became a close friend of Mark Twain. She eventually would meet every United States president, from Grover Cleveland to John F. Kennedy.

Her intellectual awakening also triggered a humanitarian spirit that would remain a focus of hers the rest of her life. It helped make Keller one of the most admired women in the world. "I resolved that whatever role I did play in life it would not be a passive one," she said. When she was ten, for example, a police officer shot her dog Lioness, presumably in confusion. The story was national and world news. Keller received letters from people offering to send her money for a new dog. She politely turned them down, but asked that money be sent instead for Tommy Stringer. Tommy was a blind and deaf child who lived in poverty in Pennsylvania, and she wanted to make it possible for him to attend Perkins. Keller also wrote letters and newspaper articles on his behalf to try to raise the money. "While other children were playing, she deliberately abstained from buying soda water and other luxuries so she might save money to give to Tommy," author Dorothy Herrmann wrote. Tommy did eventually attend Perkins.

Keller's primary goal since she was a little girl was to go to college. By October 1896, sixteen-year-old Keller was attending Cambridge School for Young Ladies in Cambridge, Massachusetts in order to gain admittance to the college of her choice, which was Radcliffe, and also in Cambridge. However, she had to overcome other people's perceptions of her limitations. That was nothing new to her.

"The thought of going to college took root in my heart and became an earnest desire, which impelled me to enter into competition for a degree with seeing and hearing girls, in the face of the strong opposition of many true and wise friends," Keller wrote in *The Story of My Life,* published in 1903—the first of her nineteen books.

> *We can do anything we want to do if we stick to it long enough.*
> —Helen Keller

Keller had learned to read braille and write it using a braillewriter, a typewriter-like machine that creates the braille alphabet of patterns of raised dots. During her classroom lectures, Sullivan would communicate what the teacher was saying to Keller by tapping out the words into the palm of her hand, using the manual alphabet (which can be done extremely fast). She would "read" Keller's course books to her in the same manner.

It was a tedious process, but a price that Keller gladly paid for her education. "It takes me a long time to prepare my lessons, because I have to have every word of them spelled out in my hand. . . . not one of the textbooks which I am obliged to use is in raised print [braille]," Keller wrote while at Cambridge. She added that while there were periods when the entirety of her studies was overwhelming, "at other times I enjoy my work more than I can say."

Keller's accomplishments were remarkable and her grades were on par with her sighted and hearing Cambridge classmates. However, Agnes Irwin, Radcliffe's dean, was skeptical about Keller's ability to succeed there. It was suggested by some that she would be better served at a school for the deaf and blind. Keller disagreed. She decided to write a letter to the chairman of Radcliffe's academic board to make her case. She drew on the determination that helped her overcome her disability and later become one of the most famous and respected women in history: "I realize that the obstacles in the way of my receiving a college education are very great— to others they may seem insurmountable; but, dear Sir, a true soldier does not acknowledge defeat before the battle."

After passing her entrance exams, Keller was admitted to Radcliffe. "I began my studies with eagerness," she wrote. "Before me I saw a new world opening in beauty and light, and I felt within me the capacity to know all things. In the wonderland of mind I should be as free as another."

She had overcome obstacles to get into Radcliffe, where she graduated with honors in 1904 with Sullivan's devoted help. "The best part of my success was having [Anne] by my side who had kept me steadfast to my purpose," Keller wrote in *Midstream*. Indeed, Keller credited her successes to Sullivan's teaching methods.

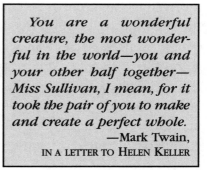

You are a wonderful creature, the most wonderful in the world—you and your other half together—Miss Sullivan, I mean, for it took the pair of you to make and create a perfect whole.
—Mark Twain,
IN A LETTER TO HELEN KELLER

She wrote: "It was my teacher's genius, her quick sympathy, her loving tact which made the first years of my education so beautiful. It was because she seized the right moment to impart knowledge that made it so pleasant and acceptable to me. . . . any teacher can take a child to the classroom, but not every teacher can make him learn."

Higher education, Keller believed, should be open to anyone who was academically qualified. When she was asked her opinion about a leading university's then discrimination against Jews, she answered, "I think when any institution of learning applies any test other than scholarship, it has ceased to be a public service institution. [That university], in discriminating against the Jew and the Negro on grounds other

The only lightless dark is the night of darkness in ignorance and insensibility.
—Helen Keller

than intellectual qualifications, has proved unworthy of its traditions and covered itself with shame."

After Keller graduated from college, she made her living as well as Sullivan's by continuing to write books about her life, and by also writing for newspapers and magazines. In addition, Keller and Sullivan went on the lecture circuit. She also received money from devoted friends for her personal needs. By 1920, however, the outside income had almost run its course. Keller and Sullivan were offered the opportunity to go on the vaudeville circuit. Sullivan didn't like the idea, just as the Kellers hadn't liked it when it was presented years before, but Keller was open to it. "We were faced with the necessity of earning more money," she wrote. She felt they could do a dignified act, while providing security for Sullivan.

"The funds my friends had provided for my support would cease with my death, and if I died before my teacher, she would be left almost destitute," Keller wrote in her book *Midstream*. During the act, Sullivan first explained the circumstances of Keller's life and how she was able to achieve the ability to communicate, then Keller spoke to the audience. She had been speaking for years, although it was a continuous work in progress, and she could be very difficult to understand. Sullivan would usually have to translate Keller's words for the audience. Keller had first resolved to learn how to speak when she was a child and heard of another blind and deaf girl who had done it.

"Without speech one is not a complete human being," she said. "Even when the speech is not beautiful, there is a fountain of joy in uttering words." To speak, Keller spent years practicing. She was taught to strengthen her vocal cords, and then to be sensitive to their vibrations so she could control her volume and pronounce letters and eventually, words.

After Keller's short talk, Sullivan fielded questions from the audience for both of them. Keller answered through Sullivan, by either signing or talking. Keller was proud of their vaudeville act, which lasted from 1920 to 1924, and brought them more money than her books or their lectures ever had. "I enjoyed it keenly," Keller said of her vaudeville days.

Those days ended in October 1924, when Keller and Sullivan signed a contract to help raise money for the American Foundation of the Blind. Keller now had regular income doing what was dearest to her heart, helping to make a difference in the lives of other people with disabilities. For the rest of her life, she traveled extensively throughout the United States, raising funds for the American Foundation of the Blind. She also traveled to other countries to raise money for the American Foundation for the Overseas Blind. She not only touched many lives personally, but her visibility and public presence helped improve the lives of the blind and deaf by bringing attention to their needs. Her activities eventually resulted in many reforms, including a uniform system of braille.

> *Helen Keller is fellow to Caesar, Alexander, Napoleon, Homer, Shakespeare, and the rest of the immortals.... She will be as famous a thousand years from now as she is today.*
> —Mark Twain

During World War II and beyond, Keller traveled to many military hospitals and visited soldiers who were wounded, paralyzed and blinded. Through Polly Thompson, who assisted Keller after Sullivan's death in 1936, Keller spread a message of hope to the soldiers who had suffered so greatly. "Face your deficiencies and acknowledge them; but do not let them master you," she said.

"When we do the best that we can, we never know what miracle is wrought in our life, or in the life of another."

"During World War II she became a symbol of hope to the thousands of blinded, deaf, and crippled soldiers," Dorothy Herrmann later wrote.

> *Faith is the strength by which a shattered world shall emerge into the light.*
> —Helen Keller

For one who had been plunged into blindness and deafness, giving into bitterness and losing all faith would have been easy. But Keller embraced God and felt that he had a reason for her handicap. "I believe that all through these dark and silent years," she said to a reporter, "God has been using my life for a purpose I do not know; but one day I shall understand and then I will be satisfied." She wrote a book about her convictions called *My Religion,* which was later revised and published as *Light in My Darkness.* "I cannot imagine myself without religion. I could as easily fancy a living body without a heart," she wrote.

For her eightieth birthday, the U.S. Senate passed a resolution in Keller's honor recognizing her contributions to humanity. The resolution read, in part: "For more than fifty years [she has] tirelessly devoted herself to the battle for the economic, cultural, and social advancement of the physically handicapped throughout the world, making her own conquest of disabilities a symbol of hope for millions. . . . and has won countless new friends for the United States of America and the cause of democracy and freedom."

"I will always—as long as I have breath—work for the handicapped," Keller said on her eightieth birthday.

Keller had strong social and political opinions and wanted to be heard. She used her public platform to speak out against child labor abuses and for female suffrage. The southern-bred Keller, whose father had been a Confederate army captain during the Civil War, was a strong supporter of the civil rights movement. "[Keller] was an activist not only for the deaf and blind, but she was also a person who was very politically aware and she also really worked throughout her long life for people who were disadvantaged in other ways," said Dorothy Herrmann in an interview. Keller was frustrated with the press because they seemed only interested in her opinions with respect "to social service and the blind," she wrote.

Many of her political views were controversial, and she considered that fair game. What she didn't consider fair was to be discounted simply because she was handicapped. "So long as I confine my activities to social service and the blind, [the press] compliment me extravagantly. . . . but when it comes to a discussion of a burning social or political issue, especially if I happen to be, as I so often am, on the unpopular side, the tone changes completely," she said. "I do not object to harsh criticism so long as I am treated like a human being with a mind of her own."

> *The public must learn that the blind man is neither a genius nor a freak nor an idiot. He has a mind which can be educated, a hand which can be trained, ambitions which it is right for him to strive to realize, and it is the duty of the public to help him make the best of himself so that he can win light through work.*
>
> —Helen Keller

In 1964 Keller was awarded the Presidential Medal of Freedom by President Lyndon Johnson, but she was too ill following a stroke to attend the ceremony. In 1965 she was elected to the Women's Hall of Fame. The number of votes she received rivaled that of Eleanor Roosevelt. In 1955, Keller became the first woman Harvard University ever recognized with an honorary degree.

Keller, with Anne Sullivan's help, had turned her dark and silent world into something that was alive, vibrant and meaningful. She didn't just exist; she lived.

She wrote, "Security is mostly a superstition. It does not exist in nature, nor do the children of men as a whole experience it. Avoiding danger is no safer in the long run than outright exposure. Life is either a daring adventure, or nothing."

How to Be Like Helen Keller

1. **Set goals.**

   After overcoming her disability, one of Keller's primary goals was to attend a college with hearing and sighted students: "The thought of going to college took root in my heart and became an earnest desire, which impelled me to enter into competition for a degree with seeing and hearing girls, in the face of the strong opposition of many true and wise friends."

2. **Don't let obstacles stop you.**

   Keller learned the manual finger alphabet to communicate and then learn. To do her school course work, Keller had to be patient and invest more hours than a sighted person. She was willing to pay the price to be educated. "It takes me a long time to prepare my lessons," she wrote, "because I have to have every word of them spelled out in my hand."

3. **Don't let others tell you what you can't do.**

   Keller wrote to the academic board at Radcliffe, who were questioning whether she'd be able to succeed there: "I realize that the obstacles in the way of my receiving a college education are very great—to others they may seem insurmountable; but, dear Sir, a true soldier does not acknowledge defeat before the battle."

4. **Pursue an education.**

   Embrace the opportunity to be educated. Keller's words apply to all: "I began my studies with eagerness. Before me I saw a new world opening in beauty and light, and I felt within me the capacity to know all things."

5. **Thirst for knowledge.**

Read good books. "I will devour every book I can lay my hands on," Keller wrote. Michael Anagnos described Keller as having a "thirst for knowledge" in his 1888 report, "Helen Keller: A Second Laura Bridgman." He further stated: "As if impelled by a resistless instinctive force [Keller] snatched the key of the treasury of the English language from the fingers of her teacher, unlocked its doors with vehemence, and began to feast on its contents with inexpressible delight."

6. **Live a life of faith.**

Keller embraced religion and God's wisdom. It helped her be at peace with her handicap: "I believe that all through these dark and silent years, God has been using my life for a purpose I do not know; but one day I shall understand and then I will be satisfied." She also said, "I cannot imagine myself without religion. I could as easily fancy a living body without a heart."

7. **Help others.**

After learning to communicate, Keller's mission from the time she was a little girl was to help others. From little Tommy Stringer to the soldiers who were the heroes of World War II, Keller tried to make other people's lives better. "I will always—as long as I have breath—work for the handicapped," Keller said on her eightieth birthday.

8. **Make your own decisions.**

Keller's friends felt vaudeville was beneath her dignity, but Keller needed to earn a living and wanted to provide something for Sullivan should she die first. Rather than listen to others, Keller evaluated the opportunity herself and developed what she felt was a dignified act. The world hasn't thought less of her because of what she did.

9. **Dare to do the impossible.**

Keller resolved to learn to speak—and worked hard to do so. Although she was never able to perfect her speaking ability, she never stopped trying. That same resolve served Keller well in other areas that she was able to master.

MARIE CURIE
1867–1934

PERSISTENCE

My work is very much my life. . . .
scientific research has its great beauty
and its reward in itself; and so I have found
happiness in my work.

—*Marie Curie*

**M**arie Curie was the first prominent female scientist, and the only woman to win two Nobel Prizes. Curie's groundbreaking work led to radiation being harnessed to fight disease, and contributed greatly to the field of atomic physics and to the application of nuclear power.

Marie Curie had to fight and even risk her life for what most of us today take for granted: the right to an education. She was born Manya Sklodowska in Poland in 1867, a nation that was under the domination of Russia, Austria and Prussia. She grew up in Warsaw, a city ruled by the Russians. They took over the school system, ordered that classes be taught only in Russian and decided the curriculums.

Women in that Poland not only weren't allowed to go to college, they weren't even allowed to take the needed courses to pass an entrance exam. Her father, Vladislav, extolled the value of education and intellectual curiosity to his daughter. He had been a professor of physics before the Russian occupation; afterwards, he made his living as a tutor. Vladislav was a highly educated man and spoke many languages. He supplemented his five children's state-controlled education with one at home as well. Through her father, she was introduced to science.

After graduating from high school, she had her mind set

on becoming a scientist. Since attending college in Poland wasn't a possibility, she risked her life to go to the "floating university." The floating university was an underground meeting place where altruistic teachers helped ambitious students like her continue their education. The university "floated" because one night the teachers and students might meet in someone's attic and the next night in someone's basement. The students managed to get Polish books and pamphlets that had been banned by the Russians. Everyone had to be extremely careful: Prison was the penalty if the Russian police caught them.

The floating university added to her education and allowed her to fight back against the Russians. While the university had many well-educated students, there were also women who had never been taught to read or write. Years later, she wrote about how the floating university instilled feelings of empowerment and justice in her: "I have a lively memory of that sympathetic atmosphere of social and intellectual comradeship. . . . I persist in believing that the ideas that then guided us are the only ones which can lead to sure social progress. We cannot hope to build a better world without improving the individual. Towards this end, each of us must work toward his own highest development, accepting at the same time his share of responsibility in the general life of humanity—our particular duty being to help those to whom we feel we can be most useful."

> *Nothing in life is to be feared. It is only to be understood.*
> —Marie Curie

To fulfill her dream of becoming a scientist, she devised a plan. The seventeen-year-old would team up with her twenty-year-old sister, Bronya, to work and save money. When they had enough, Bronya Curie would go to Paris to study medicine at the Sorbonne (which welcomed female science students), while Marie would remain in Poland to support her sister's education. Once her sister had graduated, Marie would go to France and study at the Sorbonne while Bronya supported her.

By day, Marie earned her money as a governess and tutor. By night, she continued her self-education. She wanted to be as prepared as possible for the day she would go to the Sorbonne. She studied literature and history, in addition to science. She also found a method of study that worked best for her. "I read several things at a time," she wrote in 1886. "The consecutive study of a single subject would wear out my poor little head."

Her self-education benefited from the assistance of a cousin, Joseph Boguski. He was the director of the Museum of Industry and Agriculture in Warsaw, and gave her off-hours access to a small laboratory that had the equipment she needed to conduct scientific experiments on her own. The trials and errors that she experienced taught her a valuable lesson in patience. "Progress in such matters is neither rapid nor easy," she wrote years later.

After seven long years, Bronya's studies were complete and her time had arrived. She was going to Paris and to a real college. "So it was in November 1891, at the age of twenty-four . . . that I was able to realize the dream that had been always present in my mind for several years," she wrote.

Having overcome many obstacles to get to Paris, a new set of problems was awaiting her. She knew her classes would be taught in French. She could read the language but had trouble following her professors when they were speaking it. Now, in addition to her demanding studies, she had to study the French language.

She lived with Bronya and her husband. Their home was a two-hour ride from the Sorbonne. She recognized that the four-hour commute was draining her of the mental and physical energy she needed to absorb her classes and then do her homework. She had to move closer to the Sorbonne. With little money—forty rubles a month—she lived in small, sparse rooms that would provide her shelter and the quiet she needed in which to study. "She studied in the libraries until they closed at 10 o'clock at night," wrote Beverley Birch in *Marie Curie: Courageous Pioneer in the Study of Radioactivity*. "Then, she returned in the dark to her room to read by oil lamp until she fell asleep, totally exhausted. . . . but she was always in her place in the front row of lectures making careful, detailed, rapid notes."

All the careful planning and sacrifice paid off; within a year and a half of her arrival, she had done so well with her exams that she was the top student in the physics department. She earned a physics degree in 1893 and added a mathematics degree in 1894. In 1903, Marie Curie became one of the first women in Europe to earn a doctorate in science. She lived by the words she'd written to a friend back in 1888: "First principle: never to let one's self be beaten down by persons or by events."

In 1894, Marie met Pierre Curie at the home of a friend. Pierre, who was eight years older than the twenty-seven-year-old Marie, was an accomplished scientist and college professor. He had a vision of what their life could be together. "It would be a fine thing . . . to pass our lives near each other, hypnotized by our dreams. . . . our humanitarian dream, and our scientific dream," Pierre wrote to Marie in 1894. The two were married in 1895, and she taught alongside her husband at the School of Physics and Chemistry in Paris. It was her decision to seek a doctorate that led the Curies to their destiny. She carefully read over scientific papers in search of an exciting and groundbreaking topic.

"From childhood Marie had carried the curiosity and daring of an explorer within her. This was the instinct that had driven her to leave Warsaw for Paris and the Sorbonne. . . . in her walks in the woods she always chose the wild trail or the unfrequented road," wrote Curie's daughter Eve in *Madame Curie*.

Curie decided her doctorate would explore the new field of X rays, discovered in 1895 by Wilhelm Roentgen. She read a paper by scientist Henri Becquerel, where he reported that uranium's invisible light rays had their source in the uranium itself, rather than from previous exposure to the sun. Curie decided to make a study of the uranium rays. Marie Curie's research led her, Pierre and Henri Becquerel to win the 1903 Nobel Prize in physics for their discovery of radioactivity, as she named it.

Three years later, on August 19, 1906, tragedy struck when Pierre was killed after being hit by a horse-drawn wagon. Marie was devastated, but found strength in the memory of what Pierre had often said to her. "It is impossible for me to describe the meaning and depth of this turning point in my life, as a result of the loss of him who was my closest companion and friend," she wrote. "Crushed by the blow, I am unable to think of the future. And yet, I could not forget what my husband sometimes said, that even without him I should work on."

She did. In 1911 Curie became the only person up to that time to be awarded a second Nobel Prize. This one, in chemistry, was for her discovery a number of years earlier (before her husband's death) of the elements polonium and radium, in addition to refining a precious gram of radium. Radium was found to be one million times more radioactive than the elements uranium or thorium.

Curie's unique work ethic and intellectual curiosity made the discovery possible. When she read Henri Becquerel's paper, she questioned whether only uranium gave off what she would eventually call radiation. Curie tested other elements and minerals to see what their radioactive levels were. She used a machine called an electrometer, invented by Pierre and his brother Jacques. She discovered that the mineral pitchblende was four times more radioactive than other elements that contained the same amount of uranium. There had to be something else in the pitchblende that was causing the radioactivity.

By separating out the pitchblende, Curie found two new elements, polonium (named after her native Poland) and radium. The process of refining a gram of radium was not easy. Working with her husband, Pierre, out of a shed on the campus of the School of Physics and Chemistry in Paris, it took her four hard years—from 1898 to 1902—to complete her task.

"It took a lot of work," Curie later wrote in 1923. "I had to work with as much as 45 pounds of material at a time. It was exhausting work to move the containers about, to transfer the liquids, and to stir for hours at a time, with an iron bar, the boiling material in the cast-iron basin." Curie remembered those years fondly, however, because she was doing the work she loved with the husband she loved. That proved to be a powerful combination for achievement. "We had no money, no laboratory and no help in the conduct of this important and difficult task," she wrote. "It was like creating something out of nothing. . . . it was in this miserable old shed that the best and happiest years of our life were spent, entirely consecrated to work. I sometimes passed the whole day stirring a mass in ebullition, with an iron rod nearly as big as myself. In the evening I was broken with fatigue."

Curie's discovery led to radiation being harnessed in order to treat cancer. She also showed that radiation's origin was the atom, which led to the field of atomic physics and the application of nuclear power. Years later, Albert Einstein would write in his 1950 book, *Out of My Later Years,* that "the greatest scientific deed of her life—proving the existence of radioactive elements and isolating them—owes its accomplishment not merely to bold intuition but to a devotion . . . under the most extreme hardships imaginable, such as the history of experimental science has not often witnessed."

Curie's accomplishments and celebrity didn't change her personality and work ethic. She avoided the limelight and found her greatest professional and personal satisfaction working in her laboratory.

"Marie Curie is, of all celebrated beings, the only one whom fame has not corrupted," said Einstein, who believed that Curie's moral qualities were even greater than her intellectual ones. "Her strength, her purity of will, her austerity toward herself, her objectivity, her incorruptible judgment— all these were of a kind seldom found joined in a single individual. She felt herself at every moment to be a servant of society and her profound modesty never left any room for complacency," he wrote. "Once she had recognized a certain way as the right one, she pursued it without compromise and with extreme tenacity."

If Curie and her husband had patented their methods for producing radium, they could have become extremely

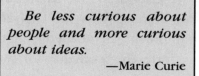

Be less curious about people and more curious about ideas.
—Marie Curie

wealthy, but they chose not to. Their interest was in the public good rather than in their own enrichment. "If our discovery has a commercial future, that is an accident by which we must not profit. And radium is going to be of use in treating disease. . . . it seems impossible to take advantage of that," Curie said.

She believed in the need of the businessman, but she believed more in the pursuit of science for the common good without financial gain. "Humanity certainly needs practical men, who get the most out of their work, and, without forgetting the general good, safeguard their own interests," Curie wrote. "But humanity also needs dreamers, for whom the disinterested development of an enterprise is so captivating that it becomes impossible for them to devote their care to their own material profit. Without the slightest doubt, these dreamers do not deserve wealth, because they do not desire it."

"Even so," Curie added, "a well-organized society should assure to such workers the efficient means of accomplishing their task, in a life freed from material care and freely consecrated to research."

During World War I, Curie's selfless attitude was evident again. Looking for a way to contribute to France and the Allied war effort, Curie took it upon herself to set up mobile

X-ray units that could travel up and down the front lines to supply aid to the wounded men. Much like Clara Barton over fifty years earlier, Curie garnered what she needed from her own efforts. She raised money and supplies from humanitarian organizations and private citizens. She got the X-ray equipment she needed from the universities.

Curie, the woman with two Nobel awards, drove one of the mobile units and personally took X rays herself—in addition to training 150 others how to do it. Curie's mobile X-ray units grew to twenty vehicles and were called "The Little Curies" by the soldiers. Another 200 stationary X-ray units were placed in military hospitals.

She believed that gaining firsthand knowledge was the best way to determine the needs of the men. "In examining the wounded in the hospital," she wrote, "I could gain information of the special needs of the region. When back in Paris, I got the necessary equipment to meet these needs and returned to install it myself, for very often people on the ground could not do it." More than one million wounded soldiers had X rays taken in these facilities. Because of a better diagnosis of their patients' wounds, doctors were able to save countless lives.

Curie's selflessness in the face of her celebrity served as an example to her daughters, Irene and Eve. Irene, seventeen at the time, assisted her mother with the mobile X-ray project, although Eve was too young. Curie raised her daughters to appreciate education and taught them to be patient and avoid mistakes when dealing with complex science or math problems. Irene went on to marry scientist Frederic Joliot, and in 1935 they were awarded a Nobel Prize for their discovery of artificial radiation.

Her accomplishments came while she was suffering from radiation sickness. In fact, both Curies had been too sick to travel in 1903 to accept their Nobel Prize. Marie Curie's symptoms included chronic fatigue and burned and peeling skin, especially on her hands, which came into direct contact with radioactive substances, such as purified radium.

For the first few years of the Curies' research, little was known about the effects of radiation on the human body. By 1901, scientists understood the danger and minimized their exposure to the harmful rays. The Curies did not take the necessary precautions, although they insisted that their assistants do so.

For the good of science and society, Curie was willing to go outside of her comfort zone. She was famous, but uncomfortable in the spotlight. Her daughter Eve wrote, "She had always fled from the crowd." When Curie became director of the Institute of Radium in 1912, it barely had a gram of radium to conduct research. A gram cost $100,000 to produce, and the Institute needed at least another gram. In 1920 an opportunity presented itself. Mrs. William Brown Meloney, an American magazine editor, met Curie in 1920 and created a committee that launched the Marie Curie Radium Fund. A year later, she wrote Curie to say, "The money has been found, the radium is yours." Meloney and the committee had one request of Curie: "Why should you not come to see us? We want to know you."

"The trials and display of a visit to America, to the one country in the world which most thirsted after publicity, terrified her," Eve Curie wrote. Meloney suggested that Curie bring her daughters with her. "We shall make it a fine journey for you," she said, "and the [symbol] of [a] gram of radium will be solemnly presented to you at the White House by the President [Warren Harding] of the United States in person." (The actual gram was too dangerous to transport and required special handling.)

The night before the ceremony, Meloney gave Curie a paper acknowledging the gift of radium. Curie read the document and said, "This paper must be modified. The radium offered me by America must belong to science. So long as I am alive, it goes without saying that I shall use it only for scientific work. . . . I want to make it a gift to my laboratory." Curie insisted that a lawyer be called that evening to change the document to reflect her wishes.

In 1929, President Herbert Hoover also presented Curie with a gram of the precious radium.

In her advancing years, plagued by radiation sickness, Curie kept working twelve- to fourteen-hour days. She loved her work and refused to rest on her accomplishments. In 1934, at age sixty-six, Curie died of leukemia—brought on by years of exposure to radiation. "She was on that last day just as gentle, stubborn, timid and curious about all things as in the days of her obscure beginnings," Eve Curie wrote.

Curie's legacy is in the field of atomic physics. Robert Reid, in his book *Marie Curie*, wrote that she was the first woman to make a "significant contribution to science."

Curie and her husband are buried in the Pantheon in France. She is the first woman buried there. In the past, it had been reserved to honor France's great men. Several countries have also recognized Curie with commemorative stamps, and she has been immortalized with a statue of her in deep thought, in front of the Cancer Research Institute in Warsaw.

Eve Curie described her mother's unique character in moving words: "Marie Curie was even more rare than her work or her life: the immovable structure of a character; the stubborn effort of an intelligence; the free immolation of a being that could give all and take nothing, could even receive nothing; and above all the quality of a soul in which neither fame nor adversity could change the exceptional purity. Because she had that soul, without the slightest sacrifice Marie Curie rejected money, comfort, and the thousand advantages that genuinely great [people] may obtain from immense fame. . . . she did not know how to be famous."

In 1894, long before her historic accomplishments, Marie Curie wrote these prophetic words: "Life is not easy for any of us. But what of that? We must have perseverance and above all confidence in ourselves. We must believe that we are gifted for something, and that this thing, at whatever cost, must be attained. Perhaps everything will turn out very well at the moment when we least expect it."

How to Be Like
Marie Curie

1. **Decide what you want from life.**

    For Curie, education and the opportunity to contribute to society was what she wanted. "We cannot hope to build a better world without improving the individual," she wrote. "Towards this end, each of us must work toward his own highest development, accepting at the same time his share of responsibility in the general life of humanity—our particular duty being to help those to whom we feel we can be most useful."

2. **Devise a plan to make your dreams happen.**

    Curie first determined that she needed a partner, and found one in her sister Bronya. They then combined their resources to send each other to college.

3. **Be persistent.**

    Curie wrote that success in science was "neither rapid nor easy." It was that attitude that led to her discovery and isolation of radium. She advised her daughters that her secret to avoiding mistakes when dealing with complex science or math problems was persistence.

4. **Mentally prepare yourself for obstacles.**

    In the face of a repressive Russian occupation of Poland, Curie risked her life to attend the floating university. At the Sorbonne, she had to learn French to understand her professors, and lived an austere existence. She graduated at the top of her class. Curie wrote: "[The] first principle: never to let one's self be beaten down by persons or by events."

5. **Be intellectually curious.**

Curie asked questions and worked to find the answers. By asking herself if uranium was the only element that emits energy, she began the process that led to the discovery and refinement of radium, which resulted in her second Nobel Prize.

6. **Never give up.**

Curie lost her mother to tuberculosis when she was only ten, and when she lost the love of her life, Pierre, she felt like giving up. "I am unable to think of the future," she wrote. "And yet, I could not forget what my husband sometimes said, that even without him I should work on."

7. **Stay humble—regardless of your accomplishments.**

"Marie Curie is, of all celebrated beings, the only one whom fame has not corrupted," Albert Einstein said. "She felt herself at every moment to be a servant of society and her profound modesty never left any room for complacency." Eva Curie wrote of her mother: "She did not know how to be famous."

8. **Consider the public good before thinking of yourself.**

Curie and Pierre could have become fabulously wealthy, but chose not to patent their process of refining radium. Curie said: "If our discovery has a commercial future, that is an accident by which we must not profit. And radium is going to be of use in treating disease. . . . it seems impossible to take advantage of that."

9. **Contribute to society.**

During World War I, Curie set up mobile X-ray units that could travel up and down the front lines to help the wounded men. She also had 200 stationary units put into military hospitals. Curie, the recipient of two Nobel Prizes, drove one of her mobile X-ray units to help the wounded soldiers.

10. **Believe in yourself.**

"Life is not easy for any of us. But what of that?" Curie wrote. "We must have perseverance and above all confidence in ourselves. We must believe that we are gifted for something, and that this thing, at whatever cost, must be attained."

BABE DIDRIKSON ZAHARIAS
1911–1956

COMPETITIVENESS

You have to get yourself all fired up to win these (golf) tournaments. It's even harder to stay at the top in sports than it is to get there.

—*Babe Didrikson Zaharias*

Babe Didrikson Zaharias is considered the greatest female athlete in history. Her achievements helped open the door and create more opportunities for women athletes.

For Mildred "Babe" Didrikson, the path to success and influence was simple: She knew exactly what she wanted out of life and was willing to pay the price to get there. "Before I was even into my teens," Didrikson said in her autobiography *This Life I've Led,* "my goal was to be the greatest athlete that ever lived."

At a time when women athletes were few, and opportunities for them rare, Didrikson ignored the obstacles and her critics to excel in basketball, tennis, diving, bowling, track and field, and the sport she is most remembered for, golf. She took her God-given, natural athletic ability and refined it through a relentless work ethic.

"I'm convinced that Babe is the single, finest, most important athlete in the history of the United States. Babe was a trailblazer. She raised women's sports to a new level with her fierce competitiveness," said Susan E. Cayleff in an interview. Cayleff is the author of *Babe: The Life and Legend of Babe Didrikson Zaharias,* which was nominated for a Pulitzer Prize.

All her life, Didrikson refused to be defined by others'

perceptions of her. The first organized sport she wanted to play was basketball, for her Beaumont (Texas) High School girls' team, but she was told that at five feet, six inches, she was too small. "I couldn't accept the idea that I wasn't good enough for the basketball team," Didrikson said, whose adult height was five feet six inches. "I was determined to show everybody." To improve, Babe went to Coach Lilburn Dimmit of Beaumont's boys' basketball team, and asked him to teach her how to be a better player. She showed Dimmit her commitment by practicing on her own. "He took the time to help me, because he could see I was interested," Didrikson said.

> *Oh, how that girl would work for the things she wanted.*
> —Lillie Didrikson,
> BABE DIDRIKSON'S SISTER

Babe became an all-city and Texas all-state high school basketball player. She was so good that she attracted the attention of Melvin J. McCombs, who was a manager with the Employers Casualty Company, located in Dallas. McCombs wanted Didrikson to become a secretary/typist for the company so she could play on its Amateur Athletic Union (AAU) team, the Golden Cyclones. After talking it over with her parents, Didrikson left school immediately to play and work for Employers Casualty. After the season, she returned to school to finish her studies and graduate.

Didrikson was a prolific scorer, averaging around thirty points a game at a time when entire women's teams didn't score that many points in a game. She averaged thirty-two points per game during the 1931 season, when she led her Golden Cyclone team to the AAU National Championship. Didrikson was named to the women's All-American basketball team in 1930, 1931 and 1932.

After achieving so much success in basketball, Didrikson started looking for a new challenge. After McCombs took Didrikson to her first track meet, they agreed that Employers Casualty should have a women's track and field team. While other women candidates for the team picked an individual sport, such as the javelin, discus or hurdles, Didrikson decided she wanted to compete in all of them.

The Olympics had been a goal of hers since 1928. Didrikson's father had been following the Olympic games that year, held in Amsterdam, when Didrikson announced to him, "Next year I'm going to be in the Olympics myself." Her father had to explain to her that since the Olympics were held every four years, she'd have to wait.

Didrikson set her sights on the high hurdles. She began to practice by hurdling the hedges that separated the neighbors' houses on her block. There were seven of them, but one of them was too high for Didrikson. So she knocked on that neighbor's door and asked the owner, Mr. King, if he wouldn't mind cutting down his hedge a little for her. He obliged.

With the support of Employers Casualty, Didrikson's Olympic goal had a real chance, and she took full advantage of it. "I really worked hard at that track and field," Didrikson said. "I trained and trained and trained. I've been that way in every sport I've taken up. After dinner . . . I'd go out to Lakeside Park at night and practice by myself until it got dark, which wasn't until nine or nine-thirty at that time of year. If there was good clear moonlight, I might keep going even longer."

In July 1932, Employers Casualty sent their entire team, which consisted of only Didrikson, to the AAU Women's Track and Field National Championships, in Evanston, Illinois. This event also doubled for the Olympic tryouts. When it was over, Didrikson had won six of the eight events she entered. She won first place in the broad jump and shot put, and set world records for women in the javelin throw (139 feet, 6¼ inches), baseball throw (272 feet, 2 inches), and 80-meter hurdles (12.1 seconds). She tied another competitor, Jean Shiley, for first place in the high jump. Their jumps of 5 feet, 3³/₁₆ inches established a new world record in that event.

Didrikson's incredible performance earned her thirty points, which meant she had singlehandedly won the AAU Championship for the Golden Cyclones—which should have been called the "Golden Cyclone" that day! George Kirksey covered the meet for the United Press and wrote that Didrikson's achievements were "the most amazing series of performances ever accomplished by any individual, male or female, in track and field history."

She was now headed for the Olympic games, held that year in Los Angeles. At the games, Didrikson won the gold medal in the javelin throw, while establishing a new world record of 143 feet, 4 inches. She also wound up with torn cartilage in her shoulder because of the throws, and had to endure the rest of her Olympic events with constant pain.

In the 80-meter hurdles, Didrikson set a new world record with a time of 11.7 seconds and won her second gold medal. In the high jump, Didrikson appeared to have tied Jean Shiley again, with a jump of 5 feet, 5¼ inches. But because the judges determined that Didrikson cleared the bar head first, which violated the women's rule of having to clear it feet first, Shiley was declared the winner, and Didrikson was given second place and the silver medal. The next year, however, the women's "feet first" rule was eliminated to conform with the men's rule, which had no such restriction. Didrikson was retroactively made the coholder of the high-jump world record with Shiley.

Concerning Didrikson's Olympic performance, the legendary sportswriter Grantland Rice wrote:"She is beyond all belief until you see her perform. Then you finally understand that you are looking at the most flawless section of muscle harmony, of complete mental and physical coordination the world of sport has ever known. . . . There is only one Babe Didrikson and there has never been another in her class—even close to her class."

In recognition of the way Didrikson dominated track and field in 1932, she was named the outstanding Woman Athlete of the Year by the Associated Press (AP) poll of sports editors. It was the first of an unprecedented six times that AP honored her with that award. The next five times would be for her dominance of women's golf. In 1950, AP named Didrikson the Outstanding Woman Athlete of the Half-Century. In 1999, AP, ESPN and *Sports Illustrated* named Didrikson the greatest female athlete of the twentieth century.

The Olympic games that Didrikson competed in were held at a time when female participation in the games was minor and almost scoffed at by some men. Avery Brundage, president of the AAU, was quoted as saying,"You know, the ancient Greeks kept women out of their athletic games. . . . They wouldn't even let them on the sidelines. I'm not so sure but they were right." Others who disparaged the inclusion of women competitors included the founder of the modern Olympic movement, Baron Pierre de Coubertin.

Didrikson never allowed herself to be beaten down by prevailing opinions. She competed in sports because she loved competition. Didrikson charmed the media by just being herself. Because she was colorful, charismatic and good-natured, even her extreme boastfulness was acceptable to the media and public that embraced her. "[Her] honesty . . . is uninhibited either by vainglory or false modesty," wrote sportswriter Harry Paxton, who helped Didrikson write her autobiography. "[Babe] lays it right on the line, without striving for any calculated effect. The Babe doesn't pretend to be anything more than what she is. Nor does she pretend to be anything less."

With respect to the writing of her book, Paxton said Didrikson "never stopped to calculate her words so as to put the best possible construction on potentially controversial matters. On all phases of her life, the details flowed out with the characteristic spontaneity of this woman who doesn't try to fool anybody—including herself."

But Babe did know, for the good of her career, when it was time to conform. It was her friend, golfer and socialite Bertha Bowen, Cayleff said, who began the feminization of the tomboyish Babe. "It was their project," Cayleff said. "Bertha is the one who took Babe to Neiman Marcus and bought her $700 worth of clothes and said to Babe 'You're never going to get endorsements, people aren't going to take you seriously . . . if you keep looking like a boy.'" (At the height of her career and popularity, in 1948, Babe did make over $100,000 in endorsements, appearances and exhibitions, Cayleff wrote.)

Despite her popularity with the public, after the Olympics Didrikson had to scramble in order to make a living. She did have some endorsement opportunities,

> *Winning has always meant much to me, but winning friends has meant the most.*
> —Babe Didrikson

then, but nothing on a par—in 1930s' dollars—with what top athletes are paid today. For a week she did a vaudeville act consisting of four or five shows a day, that showed off her athletic prowess. She was partnered with a professional entertainer, George Libbey.

Didrikson started her portion of the act by playing her harmonica and singing. Then she jumped on a treadmill that was connected to a large clock to display her speed. She also jumped hurdles and hit plastic golf balls. Her act was successful, she was a hit and the audiences wanted encores. The show apparently paid her well and had advance bookings for other cities, but she canceled all of them after only one week because she wasn't enjoying herself. Didrikson wasn't an entertainer; she was an athlete. "I don't want the money if I have to make it this way," Didrikson told her sister Nancy. "I want to live my life outdoors. I want to play golf."

Didrikson went back to her old formula for success: working hard and setting goals. She set her sights on winning the Texas State Women's Golf Championship for amateurs. During the week when she was working, Didrikson would practice from 5:30 A.M. to 8:30 A.M., then leave for the office. After work, at around 3:30, she resumed practicing until it became too dark to continue. On the weekends, she devoted twelve to sixteen hours a day practicing her golf swing. "I'd hit 1,500 golf balls until my hands were bloody and sore," Didrikson wrote. "I'd have tape all over my hands, and blood all over the tape." The hard work resulted in the attainment of her goal: Didrikson won the Texas State Women's Golf Championship in April 1935.

A few days later, however, the United States Golf Association (USGA) declared that Didrikson was ineligible to participate as an amateur because they deemed her a professional athlete. Their decision was supposedly made on the basis that Didrikson had taken money for baseball, basketball and billiards exhibitions. Many sportswriters pointed out the ruling made no sense, but Didrikson rolled with the punches.

"When you get a big setback like that, there's no use crying about it," Didrikson said. Harry Paxton wrote that in interviewing Didrikson for her book, he was struck by her "lack of animosity toward the occasional persons and organizations whose actions have impeded her progress. She seldom expresses even mild resentment, and in no case does she indicate any lasting feeling of ill will. She's the same way in private conversation. She doesn't go in for backbiting and running people down. Malice and spite are not part of her make-up."

After her amateur status was revoked, Didrikson regrouped and continued to work to improve her game by entering golf tournaments that were open to anyone. She made money playing exhibitions with the top male pro golfer of the day, Gene Sarazen, and took advantage of the opportunity to learn from him. "I kept asking him questions and questions. If I was going to be the best, I wanted to learn from the best," Didrikson wrote.

"She was very intense and wanted to learn," Sarazen recalled. "We'd play an eighteen-hole exhibition and then she'd go right back out and practice what she saw. She learned all her golf by watching. She'd stand ten feet away from me and watch everything I did. Then she'd go out and practice it for hours. If she couldn't do it, she'd ask me about it. She was a very heady golfer."

Didrikson pushed on. She won the Western Women's Open in 1940, and in 1943 the USGA reinstated her amateur status so she could begin competing again. Between 1946 and 1947, Didrikson won seventeen straight tournaments. In 1949, after dominating the women's golf circuit, Didrikson helped to start the Ladies Professional Golf Association (LPGA). She and others wanted to begin laying the foundation so that in time women, too, could compete for substantial cash awards. Up to that time, prize money was meager for women who won tournaments. During its first three years, Didrikson won the most tournaments and prize money of anyone on the LPGA tour. She was one of four inducted into the first LPGA Hall of Fame in 1951.

Didrikson was colorful and cocky from the time she was a teenager. "Okay, Didrikson's here! Now who's gonna finish second," she'd ask her fellow competitors in the locker room before the start of a tournament. While her attitude didn't always endear her to her fellow competitors, it was a boast and a confidence that was born of preparation and practice.

The way Didrikson's life ended was indicative of the way she lived it, and why she was able to become the greatest woman athlete of all time. At the height of her career in April 1953, Didrikson was diagnosed with colon cancer. An operation followed and a colostomy was performed. Didrikson resolved to stay emotionally strong. "All my life I've been competing—and competing to win," Didrikson said. "I came to realize that in its way, this cancer was the

> *I liked [Babe] very much. ...She was friendly, and she was confident and fun loving. Babe was just unique. She was kind of cocky, it's true, but I guess she had every reason to be, because as far as sports went, she was outstanding.*
> —Bea Smith,
> HIGH SCHOOL FRIEND AND ATHLETE, AS QUOTED IN
> *BABE DIDRIKSON ZAHARIAS*

toughest competition I'd faced yet. I made up my mind that I was going to lick it all the way. I not only wasn't going to let it kill me, I wasn't even going to let it put me on the shelf. I was determined to come back and win golf championships just the same as before. You just have to face your problem and figure out what to do next."

Ten days after her operation, Didrikson was walking around the hospital and visiting children—and any other patients she could find—to cheer them up. A little more than three months after her surgery, Didrikson entered the All-American Golf Tournament, held at the Tam O'Shanter Country Club near Chicago. After playing poorly the first and second day, Didrikson started off the third day the same way. She was demoralized. "I was beginning to think it was true what so many people had said," she wrote. "That I'd never be able to play championship golf again. . . . I walked on to the sixth tee, and sat down on my seat cane. And then—I couldn't stop myself—I put my face in my hands and just bawled."

Her husband and manager, George Zaharias, along with her friend and fellow golfer, Betty Dodd, went over to

> *I don't guess I have to tell you that I was a pretty competitive type myself.*
> —Babe Didrikson Zaharias

her. They both told Didrikson that if she wanted to, she should just pick up her ball and go back to the clubhouse. Everyone would understand given what she had been through with her illness. "I told them, 'I don't pick up the ball!' I went on and played out the round, and my game began coming back." In 1954, Didrikson won four major tournaments. She was again named the AP Woman Athlete of the Year.

"There are several reasons why I didn't retire from golf after that 1953 cancer business," Didrikson said. "One reason is that every time I get out and play well in a golf tournament, it seems to buck up people with the same cancer trouble I had. I can tell that from the letters I keep getting."

Didrikson became a highly visible spokesperson for the American Cancer Society. She helped to raise money to fight the disease and to help people with cancer. Didrikson made it a point to visit cancer patients in the cities where she played tournaments, and she eventually started the Babe Didrikson Zaharias Cancer Fund.

"I think that [her cancer] really was a time in her life when she distinguished herself with some very significant humanitarian aspects, because people didn't go public with cancer in the early mid 1950's," Cayleff said. "She did something that really nobody had done and I [compare] it to Rock Hudson going public with AIDS and Magic Johnson going public with HIV." Didrikson's decision helped bring needed funding to fight the disease.

In 1955, tests determined that Didrikson had cancer again. "[Babe] took the bad news like the mighty champion she has always been. . . . She's not giving up. . . . She never flinched when told she had another cancer," George Zaharias told the media. While she made her last stand, Didrikson again used her time in the hospital to cheer up children and other adults.

Her fight ended on September 27, 1956 when Didrikson died. She was forty-five years old. Bertha Bowen, her close friend and fellow golfer, said, "I guess she never gave up. She kept her gold clubs in the room right to the end."

Too weak to talk near the end, Didrikson whispered to George, "I hate to die. . . . I'm just learning to play golf."

Her optimistic spirit was evident in the last line of her autobiography, which she wrote after the return of her cancer and about a before her death. "In the future, maybe I'll have to limit myself to just a few of the most important tournaments each year. But I expect to be shooting for championships for a good many years to come. My autobiography isn't finished yet."

In a sense, her words are true. Largely because of what Didrikson accomplished, greater athletic opportunities for women, in high school, college and professionally, were set into motion and have continued. In a 1982 poll of America's leading sports historians, who were asked to rank the ten most outstanding and influential athletes or administrators in sports history, Didrikson came in second—to Babe Ruth.

Didrikson's life was one of a single-minded pursuit of excellence. "All my life I've always had the urge to do things better than anybody else," she said.

> *I should like to take one minute to pay a tribute to Mrs. Zaharias, Babe Didrikson. She was a woman who, in her athletic career, certainly won the admiration of every person in the United States, all sports people over the world . . . and in her gallant fight against cancer, she put up one of the kinds of fights that inspired us all.*
> —President Dwight D. Eisenhower, speaking in a press conference on the day of Didrikson's death

How to Be Like
Babe Didrikson Zaharias

1. **Develop clear goals.**

   Didrikson said: "Before I was even into my teens . . . My goal was to be the greatest athlete that ever lived."

2. **Be willing to pay the price to improve.**

   Whether it involved basketball, track and field, or golf, Didrikson's intense desire to practice and improve was relentless. "I trained and trained and trained," she said. "I've been that way in every sport I've taken up."

3. **Don't allow others to define who you are.**

   Didrikson never listened to critics or to society's perception of what she should be. As a teenager trying to make her high school girls' basketball team, she was told she was too small. "I couldn't accept the idea that I wasn't good enough for the basketball team," Didrikson said, and went on to excel in the sport.

4. **Recognize when you're being sidetracked.**

   Didrikson was making good money doing her vaudeville act, but canceled it after only one week. She knew she wasn't an entertainer; she was an athlete. "I don't want the money if I have to make it this way," Didrikson said to her sister Nancy. "I want to live my life outdoors. I want to play golf."

5. **Seek out experts and learn from them.**

   Didrikson made money playing exhibitions with the top male pro golfer, Gene Sarazen, and took advantage of the opportunity to learn from him. "I kept asking him questions and questions. If I was going to be the best, I wanted to learn from the best," Didrikson said. At Beaumont High School, it was the boys' basketball coach, Coach Lilburn Dimmit, that Didrikson asked to work with her to improve her game.

6. **Be yourself.**

Didrikson connected with the media and the public because she was always just herself. Harry Paxton wrote of Didrikson in the introduction to her autobiography that she had an "honesty that is uninhibited either by vainglory or false modesty. [Didrikson] lays it right on the line, without striving for any calculated effect."

7. **Stay mentally tough.**

After the United States Golf Association stripped Didrikson's amateur status from her, and she was declared ineligible to play, she entered open tournaments and played in exhibitions with Gene Sarazen. "When you get a big setback like that, there's no use crying about it," Didrikson said.

8. **Guard against bitterness.**

Bitterness is a negative emotion that prevents you from overcoming injustices, and it gives power to those who caused the situation. Harry Paxton wrote that he was struck by Didrikson's "lack of animosity toward the occasional persons and organizations whose actions have impeded her progress. She seldom expresses even mild resentment, and in no case does she indicate any lasting feeling of ill will. . . . Malice and spite are not part of her make-up."

9. **Be courageous.**

Find the courage within you, although this may be easier said than done—especially when confronted by the kind of illness that Didrikson faced. Her example and formula for courage was straightforward: "You just have to face your problem and figure out what to do next," she said of her cancer diagnosis. While Didrikson was never particularly religious, she turned to God for strength to help her cope with her illness.

10. **Keep doing what you love.**

After her cancer diagnosis, Didrikson said: "I was determined to come back and win golf championships just the same as before." In 1954, the year after her first cancer diagnosis and subsequent surgery, Didrikson won four major tournaments. She was again named the AP Woman Athlete of the Year.

11. **Give back to society.**

Didrikson did this by helping make life better for those suffering from cancer. She became a highly visible spokesperson and fund-raiser for the American Cancer Society, and started the Babe Didrikson Zaharias Cancer Fund.

12. **Strive to be the best at whatever you do.**

"All my life I've always had the urge to do things better than anybody else," Didrikson said.

AMELIA EARHART
1897–1937

DARING

The most difficult thing is the decision to act, the rest is merely tenacity. The fears are paper tigers. You can do anything you decide to do.

—Amelia Earhart

melia Earhart was the most famous woman aviator of the 1920s and 1930s. Her achievements made her a household name that endures to this day. Indeed, by June 1928, it seemed as though almost everyone in America was impressed with Amelia Earhart. There was one notable exception: Amelia Earhart herself.

She was lauded by press and public as the first woman to fly across the Atlantic Ocean. Earhart had been part of the *Friendship* crew, one of the first airplanes to make the crossing successfully. *Friendship* took off from Trepassey Bay, Newfoundland, on June 17, 1928, and arrived twenty hours and forty minutes later in Wales. The flight was put together and financed by Amy Guest, who believed it would make a show of goodwill and friendship between the United States and Great Britain.

When Guest decided that she wanted an "American girl of the right image" included in the crew, the thirty-one-year-old Earhart was selected. She was already an accomplished pilot who at one time had held the women's altitude record (14,000 feet) and had more than 500 solo hours in the air. She was named the commander of the flight, but Earhart didn't do any of the actual flying because she wasn't trained in instrument navigation. In addition to supervising the flight, she recorded events in a logbook.

Upon *Friendship's* landing, Hilton Railey, who was in charge of public relations for the flight, asked Earhart how it felt to be the first woman to have flown across the Atlantic. Earhart said she felt like a sack of potatoes, because she was just baggage. She later told the *New York Times* on June 19: "I was just a passenger on the journey—just a passenger. Everything that was done to bring us across was done by [pilot] Wilmer Stultz."

When President Calvin Coolidge sent a telegram congratulating her and "co-pilot" Mr. Wilmer Stultz, Earhart sent a telegram back to the president that read, "SUCCESS ENTIRELY DUE [TO] GREAT SKILL OF MR. STULTZ."

Earhart was smart, talented and attractive. She received some criticism that only mirrored what she'd already said about her flight contributions, but her press was overwhelmingly favorable. The modest Earhart was now a celebrity. She received a book offer from publisher George Putnam (whom she later married) to write her account of the *Friendship* flight. The book was called *20 Hrs., 40 Min.* Then *Cosmopolitan* magazine hired Earhart to write a regular column on flying. She was in demand on the lecture circuit, and she was asked to promote such things as clothing and luggage.

Still, there was something missing for Earhart. She wanted to be worthy of the admiration she was now receiving. Earhart was a pilot, not a passenger. She soon set an ambitious goal for herself: to become the first woman pilot to solo across the Atlantic Ocean. It would be an extremely dangerous flight, and Earhart gauged her chances of successfully completing it at "one in ten."

Success didn't come to Earhart by accident. She had been studying the topic from the time she was a teenager in college.

> *Courage is the price that*
> *life exacts for granting peace.*
> —Amelia Earhart,
> IN HER 1927 POEM "COURAGE"

Earhart cut out articles on successful women who were making their mark in areas that had been reserved for men, such as business and law. She kept the articles in a scrapbook for reference. She also had definite ideas about what women had to do to succeed in life. When she came across an article about a proposed law that would guarantee women their property and inheritance rights, Earhart expressed her disagreement with the need for women to depend on legal remedies as the sole way to protect their rights. "This method is not sound," she wrote. "Women will gain economic justice by proving themselves in all lines of endeavor, not by having laws passed for them."

At a young age, Earhart showed the type of character, kindness and social responsibility that allowed her to later meet Amy Guest's requirement for an "American girl of the right image." At Ogontz College in Pennsylvania, she was upset that some girls couldn't get into one of the three sororities. She tried to change that by asking the faculty to approve a fourth one, and eventually quit her own because she didn't like it that some girls were excluded from sororities in general.

Earhart's compassion for people also led her to become a nurse's aide during World War I. She was serving in Toronto, Canada, in 1917 when she came face-to-face with the realities of war. "There for the first time I realized what world war meant," Earhart wrote. "Instead of new uniforms and brass bands I saw only the results of four years' desperate struggle; men without arms and legs, men who were paralyzed and men who were blind."

Earhart took her first plane ride in 1920 when she was twenty-three years old. She liked air shows and after attending a show in Los Angeles, where her family had moved, her father paid a pilot ten dollars for a ten-minute plane ride for her. From the first time Earhart soared in an airplane, she knew she'd found her life's passion. "As soon as we left the ground I knew I myself had to fly," Earhart wrote in her book *The Fun of It*. She soon learned that in order to fly, she would have to work hard to pay for it. Her first twelve hours of instruction would cost $500. Earhart and her family, with whom she was living, couldn't afford that. So Earhart got a job to pay for her lessons herself.

She sought out the best flight instructors, such as Anita "Neta" Snook and a former army flight instructor, John Montijo. Neta recalled Earhart's words when they first met: "I'm Amelia Earhart. . . . I want to learn to fly. . . . Will you teach me?" Snook taught Earhart, among other things, to check things for herself and not take little things for granted—right down to making sure that she had a full tank of gas in the airplane, rather than taking someone else's word for it.

When she was not flying or working, Earhart spent time peppering experienced pilots with questions. She possessed an intellectual curiosity that was evident from the time she was a student. "Earhart was always pushing into unknown seas in her reading," said her headmaster at Ogontz College.

In 1926, Earhart became a social worker and helped immigrant families learn English and receive proper health care. In April 1928 Hilton Railey called her about joining the crew of the *Friendship*. In addition to her own personal need to try to solo across the Atlantic, she also believed it would be a positive thing for the entire women's movement, which she supported. Her celebrity after the *Friendship* flight gave her a voice in the movement.

"After the pleasant accident of being the first woman to cross the Atlantic by air," Earhart wrote in her book *Last Flight*, "I was launched into a life full of interest.... With these activities came opportunity to know women everywhere who shared my conviction that there is so much women can do in the modern world and should be permitted to do irrespective of their sex. Probably my greatest satisfaction was to indicate by example now and then, that women can sometimes do things themselves if given the chance."

Earhart hoped that her accomplishments in the air would inspire women and girls on the ground. She wanted them to try to achieve things that had previously only been in the domain of males. "There are no heroines following the shining paths of romantic adventure, as do the heroes of boys' books," she said. "Of course girls have been reading the so-called boys' books ever since there was such. But consider what it means to do so. Instead of closing the covers with shining eyes and the happy thought, 'That might happen to me someday!', the girls turning the final page can only sigh regretfully, 'Oh, dear, that can never happen to me—because I'm not a boy.'"

With the money Earhart was making from writing and lecture tours, she put her plan into action to solo the Atlantic and began honing her flying skills. She hadn't been able to pilot the *Friendship* flight because she had no experience with instruments and multiengine airplanes. Now she sought out navigation instruction from an expert, James Kimball. Earhart prepared for her transcontinental flight by practicing the things she needed to know in order to make the journey successfully.

On May 20, 1932, after five years of preparation, Earhart took off from Harbor Grace, Newfoundland, in the evening. The first few hours of the flight were routine. Then suddenly, at 12,000 feet, her altimeter failed. For the rest of the flight she never knew what her altitude was. She did have a barograph, however, which told her when she was gaining or losing altitude. Earhart also encountered a severe storm, complete with lightning. Ice built up on the plane, sending it into a dangerous spin. Earhart, however, was prepared for this: She had studied stunt flying with John Montijo.

Earhart didn't study stunt flying because she wanted to be a stunt pilot, but because she wanted to be a live pilot. "A knowledge of some stunts is judged necessary to good flying," she wrote in *The Fun of It*. "Unless a pilot has actually recovered from a stall, has actually put his plane into a spin and brought it out, he cannot know accurately what those acts entail. He should be familiar enough with abnormal positions of his craft to recover without having to think how."

Earhart straightened her plane out, and soon she flew into daybreak. When she finally saw a small fishing boat, she knew she was close to land. When she reached it, she looked for an airfield to land. When she couldn't find one, she put her Lockheed down in a large pasture. Earhart had landed in Culmore, Northern Ireland. Her "audience" included some grazing cows and a man named Danny McCallion. She had become the first woman to fly solo across the Atlantic, and she joined Charles Lindbergh as the only other person in the world to have accomplished this feat.

Earhart, who was also the first person to cross the Atlantic twice in an airplane, had traveled 2,026 miles in record time: 14 hours and 56 minutes. She said her accomplishment served as a lesson learned: "To want in one's heart to do a thing, for its own sake; to enjoy doing it; to concentrate all one's energies upon it—that is not only the surest guarantee of its success, it is also being true to oneself. If there is anything I have learned in life it is this: If you follow the inner desire of your heart, the incidentals will take care of themselves."

Earhart mania was now in full throttle. In Europe, after the flight, the pope and other dignitaries greeted Earhart and her husband, George Putnam. Wherever she went, adoring crowds were waiting to mob her. When she returned to America, her ticker-tape parade in New York was as big as the one given for Charles Lindbergh years before. She met with President Herbert Hoover and received from him the National Geographic Society's Gold Medal in recognition of her accomplishment. Hoover praised Earhart by saying that she wanted "to help others share in the rich opportunities in life." He added that the publicity from her accomplishments helped to "enlarge those opportunities by expanding the powers of women."

> *I can give you a six-word formula for success: Think things through—then follow through.*
> —Eddie Rickenbacker, AVIATOR

"I shall be happy if my small exploit has drawn attention to the fact that women are flying, too," Earhart said at the White House ceremony.

Her torrent of awards included the Distinguished Flying Cross and a congressional citation, presented to her by Vice President Charles Curtis. Earhart's year was capped off when she was named Outstanding American Woman of the Year for 1932.

Just as she did after her *Friendship* flight, Earhart soon began looking for new challenges. In August of 1932, Earhart set the women's transcontinental speed record when she flew from Los Angeles, California to Newark, New Jersey. She broke her own record in July of 1933 flying the same route. Next, she planned to become the first person to fly solo from Honolulu, Hawaii to Oakland, California. This time she gauged her chances of success to be "fifty-fifty." A successful completion of the flight would again require top navigation skills using instruments. Another pilot, Charles Ulm, had lost his life a month earlier attempting such a flight. On January 11, 1935, Earhart took off from Hawaii. Eighteen hours and fifteen minutes later, Earhart landed safely in Oakland, California. She and her plane were mobbed by 10,000 of her fans.

Her next mission was to fly from Los Angeles to Mexico City, then fly on to Newark, New Jersey. The 2,185-mile flight would be so dangerous that her friend and fellow pilot, Wiley Post, argued against her going. (Post, who'd flown around the world previously, lost his life and that of his passenger, Will Rogers, when his plane crashed in Alaska in 1935.) Earhart's flight to New Jersey would again require the test of flying over water, in this case the Gulf of Mexico. She made the flight successfully—and was met by her usual mob of fans.

Earhart was now ready to go for what she felt would be the crowning achievement in her career: a flight around the world. This was something no woman had ever accomplished. The route she chose conjures up an Indiana Jones-type of excitement: She would fly to South America; Senegal in Africa; Calcutta in India; Asia; and Australia. Over the vast Pacific Ocean, she would head for New Guinea and Howland Island, Hawaii, and then finish up in Oakland, California. As Earhart said: "Adventure is worthwhile in itself."

Her husband, George Putnam, recalled her words regarding danger in the Introduction of *Last Flight*. "Please don't be concerned," Earhart said. "It just seems that I must try this flight. I've weighed it all carefully. With it behind me, life will be fuller and richer. I can be content. Afterward it will be fun to grow old."

While others were worried about her, Earhart felt that worrying about danger was counterproductive, Putnam recalled. "The time to worry," she said, "is three months before a flight. Decide then whether or not the goal is worth the risks involved. If it is, stop worrying. To worry is to add another hazard. It retards reactions, makes one unfit."

Earhart also accepted full responsibility for her flight and wanted to alleviate her husband of any guilt. "I know that if I fail or if I am lost," she wrote, "you will be blamed for allowing me to leave on this trip; the backers of the flight will be blamed and everyone connected with it. But it's my responsibility and mine alone."

On June 1, 1937, Earhart, along with navigator Fred Noonan, took off in her Lockheed Electra and began her trip around the world. The world closely followed Earhart's exploits. At her stops she wrote articles for the *New York Herald Tribune* about the flight and the places she visited and people she met.

Thirty-two days after taking off, Earhart was heading for the home stretch—tiny Howland Island (less than two square miles) in the Pacific. She left from New Guinea. The 2,556-mile route she was taking to Howland Island had never before been traveled by an airplane. At six in the morning, Earhart was in radio contact regarding weather conditions. Her last communique was "KHAQQ calling

Itasca. We must be on you, but cannot see you. Gas is running low." After that, nothing was ever heard from the plane again. Earhart and Fred Noonan were presumed lost at sea. Many of her biographers have concluded that her plane ran out of fuel and crashed.

Her loss was worldwide news. A massive search party of sixty planes and ten ships looked for Earhart and her plane for two weeks, but she was never found.

"When I go," Earhart once told her husband, "I'd like best to go in my plane. Quickly." In all likelihood she did, but her legacy as a courageous pioneer endures and will continue to do so. Her attempt to fly around the world symbolized her philosophy about life. As she wrote in her last letter to her husband: "I want to do it because I want to do it. Women must try to do things as men have tried. If they fail, their failure must be but a challenge to others."

> *Those of us who knew Amelia and realized her value cannot help but regret our loss. I only hope it will spur us on to do something in her memory which will carry on the influence which her personality and spirit brought everyone with whom she came in contact.*
> —Eleanor Roosevelt

How to Be Like Amelia Earhart

1. **Don't allow others to define you.**

   Earhart was praised after her *Friendship* flight, but she didn't believe her press clippings. She looked for a way to earn that praise, and if she hadn't, her name might have been forgotten a long time ago.

2. **Be honest with yourself.**

   Earhart wouldn't allow herself to take credit for what *Friendship* pilot, Wilmer Stultz, had done, even if the credit came from the president of the United States. "I was just a passenger on the journey—just a passenger," she told the *New York Times*.

3. **Set clear-cut goals.**

   After the accolades she received from being part of the *Friendship* crew, Earhart wanted to be worthy of the admiration she was receiving. She was a pilot, not a passenger. She soon set an ambitious goal for herself: to become the first woman pilot to solo across the Atlantic Ocean. It would be an extremely dangerous flight, and Earhart gauged her chances of successfully completing it at "one in ten." She also said: "Courage is the price that life exacts for granting peace."

4. **Study successful people.**

   Earhart kept a scrapbook of successful women and studied their lives carefully. She also developed her own philosophy about being successful. "Women will gain economic justice by proving themselves in all lines of endeavor, not by having laws passed for them," she wrote.

5. Do what you love.

Earhart said that from the first time she was in an airplane "I knew I myself had to fly. . . . To want in one's heart to do a thing, for its own sake; to enjoy doing it; to concentrate all one's energies upon it—that is not only the surest guarantee of its success, it is also being true to oneself. If there is anything I have learned in life it is this: If you follow the inner desire of your heart, the incidentals will take care of themselves."

6. Don't take things for granted.

Anita Snook taught Earhart to check everything on her airplane. This included being sure the plane had a full tank of gas.

7. Prepare for worst-case scenarios.

Earhart studied stunt flying so she'd be familiar with the unexpected. This was needed when her plane went into a spin during her solo flight across the Atlantic. "A knowledge of some stunts is judged necessary to good flying," she said. "Unless a pilot has actually recovered from a stall, has actually put his plane into a spin and brought it out, he cannot know accurately what those acts entail. He should be familiar enough with abnormal positions of his craft to recover without having to think how."

8. Ask questions.

Earhart learned from asking questions of experienced pilots.

9. Care about others.

Whether it was girls excluded from sororities or soldiers wounded in battle, Earhart gave of herself and helped others. This helped her become the kind of person that Amy Guest was looking for. She wanted a girl of the "right image" for the *Friendship* flight, and Earhart was selected.

10. **Keep challenging yourself.**

Earhart may have lost her life doing what she loved to do, but this was the way she needed to live her life.

11. **Evaluate risks.**

Most of our daily decisions aren't about life and death, but even so, evaluate the risks of anything you do. Earhart's formula was to "decide then whether or not the goal is worth the risks involved. If it is, stop worrying. To worry is to add another hazard. It retards reactions, makes one unfit."

12. **Accept responsibility for your decisions and actions.**

Earhart accepted full responsibility for her attempt to fly around the world and wanted to alleviate her husband of any guilt. She wrote: "I know that if I fail or if I am lost you will be blamed for allowing me to leave on this trip; the backers of the flight will be blamed and everyone connected with it. But it's my responsibility and mine alone."

13. **Don't worry about failing—just try.**

Earhart's attempt to fly around the world was the perfect expression of her life's philosophy. Earhart said: "I want to do it because I want to do it. Women must try to do things as men have tried. If they fail, their failure must be but a challenge to others."

FLORENCE NIGHTINGALE
1820–1910

STEADFASTNESS

Every woman, or at least almost every woman, in England has, at one time or another of her life, [been in] charge of the personal health of somebody, whether child or invalid—in other words, every woman is a nurse.

—*Florence Nightingale, from the preface to* Notes on Nursing

lorence Nightingale's name is synonymous with nursing and compassion. Her heroic efforts during and after the Crimean War ushered in the era of modern nursing and encouraged army medical reforms.

Florence Nightingale was given the world on a silver platter, but going through life as a pampered society woman wasn't her idea of living a meaningful life.

Her father, William, and mother, Fanny, came from wealthy families. What William gained in inheritance, however, he lost in ambition. "My father is a man who has never known what struggle is," Nightingale noted. Her mother said that she and her nine siblings were raised to think only of their own material needs and comforts. William and Fanny's honeymoon was an extended vacation, as they traveled in luxury throughout the European continent. It lasted long enough for them to see their daughters, Parthe and Florence, born.

When William and Fanny decided their fifteen-bedroom house, Lea Hurst, in Derbyshire, England, was too small, it became their summer residence. The family moved to new quarters, a mansion called Embley Park in Hampshire, near London, situated on a "mere" four thousand acres.

Despite being surround by such wealth, the young Florence Nightingale had a zeal to help the downtrodden. Perhaps she inherited this instinct from her maternal grandfather, William Smith, who spent forty-six years in Britain's House of Commons, establishing his credentials as an abolitionist and advocate for the poor. Her father, William, was well educated and stressed education to his daughters. He had attended Cambridge University and personally saw to all facets of their education and nurtured their intellectual curiosity.

At seventeen, Nightingale felt divinely inspired. "God spoke to me . . . and called me to His service," she said. From that moment, she was driven to do something meaningful with her life. "I see so many of my kind who have gone mad for want of something to do," she wrote when she was thirty. Nightingale decided to devote her life to health care, which emcompassed nursing, but at that time, hospital nursing was considered scandalous. It was looked down upon as menial work, performed by women who were labeled "lower class."

In a Victorian England that didn't recognize the rights of women to own property or be educated, women who were not cared for by families or husbands, or who were widows, had few opportunities to earn a living. Many turned to prostitution to survive, alcohol to cope, and what was called nursing to get themselves a few hours of shelter and a hot meal. The prevailing societal perception that nurses (meaning women minimally trained in health care) were alcoholics and of low character was because so many found themselves going down this dark road. The only nurses considered respectable were nuns who worked at church hospitals.

Nightingale started nursing in acceptable settings, by providing care for relatives and neighbors who were ill and by assisting women who needed help with childbirth. Nursing others back to health brought great happiness to Nightingale.

"My heart was filled. My soul was at home. I wanted no other heaven. May God be thanked as He never yet has been thanked for that glimpse of what it is to live," she said about nursing and teaching the poor near her family's summer home in Derbyshire.

> *The misconceptions about Nightingale are that she was a mean, vindictive, hateful person. She wasn't that. She was driven. She was a woman working in a man's time.*
>
> —Louise Selanders,
> NIGHTINGALE HISTORIAN

When Nightingale told her parents that she wanted to study health care and nursing at a hospital, they were shocked and extremely worried about her safety and health. They also worried about the disgrace they felt she would bring upon the family. Nightingale was devastated by her parents' resistance and felt that life wasn't worth living if she wasn't free to help people the way she wanted. She emerged from this crisis, however, with increased resolve, and began to study nursing on her own in the evening.

Soon, Nightingale looked into a nursing school, at the Institution of Deaconesses, in Kaiserswerth, Germany. Because of its strong reputation, Nightingale felt that the school would be acceptable to her parents. Eventually, her sheer determination prevailed, and a compromise was reached. She could attend Kaiserwerth, but no one was to know.

Nightingale went from a life of affluence to the life of a nursing student. Private quarters and maids were gone, replaced by roommates and chores beginning at five in the morning. This was Nightingale's first step toward the life she wanted, even if her parents didn't understand her need to be useful. When she finished her three-month training and returned home, she wrote that her family treated her "as if I had come from committing a crime."

Thanks to a friend's recommendation, Nightingale became superintendent of a new hospital for poor women in London. While her mother and her sister never approved of her occupation, her father did to a degree. He provided her with a generous allowance so that she could focus totally on her work. Her father's generosity allowed Nightingale to decline her salary, so that the hospital could use it for the patients.

Nightingale immediately put her imprint on the hospital's policy. When the committee decided that only Anglican women would be admitted, she was adamant that women from all religious denominations be welcomed or she would resign. Nightingale's stance prevailed.

Her greatest impact was in hospital administration. Throughout her career, Nightingale diligently maintained accurate records and relied on statistical information to help make the best decisions. In six months, through hard work and attention to detail, Nightingale created a model of hospital efficiency while never forgetting that the mission of the facility was to serve the patients. "She spread happiness among her patients, too, caring for more than just their medical treatment," wrote Gena K. Gorrell in *Heart and Soul: The Story of Florence Nightingale*. "She worried about them, found money for them, arranged holidays for them before they returned to work. Their letters spoke of love and admiration: 'How gratefully I accept your offer' . . . 'I cannot thank you enough' . . . 'You are sunshine.'"

During England's cholera epidemic of 1854, Nightingale labored in the slums and public hospitals. She nursed the poor and sick. Once she mastered hospital administration,

Nightingale resigned her position to set up a proper teaching program for prospective nurses. In the fall of 1853, however, Turkey declared war on Russia. England and France declared war on Russia in March 1854. The Crimean War was underway, and Nightingale would soon find herself nursing in the trenches.

In September 1854, British forces landed in Turkey and the ensuing battles left many dead in the Crimean. The wounded soldiers were transported three hundred miles by ship to Barrack Hospital in Scutari, Turkey. William Howard Russell of the *London Times* newspaper was on the scene as England's first war correspondent. He reported that the facilities for wounded soldiers were disgraceful, and that there weren't even essential medical supplies such as bandages, splints, chloroform and morphia. Soldiers endured amputations without the benefit of sedation. The British public was outraged. "No sufficient preparations have been made for the care of the wounded," Russell wrote in a dispatch. "[N]ot only are there no dressers and nurses ... there is not even linen to make bandages. Men must die [because] the medical staff of the British Army has forgotten that old rags are necessary for the dressing of wounds."

Nightingale was making preparations to go to the military hospital at Scutari, Turkey, with three other nurses as private citizens to care for the wounded, when a letter arrived from the secretary for war, Sidney Herbert. In the face of the terrible publicity that the British medical facilities were creating, he asked Nightingale, who was an old friend of his, to go to Scutari as Superintendent of the Female Nursing Establishment of the English General Hospitals. Her first duty was to find forty qualified nurses to join her.

Herbert's offer presented Nightingale with an opportunity to change the face of nursing, and she seized it. He wrote: "If this succeeds, an enormous amount of good will be done now. . . . and a prejudice will have been broken through, and a precedent established, which will multiply the good to all time."

Nightingale was risking her life to go into a war zone, exposing herself to disease on a mass scale. Her focus, though, was on the mission. Her sister Parthe wrote that on the eve of her departure, Nightingale was "as calm and composed as if she was going for a walk."

In early November 1854, Nightingale arrived at Barrack Hospital in Scutari. The massive structure, running 200 yards long on each of its four sides, was described by the Sanitary Commission a few months later as "murderous."

"Beneath the magnificent structure were sewers of the worst possible construction, mere cesspools, choked, inefficient, and grossly over-loaded," wrote Cecil Woodham-Smith in *Florence Nightingale*. "The whole vast building stood in a sea of decaying filth. The very walls, constructed of porous plaster, were soaked in it. Every breeze, every puff of air, blew poisonous gas through the pipes of numerous open privies into the corridors and wards where the sick were lying."

There was very little fresh water, and no furniture or beds. The wounded slept on straw mats laid on filthy floors that were crawling with vermin. The wounded were also poorly fed, which hampered their recovery. "Animal carcasses were hacked into portions and thrown into boiling water, and then the pieces were handed out to the soldiers," Gorrell wrote. "Some got meat; some got bone and gristle. Some got tough, overboiled scraps; some got the last lumps thrown into the pot, still oozing blood. Many of the men were far too sick to gnaw the meat, let alone digest it, but there was almost nothing else. . . . these men were starving to death."

What Nightingale discovered at Barrack Hospital was in direct contrast to the famous words she would write in her 1859 book, *Notes on Nursing*. "It may seem a strange principle to enunciate as the very first requirement in a hospital that it should do the sick no harm."

Efforts to improve the hospital's condition were difficult because British officers and their medical officers found the conditions at Barrack Hospital acceptable. This was due in part to their low regard for the average soldier during that war and previous ones. "The Duke of Wellington described his army, the army which won the victories of Peninsula and Waterloo, as 'the scum of the earth enlisted for drink,'" Woodham-Smith wrote. "Officers had no feeling of responsibility toward their men." A doctor on the scene wrote to the Hospital Commission: "During the time I have been in the Crimea . . . no general officer has visited my hospital nor, to my knowledge, in any way interested himself about the sick."

Nightingale immediately directed orderlies and her nurses to clean up the filth of Barrack Hospital. She ordered around 200 scrubbing brushes for the floors and enough supplies for each patient's filthy clothes to be washed.

Next, she commandeered the kitchen in the nurses' quarters and any other kitchen she could, to direct the preparation of edible food. She recruited assistance from an accomplished young French cook, Alexis Soyer. To help his countrymen and their allies, Soyer transferred his skills from cooking for the wealthy at a stylish London club to preparing food for the wounded at Scutari. He took what little was available and prepared it so that the men could gain strength. "As Soyer walked the wards with his tureens of soup, the men cheered him," Woodham-Smith wrote.

The sheer number of seriously wounded soldiers created a massive challenge for Nightingale and her nurses. In addition, she was treated by army doctors as a society nuisance, rather than being respected as a trained nurse who could help save lives. Her compassion, including her desire to help illiterate wounded soldiers learn how to read during their recovery, was met with disdain. One officer told her: "You will spoil the brutes."

Nightingale created a plan for the eventual acceptance of her and her nurses as trained professionals. "She realized that before she could accomplish anything she must win the confidence of the doctors," Woodham-Smith wrote. "She determined not to offer her nurses ... but to wait until the doctors asked her for help."

While Nightingale could be stubborn and difficult to deal with when she felt the situation warranted it, she rarely, if ever, raised her voice or lost her composure. Instead, she relied on her steely resolve to elicit change.

To bring about improvements at Barrack and other hospitals, Nightingale also relied on her pen. During her time in the Crimea, from

> *No man, not even a doctor, ever gives any other definition of what a nurse should be than this— "devoted and obedient." This definition would do just as well ... for a horse. It would not do for a policeman.*
> —Florence Nightingale

November 1854 to July 1856, she wrote about 300 detailed letters. (Throughout her life Nightingale authored over 200 books and pamphlets and around 13,000 letters.) Many of her letters from the Crimea were sent to government officials, such as Sidney Herbert.

Nightingale wrote in weather so bitterly cold that the ink in her inkwell froze. She wrote so late into the night that the staff reported the light in her room was never out. She wrote not only to officials, but also to families of deceased soldiers who had asked her to deliver a final message to their loved ones. "It is almost incredible that in addition to the unceasing labor she was performing [twelve to fifteen hours a day], when she was living in the foul atmosphere of the Barrack Hospital, incessantly harried by disputes, callers, complaints and overwhelmed with official correspondence which had to be written in her own hand, she should have found time and energy to write this long series of vast, carefully thought-out letters, many as long as a pamphlet," Woodham-Smith wrote.

Nightingale's letters on reforms, packed with facts and statistical information to support her points, were used by Sidney Herbert and other cabinet officials to make "important changes in the British Army organization during the course of the Crimean War," Woodham-Smith also wrote. Still, Nightingale never fell into the trap of believing that words alone were enough to get things done. Words, she said, "ought all to be distilled into actions and into actions which bring results."

The enduring image of Nightingale as a war heroine was born at night in the darkened corridors of Barrack Hospital. Making her rounds with a lantern in hand, she worked her way around the 800 square yards of each of the hospital's three floors, comforting countless patients and assessing their needs. Most of the time Nightingale was alone, but sometimes a nurse would accompany her. One nurse described the scene: "It seemed an endless walk. . . . A dim light burned here and there, Miss Nightingale carried her lantern which she would set down before she bent over any of the patients. I much admired her manner to the men—it was so tender and kind."

"What a comfort it was to see her pass even," a soldier wrote, as quoted by Woodham-Smith. "She would speak to one, and nod and smile to as many more; but she could not do it all you know. We lay there by the hundreds; but we could kiss her shadow as it fell and lay our heads on the pillow again content."

Nightingale was immortalized in Henry Wadsworth Longfellow's 1857 poem about her, called "Saint Nightingale." She would forever be known as "The Lady with the Lamp." Longfellow wrote:

Lo! In that hour of misery
A lady with a lamp I see
Pass through the glimmering gloom,
and flit from room to room.
And slow, as in a dream of bliss,
The speechless sufferer turns to kiss
Her shadow, as it falls,
Upon the darkening wall.

The wounded soldiers revered Nightingale. "The surgeons were amazed at her ability to strengthen men doomed to an operation," Woodham-Smith wrote. A veteran recalled: "She was wonderful at cheering up anyone who was a bit low." The men termed her energy and ability to effect positive changes as "Nightingale power." They believed strongly that with her resolve, if she were at the head of the army, the war might be over.

In turn, Nightingale drew strength from the men. "In the troops she found the qualities which moved her most," Woodham-Smith wrote. "They were victims; her deepest instinct was to be the defender of victims. They were courageous, and she instantly responded to courage. Their world was not ruled by money, and she detested materialism. The supreme loyalty which made a man give his life for his comrade, the courage which enabled him to advance steadily under fire, were displayed by men who were paid a shilling a day."

Reverend Sidney Godolphin Osborne, who was on the scene a few weeks after Nightingale arrived in Scutari, also wrote of her devotion to the men: "She had an utter disregard of contagion. . . . I have known her [to] spend hours over men dying of cholera or fever. The more awful to every sense any particular case, especially if it was that of a dying man, the more certainly her slight form [would] be seen bending over him, administering to his ease by every means in her power and seldom quitting his side until death released him." Nightingale's rule, according to Woodham-Smith, was that she would not allow any man to die alone who was under her observation.

After roughly six months, Nightingale and her nurses helped dramatically decrease the death rate at the hospital. This was due primarily to her strict attention to cleanliness and her administration of supplies. Hugh Small, in his book *Florence Nightingale: Avenging Angel,* wrote that 10,000 soldiers died of sickness during a five-month fall/winter period during the first year of the war. During that same period a year later, the number of men who died from sickness was reduced to 500, thanks in large part to Nightingale and her nurses.

Nevertheless, thousands of men had died needlessly. Nightingale wrote of a 73 percent mortality rate in six months in eight divisions. The horror of all the dead stayed with Nightingale her entire life. In all, out of 250,000 men who died for the allied cause, about two-thirds of them died from infections and disease.

Nightingale, through her work and success in the Crimean War, and the resulting publicity, single-handedly changed the image of nurses, giving the profession respectability around the world. Her influence on medical treatment of soldiers would be felt particularly in the American Civil War (roughly five years away), and be personified in women such as Clara Barton and Dorothea Dix. The wounded who survived that war, in both the Union and Confederate armies, owed a huge debt of gratitude to "the blueblood from England."

By 1855, Nightingale began to inspect other military hospitals in the Crimean theater of war. She visited troops at the war's front without any concern about the dangers to herself. While visiting the other hospitals, she became seriously ill with Crimean fever, and was bedridden

> *Never lose an opportunity of urging a practical beginning, however small, for it is wonderful how often in such matters the mustard-seed germinates and roots itself.*
> —Florence Nightingale

with high fevers for many weeks before finally recovering.

After the war ended on March 30, 1856, she was celebrated as a national hero, but didn't join in the festivities. Instead, Nightingale stayed in the Crimea until every soldier had left, declining the British government's offer to sail home on a warship and attend parades planned in her honor. She couldn't forget those left behind, and didn't want others to either. "I stand at the altar of the murdered men," she said in 1856, "and, while I live, I fight their cause."

"She said she had seen Hell, and because she had seen Hell she was set apart," Woodman-Smith wrote. "Between her and every normal human pleasure, every normal human enjoyment, must stand the memory of the wards at Scutari. She could never forget. She wrote the words again and again, in private notes, on the margins of letters, on scraps of blotting-paper; whenever her hand lay idle the phrase formed itself—'I can never forget.'"

Throughout her life, Nightingale received credit for the men who had been saved at Barrack Hospital, and throughout her life she sought to share this credit. "I often think, or rather do not like to think . . . how all the people who were with me in the Crimea must feel how unjust it is that all the 'Testimonial' went to me," she wrote in 1888.

Upon returning home, the thirty-seven-year-old Nightingale was exhausted from her eighteen months of hard work in the Crimea. She had been exposed to so much sickness that her emaciated appearance was a cause of great concern to her family. Her father and sister both felt she wasn't going to live much longer. She did live—for many more years—but spent

> *Nightingale led a very principled life. She had a set of principles, which drove her to accomplish the things that she wanted to do. She was a very spiritual woman. Her guiding principles were based on her spirituality and her Christianity.*
>
> —Louise Selanders,
> NIGHTINGALE HISTORIAN

the next ten years of her life as an invalid and was rarely seen in public after that. Seeing so much death and not being able to do more about it left her with emotional scars.

Nightingale's legend as a saintly nurse was advanced by Longfellow's poem and by songs written about her. In addition, there were portraits painted, books written and Staffordshire figurines produced. Many newborn baby girls received the name Nightingale in her honor. She, however, had no interest in being a celebrity and worked fervently to defuse the notion. She was far more interested in helping fully investigate the failure of British military hospitals during the Crimean War. Nightingale helped set up a government commission to correct the problems that caused so many soldiers to die in the hospitals. She provided detailed reports to the commission, based on her firsthand knowledge of the events. "If I could only carry one point which would prevent one part of the recurrence of the colossal calamity, then I should be true to the brave dead," she wrote.

"[Nightingale] used the truth to push Victorian England into a burst of social progress that may justify a claim that the pioneering National Health Service was born on the floor of the Scutari Barrack Hospital," Hugh Small wrote.

While she was in the Crimea, a charity organization had been set up in her name—the Nightingale Fund. Grateful British citizens contributed millions of pounds and Nightingale used the money to start a nursing school in 1859. She personally selected the superintendent, Sarah Wardroper. Wardroper was the head nurse of St. Thomas's Hospital in London, where the Nightingale Training School was located. The Training School's one-year course was to be followed by three years of hospital experience.

To begin permanently erasing the prewar image of nurses, students had to meet certain standards before being admitted to the school. They also had to pass a personal interview with Nightingale. During the training, a student's positive evaluation was dependent as much on her personal traits, such as honesty and sobriety, as it was on her grasp of nursing skills. The Nightingale Training School was, Nightingale wrote, "a place of training of character, habits, and intelligence, as well as of acquiring knowledge."

Nightingale also focused on new causes, such as helping to reform the health system of the British Army in India, which was then under Britain's control. She sent a detailed questionnaire to the British military bases there, and wanted to learn about their sanitation facilities, medical care and diet. Nightingale and two doctors analyzed the mass of information and the result was a 2,000-page report on the state of health conditions of the British troops in India.

The full report was only to be seen by members of parliament. Afraid that they would hide the full truth from the British public, as they had the number of Crimean War dead, Nightingale published the parts of the report she had written to help bring public pressure for reforms. She exposed the fact that the military personnel were living in filth and drinking unpure water. She drew up a plan to reform health conditions for the entire country of 200 million people. While she only made a dent in such a massive undertaking, Nightingale pushed for reforms in India the rest of her life. The country was better off for her efforts and did eventually make some progress. "If she didn't always succeed, at least she always tried," Gena Gorrell wrote.

In 1907, King Edward VII bestowed upon Nightingale the

medal of the Order of Merit. She was the first woman in England's history to receive this prestigious honor.

Nightingale requested that, upon her death, a simple cross mark her grave, with her initials and the years she lived. Her family, in accordance with her wishes, declined Britain's offer of a national funeral. She was laid to rest at the family gravesite, her coffin carried by members of the British Army while Crimean War veterans looked on.

The Crimean veterans sang a song about Nightingale for many years at regimental reunions. One of the verses of "The Nightingale in the East," states:

Her heart it means good for no bounty she'll take,
She'd lay down her life for the poor soldier's sake.
She prays for the dying, she gives peace to the brave,
She feels that the soldier has a soul to be saved.
The wounded they love her as it has been seen,
She's the soldier's preserver, they call her their Queen.
May God give her strength, and her heart never fail,
One of heaven's best gifts is Miss Nightingale.

How to Be Like Florence Nightingale

1. Decide how you will impact the world.

Nightingale was born into wealth and the Victorian role of a society woman. She didn't need to work and didn't need to accomplish anything by the norms of that society. However, she demanded more of herself. "I see so many of my kind who have gone mad for want of something to do," she wrote.

2. Follow your heart and religious faith.

When Nightingale was seventeen, she felt a divine inspiration. "God spoke to me . . . and called me to His service," she said. She listened and then moved into action.

3. Ignore society's stereotypes.

In Nightingale's time, nursing was considered a disreputable occupation performed by women who were alcoholics and prostitutes. That didn't stop Nightingale from pursuing her career in health care and, in the process, helping to legitimize the nursing profession.

4. Stand up for yourself.

Sometimes you have to stand up to those you love most in order to turn your dreams into realities. Nightingale's parents were strongly opposed to her pursuit of a nursing career. It would have been easy to buckle under that kind of pressure, or to substitute their judgment for hers, but Nightingale didn't allow that to happen. She took the initiative and studied nursing on her own, eventually convincing her family that she was doing the right thing.

5. Be courageous.

Nightingale risked her life by going into a war zone and exposing herself to disease on a mass scale, but her focus was always on her patients. Her courage had its roots in her commitment to her cause. Because she was so committed, the cause was more important than the risks involved. On the eve of her departure for the Crimea, her sister Parthe wrote that Nightingale was "as calm and composed as if she was going for a walk."

6. When one road is blocked, take another.

When those in authority try to block your path, seek an alternative. Upon arriving at Barrack Hospital, Nightingale met opposition from army doctors who resented her presence. She made progress in the areas of cleanliness and food preparation, and in time won the respect of the soldiers and eventually the doctors.

7. Learn to write well.

Nightingale, like Clara Barton, Eleanor Roosevelt, Margaret Thatcher and Mother Teresa, depended on letter writing to advance her cause. During her time in the Crimea, from November 1854 to July 1856, she wrote about 300 detailed letters, many of them to government officials, such as Sidney Herbert. Nightingale's letters on reforms, packed with facts and statistical information to support her points, were used by Sidney Herbert and other cabinet officials to make "important changes in the British Army organization during the course of the Crimean War."

8. Move into action.

Nightingale said, "Words ought all to be distilled into

actions and into actions which bring results." Nightingale always followed that path.

9. **Pay attention to details.**

Throughout her career, Nightingale maintained records and relied on statistical information to make the best decisions as a hospital administrator, and later as a head nurse during the Crimean War.

10. **Don't be lured by materialism.**

There is nothing wrong with the pursuit of wealth, but don't love things more than you love people. That's the Florence Nightingale way.

11. **Be honest about your accomplishments.**

After returning from the Crimea, Nightingale became a media celebrity and was praised in poems, songs, portraits and figurines. She could have easily brushed aside the failures of the Crimea, but she didn't. Instead, she honored the dead by highlighting the medical failures, and used that as the starting point for medical reforms in the British Army. "[Nightingale] used the truth to push Victorian England into a burst of social progress that may justify a claim that the pioneering National Health Service was born on the floor of the Scutari Barrack Hospital," Huge Small wrote. Nightingale said: "I stand at the altar of the murdered men, and, while I live, I fight their cause."

12. **Avoid false praise.**

Regarding the praise she received for her nursing efforts, Nightingale wrote in 1888: "I often think, or rather do not like to think . . . how all the people who were with me in the Crimea must feel how unjust it is that all the 'Testimonial' went to me."

13. **Remember that all progress, however small, is valuable.**

As many as 14,000 British soldiers died needlessly from disease during the Crimean War. Out of that catastrophe, however, came the reforms that led to improved care for the war wounded and sick. "Never lose an opportunity of urging a practical beginning, however small, for it is wonderful how often in such matters the mustard-seed germinates and roots itself," Nightingale said.

14. **Be a hands-on person.**

To assess the needs of patients at Barrack Hospital, Nightingale, after working hard all day, personally made her rounds at night in the massive structure to talk with the soldiers. When Nightingale opened the Nightingale Training School for Nurses, she personally selected the superintendent and interviewed the prospective students. In order to help change the image of nurses, Nightingale wanted to make certain her students were of the highest moral character.

15. **Don't rest on your laurels.**

After the Crimean War, Nightingale could have stopped working because her place in history was assured. However, like so many women of influence, she looked for new challenges and ways to be useful. As she got older, she was still able to accomplish some of her most important work. Through letters and contacts, Nightingale helped introduce health reforms in India.

16. **Defend those who can't defend themselves.**

"The soldiers were victims; her deepest instinct was to be the defender of victims," Woodham-Smith wrote.

HARRIET BEECHER STOWE
1811–1896

EMPATHY

It may truly be said that I write with my
heart's blood. Many times in writing
Uncle Tom's Cabin I thought my health
would fail utterly; but I prayed earnestly
that God would help me till I got through,
and still I am pressed beyond measure
and above strength.

—*Harriet Beecher Stowe*

arriet Beecher Stowe wrote *Uncle Tom's Cabin,* one of the most historically important novels ever written.

President Abraham Lincoln, upon meeting Stowe in 1862, greeted her by saying, "So you're the little woman who wrote the book that started this great war!" While Lincoln was only saying in jest that the diminutive Stowe's mammoth bestseller, *Uncle Tom's Cabin* (published in 1852), had started the Civil War, it is remembered as an ingredient that helped ignite the conflict that began in April 1861.

Uncle Tom's Cabin was the story of people living amidst the cruelty of slavery while attempting to maintain their dignity. It humanized slaves to those who were indifferent about their plight like nothing had before, by showing that they, too, had a face, a voice and most importantly, a soul. *Uncle Tom's Cabin* polarized the slavery issue for the free North and infuriated the slave-holding South.

Stowe, the daughter of a minister, had a strong religious faith that was heard in the voices of the people she depicted. In *Uncle Tom's Cabin,* she attacked slavery by subjecting it to a moral test, as defined by the tenets of religion and God. "How could those who professed to be followers of Christ justify the enslaving of human beings?" she in effect asked.

Overnight, after its release in March 1852, *Uncle Tom's*

Cabin was a runaway bestseller. It broke all existing book-sale records. In its first week of release, it sold 10,000 copies. Within a year, 300,000 copies had been sold in the United States. It was extremely popular in Great Britain as well. Queen Victoria read it and was so touched she arranged to meet Stowe when she visited England in 1856, although they never actually met. It has been translated into over sixty different languages. The only book that outsold *Uncle Tom's Cabin* during the nineteenth century was the Bible.

The lead character, the saintly and kind Uncle Tom, was Stowe's protagonist. Unfortunately, the name "Uncle Tom"— because of unflattering portrayals of him in stage plays of the book—became in time a derogatory term used to describe a black man who was submissive to white people. Stowe's Uncle Tom wasn't that; he was a principled hero living his life fully by the teachings of Jesus Christ.

Stowe's journey from unknown author to voice of a people held in bondage began in many different ways. It started as a child growing up in a prominent family of abolitionists. It continued as a woman helping a runaway slave to stay free. And it most certainly reached its zenith as a brokenhearted mother standing over the grave of her infant son, Charles, who died in July 1849, during the cholera epidemic that had hit Cincinnati, Ohio.

"It was at his dying bed, and at his grave that I learned what a poor slave mother may feel when her child is torn away from her," Stowe wrote.

Harriet was one of Lyman Beecher's thirteen children. She was the seventh child born to him and her mother, Roxana. When she was only five, she lost her mother to tuberculosis. Lyman, a well-known minister and abolitionist, remarried. He encouraged his children to be educated, and to take an interest in the great issues of the day. Harriet loved to read from the time she was a little girl. She enjoyed books such as *The Arabian Nights* and *Ivanhoe*, and read the poetry of Lord Byron.

Harriet Beecher, who was born in Litchfield, Connecticut, learned the realities of slavery when she moved with her family to Cincinnati, Ohio, in 1832. Across the Ohio River lay the slave state of Kentucky. Since Ohio was a free state, many a fleeing slave made his escape to Cincinnati. Wanted posters of the runaway slaves, being treated as though they were the criminals, were regular features in the city. Some posters, seemingly with pride, mentioned identifying scars left from repeated whippings by which their runaways could be recognized.

She saw slaves working like pack mules to unload the cargo that boats and barges were delivering to the port of Cincinnati. While traveling through Kentucky over the course of a weekend to visit friends, Stowe saw with her own eyes the faces of slaves who'd had their freedom brutally taken away from them.

Her choice in a husband was Calvin Stowe, a theology professor and fellow abolitionist, whom she married in 1836. Stowe gave birth to seven children over the next fourteen years. To help bring in extra income for her family, she began writing stories and articles for different publications. Calvin encouraged her writing career, telling her

> *Did you ever think of the rhythmical power of prose? . . . How every writer when they get warm fall into a certain swing [and] rhythm peculiar to themselves, the words all having their place and sentences their cadences.*
>
> —Harriet Beecher Stowe

in a letter, "My dear, you must be a literary woman. It is so written in the book for fate . . . Make all your calculations accordingly." In 1843, her stories were published in the form of a book titled *The Mayflower: Sketches of Scenes and Characters Among the Descendants of the Pilgrims.*

In 1850, the United States Congress passed the Fugitive Slave Law. It gave federal officials absolute legal authority to track down escaped slaves and return them to their "masters" without even a trial. Many free blacks were sold into slavery because of this. In addition, the new law made it a crime for anyone to assist a runaway slave. The United States government was now forcing people in the free northern states to assist the southern slave-holding states to keep men, women and children in chains.

The Fugitive Slave Law especially outraged abolitionists. Stowe, now living with her family in Brunswick, Maine, wrote an article in 1850 for the *National Era,* a weekly abolitionist newspaper. In her article she stated there was a higher authority than the politicians who sat in Washington. Stowe condemned all people "who seem to think that there is no standard of right and wrong higher than an act of Congress, or an interpretation of the United States Constitution." The paper's editor, Gamaliel Bailey, liked Stowe's writing so much he asked her to do more articles. She did, sending him three new ones and earning $100.

Isabella Beecher, Harriet's sister-in-law, wrote a letter encouraging her to harness her writing talent to fight slavery. "Now, Hattie, if I could use a pen as you can, I would write something that would make

> *That which is not just is not law.*
> —William Lloyd Garrison

this whole nation feel what an accursed thing slavery is."

"I will write something," Stowe announced to her family after Isabella's letter was read aloud. That "something" began to take form in early 1851. The sentiments came from her heart; the story took shape from actual people and events. She was inspired by the slave narratives of Frederick Douglass, Henry Bibb and Josiah Henson (who claimed Uncle Tom was modeled after him). One true story she heard firsthand in Ohio particularly moved Stowe: that of a young runaway slave mother, clutching her child in her arms as she crossed the Ohio River on ice floes trying to make her way to Ohio. Freedom, to this young slave mother, was worth risking their lives.

"I have begun a set of sketches in the *National Era,* to illustrate the cruelty of slavery: I call it *Uncle Tom's Cabin,*" Stowe wrote to her brother, Henry, who was a nationally known clergyman and abolitionist. Looking for an outlet for *Uncle Tom's Cabin,* Stowe wrote to Bailey to see if the *National Era* would be interested in publishing her story in three to four installments. Writing, one of the few vocations open to women, gave her the opportunity to make a difference.

"I feel now that the time [has] come when even a woman or a child who can speak a word for freedom and humanity is bound to speak," Stowe wrote in her letter to Bailey. "The Carthaginian women in the last peril of their state cut off their hair for bowstrings to give to the defenders of their country; and such peril and shame as now hangs over this country is worse than Roman slavery, and I hope every woman who can write will not be silent."

Those three to four installments of *Uncle Tom's Cabin* grew by popular demand to forty-one, running in the

National Era from June 5, 1851 to April 1, 1852. During that time Stowe pored her emotions into her work. The power of *Uncle Tom's Cabin* is not only in Stowe's beautifully crafted words, but also in the passion with which she wrote about the plight of her noble slaves. "My heart was bursting with the anguish [and] the cruelty and injustice our nation was showing to the slave, and praying [to] God to let me do a little and to cause my cry for them to be heard," Stowe wrote.

As the mother of seven children, Stowe rarely had any peace and quiet. "She tried to carve out three hours a day, with the help of servants," said Joan D. Hedrick, author of *Harriet Beecher Stowe: A Life.* Stowe described her challenge of writing and combining motherhood in this way: "Nothing but deadly determination enables me ever to write. It is rowing against wind and tide."

The installments were so popular that the *National Era* started to sell out week after week. One reader said the papers were passed from person to person and family to family, getting worn in the process and accumulating seemingly "sacred" tearstains from its readers. Stowe eventually signed a contract with a book publisher, and *Uncle Tom's Cabin* came out in book form in March 1852. It has never been out of print since.

The story begins with the introduction of Uncle Tom, who is owned by Mr. and Mrs. Shelby. They have a farm in Kentucky and treat their slaves well. However, Mr. Shelby, out of financial necessity due to debts, decides he

> *When you get into a tight place and everything goes against you, till it seems as though you could not hang on a minute longer, never give up then, for that is just the place and time that the tide will turn.*
> —Harriet Beecher Stowe

must sell Uncle Tom, his most loyal and trusted slave, along with a young boy named Harry, to a slave trader named Haley. Harry is the son of slaves, Eliza and George Harris. Mrs. Shelby promises Tom that she will buy him back, whatever the price, as soon as possible.

Eliza will not allow her son to be sold and separated from her. She decides she must escape, and one evening carries out her plan. The next morning Haley discovers that Eliza and Harry are missing. He takes off after them with two other men and a pack of search dogs. They finally catch up with Eliza and Harry at the foot of the icy Ohio River. Across the river is the free state of Ohio. Eliza picks up Harry in her arms and in what may be the most famous scene in the book, jumps into the river and lands on an ice floe.

"Right on behind they came," Stowe wrote, "and, [Eliza], nerved with strength such as God gives only to the desperate, with one wild cry and flying leap, [she] vaulted sheer over the turbid current by the shore, on to the raft of ice beyond. It was a desperate leap—impossible to anything but madness and despair; and Haley, Sam, and Andy, instinctively cried out, and lifted up their hands, as she did it."

"The huge green fragment of ice on which she alighted pitched and creaked as her weight came on it, but she staid there not a moment. With wild cries and desperate energy she leaped to another and still another cake—stumbling—leaping—slipping—springing upwards again! Her shoes are gone—her stockings cut from her feet—while blood marked every step."

Eliza is free in Ohio, but of course still subjected to the Fugitive Slave Law. She finds saviors in the form of Mr. and Mrs. Bird, who send her to a station on the Underground

Railroad located in a Quaker village. It is there she and Harry are reunited with her husband, George, who has made his own escape from his plantation. With the help of the Underground Railroad, which assisted runaway slaves, Eliza, Harry, George and two other slaves begin their journey to Canada, where they can live out their lives in freedom.

As for Uncle Tom, he has no plans to escape. As a deeply devoted Christian, Tom considers himself bound by his word not to even try. Even after he learns that he's going to be sold "down the river" to the deep South, where slavery is even worse and more brutal than in the upper South, he refuses to try to escape. He knows if he did run away, Mr. Shelby would sell his wife and children, and then they might end up in a far worse place. As he says good-bye to his heartbroken wife before being taken away, Uncle Tom tries to comfort her with faith: "Pray for them that 'spitefully use you,' the good book says."

Slave catchers track George, Eliza, Harry, and two other escaped slaves, Jim and his mother, before they reach the safety of Canada. They find the group on the crest of a hill. When the slave catchers assert their right under "the law," to recapture them, Stowe speaks through George, who she has portrayed as an educated and skilled slave. George makes it clear to the men that he will shoot anyone who tries to come up the hill.

"I know very well that you've got the law on your side, and the power," said George, bitterly. "You mean to take my wife to sell in New Orleans, and put my boy like a calf in a trader's pen . . . you want to send Jim and me back to be whipped and tortured. . . . We don't own your laws; we don't own your country; we stand here as free, under God's sky, as you are;

and, by the great God that made us, we'll fight for our liberty till we die."

George makes good on his promise by shooting and wounding one of the men as he attempts to approach. The other slave catchers decide they're not willing to risk their lives to bring back the runaways and give up their pursuit. The group eventually makes it to the free soil of Canada.

In the character of Eliza, Stowe shows that slave mothers are no different than white mothers: they love their children just as much, and will do anything to protect them. In George and Tom, Stowe shows that black men are intelligent and heroic. Both men possess a wisdom that exceeds that of their white tormentors.

Uncle Tom is taken in chains and sent down south. While on a riverboat, Tom jumps into the powerful Mississippi River to save the life of a little white girl named Eva, who had fallen overboard. Tom's act of unselfish heroism results in Eva's father Augustine St. Clare buying him.

At the St. Clare house in New Orleans, Louisiana, Tom is treated very well, as are the other slaves. Augustine and Tom become close friends, especially after little Eva dies following an illness. Tom is promised his freedom so he can return to his own wife and children. Augustine even begins the necessary legal paper work, but then is killed trying to stop a knife fight between two drunken combatants.

Augustine's widow Marie puts the house and its slaves, including Tom, up for auction. Marie knows of her husband's promise to Tom of freedom. She also knows her husband even promised their little daughter Eva on her deathbed that Tom would be given his freedom. But Marie's desire for money exceeds any concern for a slave, even one such as Tom, who had saved her daughter's life.

Stowe uses Marie to speak for all of the slaveholders, to offer their reasoning to the world for their practice of slavery. In the immoral mind of the slaveholder, they say they are actually doing the slaves a "favor" by keeping them in bondage, even if that means a slave must live in wretched conditions, endure vicious beatings, and worst of all, watch their children sold away from them or vice versa. Stowe discredits slavery in *Uncle Tom's Cabin* by using the very words and logic that the southern slave aristocracy had been espousing to perpetuate it. Marie says a "Negro" needs the care of a master because he or she can't care for him or herself. When told that Tom desires to be free, Marie answers:

"I dare say he does want it . . . they all want it, just because they are a discontented set—always wanting what they haven't got. Now, I'm principled against emancipating, in any case. Keep a Negro under the care of a master, and he does well enough, and is respectable; but set them free, and they get lazy, and won't work, and take to drinking, and go all down to be mean, worthless fellows. I've seen it tried, hundreds of times. It's no favor to set them free," Marie said.

Marie also rejects concerns that Tom will be bought by a bad master. "Most masters are good. . . . I never yet was acquainted with a master that didn't treat his servants well," Marie said. While that is easy for her to say, since she is not a slave, Tom is purchased by a man whose name will become synonymous with evil and cruelty, Simon Legree.

After buying Tom, Legree notices his "cherished Bible," and asks him if he belongs to the church. Tom proudly answers that he does, at which point Legree says: "'Well, I'll soon have that out of you. I'll have none o' yer bawling, praying, singing niggers on my place; so remember. Now, mind yourself,' he said, with a stamp and a fierce glance of his gray eye, directed at Tom.'I'm your church now! Ye won't find no soft spot in me, nowhere. So, now, mind yerselves; for I don't show no mercy!'"

Stowe presents Legree as a northerner who has come to the South as a young adult. She is not condemning southerners per se, but slaveholders and the institution of slavery. While all slaveholders are participating in an immoral practice, some are even worse than others. Mr. Shelby, for example, treats his slaves well, but is expedient about his needs and will cruelly allow families to be separated. Legree doesn't treat his slaves well. There are no limits to the corruption of his soul. He explains his philosophy to a stranger inquiring about the practice of slavery:

"'I don't go for savin' niggers. Use up, and buy more's my way; makes you less trouble, and I'm quite sure it comes cheaper in the end,'" Legree tells the man he's speaking with. "'Now, you see, I just put 'em straight through, sick or well. When one nigger's dead, I buy another.'"

While at Legree's run-down plantation, Tom is ordered one day to whip a female slave named Lucy. He refuses. Legree strikes Tom several times, then threatens him with a worse beating for disobeying him and for telling him it is wrong to harm Lucy or anyone else. Tom has challenged Legree on moral authority, and Legree responds: "'An't I yer master? Didn't I pay down twelve hundred dollars, cash, for all there is inside yer old cussed black shell? An't yer mine, now, body and soul?' he said, giving Tom a violent kick with his heavy boot; 'tell me!'

"In the very depth of physical suffering, bowed by brutal oppression, this question shot a gleam of joy and triumph through Tom's soul. He suddenly stretched himself up, and looking earnestly to heaven, while the tears and blood that flowed down his face mingled, he exclaimed. 'No! no! no! My soul an't yours, Mas'r! . . . You haven't bought it—ye can't buy it! It's been bought and paid for, by one that is able to keep it—no matter, no matter, you can't harm me!'" Legree makes good on his threat and gives Tom a savage beating for disobeying him.

Later in the story, Tom helps two female slaves escape. Legree suspects that Tom has information that could help him recapture them, but Tom refuses to divulge anything. "'Well, Tom!' said Legree, walking up, and seizing him grimly by the collar of his coat, and speaking through his teeth, in a paroxysm of determined rage, 'do you know I've made up my mind to KILL you?'

"'It's very likely, Mas'r,' said Tom, calmly. 'I have,' said Legree, with grim terrible calmness, 'done-ust-that-thing, Tom, unless you'll tell me what you know about these yer gals!'"

"'I know Mas'r, but I can't tell anything.'" Tom has no fear because of his faith, which further infuriates Legree because it lessens his perceived power over him. Legree continues to threaten Tom in graphic terms. "'You've always stood it out agin' me: now I'll conquer ye; or kill ye!—one or t' other. I'll count every drop of blood there is in you, and take 'em, one by one, tell ye give up!'"

"Tom looked up to his master, and answered, 'Mas'r, if you was sick, or in trouble, or dying, and I could save ye, I'd give ye my heart's blood, and, if taking every drop of blood in this poor old body would save your precious soul, I'd give 'em freely, as the Lord gave his for me. O, Mas'r! Don't bring this great sin on your soul! It will hurt you more than 't will me!

Do the worst you can, my troubles 'll be over soon; but, if ye don't repent, yours won't never end!'"

In a powerful statement in the next paragraph of her book, Stowe wrote that Legree takes an instant to consider Tom's words, then dismisses them. As Stowe tells us through Tom, the victim will not suffer more than the persecutor. As God says in the Bible, "Vengeance is mine." Stowe continues:

"Like a strange snatch of heavenly music, heard in the lull of a tempest, this burst of feeling made a moment's blank pause. Legree stood aghast, and looked at Tom; and there was such a silence, that the tick of the old clock could be heard, measuring, with silent touch, the last moments of mercy and probation to that hardened heart. It was but a moment. There was one hesitating pause—one irresolute, relenting thrill—and the spirit of evil came back, with seven-fold vehemence; and Legree, foaming with rage, smote his victim to the ground."

Near death, Tom offers Legree forgiveness, telling him, "'Ye, poor miserable critter . . . there an't no more ye can do! I forgive ye, with all my soul.'" Tom also forgives the two slaves who helped Legree to beat him. He tells them, "'I'd be willing to bar' all I have, if it'll only bring ye to Christ! O, Lord! Give me these two more souls, I pray!'"

In the South Stowe's name and book evoked anger and hatred. Newspapers lambasted the book as a "pack of lies," and Stowe as an irresponsible author who was giving women a bad name. In many slave states laws were passed that made it illegal to buy or sell her book. Children in Virginia sang a rhyme "Go, go, go, Ol' Harriet Beecher Stowe! We don't want you here in Virginny—Go, go, go!"

The most ridiculous criticism leveled against her was that

she'd never lived in a slave state, and because she spent only one weekend in Kentucky, she really didn't know what she was talking about. The fact was, Stowe did have much first-hand knowledge from former slaves detailing the system and their torturous physical abuse, but even if she didn't, was it really necessary to live in a slave state to understand that holding human beings against their will, and separating families, was cruel and immoral?

To answer her southern critics, who tried to dismiss her as another radical abolitionist given to doing anything to promote her cause, she painstakingly wrote a book in 1853 detailing the sources she used, called *A Key to Uncle Tom's Cabin: Presenting the Original Facts and Documents Upon Which It Is Based.* The book, which was longer than *Uncle Tom's Cabin,* contained, Stowe wrote, "all the facts and documents on which the story was founded, and an immense body of facts, reports of trials, legal documents, and testimony of people now living South, which will more than confirm every statement in Uncle Tom's Cabin."

Stowe didn't write *Uncle Tom's Cabin* to become a celebrity, but she used her newfound status and wealth (she had become the richest author in the United States) to continue to help the abolitionist movement. She also supported the women's suffrage and temperance movements. In 1853 she toured on behalf of antislavery societies in England and Scotland, and raised money for them as well. She wrote pamphlets and articles against slavery. In print, she encouraged Abraham Lincoln to issue the Emancipation Proclamation as soon as possible.

On December 31, 1862, abolitionists rang in the new year in Boston's Music Hall. On the first day of the new year, in the midst of the Civil War, the Emancipation Proclamation was to go into effect. Stowe was there, and was cheered by the crowd.

Stowe wrote around thirty books in her fifty-one-year writing career. Some were novels, some were nonfiction books on subjects such as geography for children, homemaking, child rearing and religion. But of course, it is *Uncle Tom's Cabin* for which she is most remembered. In the final paragraph of that book, Stowe offered an ominous warning of things to come:

"A day of grace is yet held out to us. Both North and South have been guilty before God; and the Christian church has a heavy account to answer. Not by combining together, to protect injustice and cruelty, and making a common capital of sin, is this Union to be saved—but by repentance, justice and mercy; for, not surer is the eternal law by which the millstone sinks in the ocean, than that stronger law, by which injustice and cruelty shall bring on nations the wrath of Almighty God!"

As Uncle Tom lies on his deathbed after his beating by Legree, the son of Mr. and Mrs. Shelby, George Shelby, shows up at Legree's plantation. He has come to buy back Uncle Tom and bring him home, but Tom dies. Finding out the circumstances of Tom's death sends George into such repentance, he decides to free all of the slaves on his plantation and offers to pay wages for their work to any who wish to stay.

As Stowe wrote: "George here gave a short narration of the scene of his [Tom's] death, and of his loving farewell to all on the place, and added, 'It was on his grave, my friends, that I resolved, before God, that I would never own another slave, while it is possible to free him; that nobody, through me, should ever run the risk of being parted from home and friends, and dying on a lonely plantation, as he died. So, when you rejoice in your freedom, think that you owe

> *The bitterest tears shed over graves are for words left unsaid and deeds left undone.*
> —Harriet Beecher Stowe

it to that good old soul, and pay it back in kindness to his wife and children. Think of your freedom, every time you see UNCLE TOM'S CABIN.'"

How to Be Like
Harriet Beecher Stowe

1. **Develop faith in God.**

   Stowe was the daughter of minister Lyman Beecher. She had a strong Christian faith that was heard in the voices of the slaves she depicted, especially Uncle Tom.

2. **Realize that out of tragedy can come triumphs.**

   Try to uncover life's lessons even in the worst of times. Stowe took the pain in her heart from losing her infant son Charles and used it to help write *Uncle Tom's Cabin,* and thus make a difference to the cause of abolition and in the lives of slaves.

3. **Read.**

   Reading improves the mind. Lyman Beecher encouraged his children to be educated, and Stowe loved to read from the time she was a little girl. As Eleanor Roosevelt said, reading helps people reach greater "intellectual attainments." Only through a book, Eleanor said, is it possible to explore "the most fascinating thing in the world—another person's mind."

4. **Choose a partner who brings out the best in you.**

   Calvin Stowe was also a committed abolitionist who supported and encouraged Stowe's writing career. "My dear, you must be a literary woman. It is so written in the book for fate . . . Make all your calculations accordingly," he wrote.

5. **Set goals.**

   It was Isabella Beecher, Stowe's sister-in-law, who wrote a letter encouraging Stowe to harness her writing talent to fight slavery. "I will write something," Stowe announced to her family after Isabella's letter was read aloud. That "something" became *Uncle Tom's Cabin*.

6. **Blaze your own trail.**

As Stowe wrote to *National Era* editor Bailey when she told him about her story of *Uncle Tom's Cabin*: "I feel now that the time [has] come when even a woman or a child who can speak a word for freedom and humanity is bound to speak. . . . I hope every woman who can write will not be silent."

7. **Work with passion; strive to make a difference.**

Mother Teresa said, "Life is not worth living unless it is lived for others." Stowe made her difference while working for the slave. "My heart was bursting with the anguish [and] the cruelty and injustice our nation was showing to the slave, and praying [to] God to let me do a little and to cause my cry for them to be heard," she wrote.

8. **Create time to follow your dream.**

As the mother of seven young children (with the oldest around fifteen), Stowe rarely had any peace and quiet during the day. She worked when she could during the day, and tried to carve out three hours a day to write. "Nothing but deadly determination enables me ever to write. It is rowing against wind and tide," she wrote.

9. **Challenge people to think.**

Uncle Tom's Cabin attacked the stereotype of black slaves. Tom and George have more wisdom, courage and goodness than their persecutors. Eliza loves her son Harry every bit as much as a white mother, and courageously protects him.

10. **Don't rest on your accomplishments.**

Stowe secured her place in history with *Uncle Tom's Cabin* and made a great deal of money from it. But she kept working for the cause of abolition. In 1853 she toured on behalf of antislavery societies in England and Scotland, and raised money for the cause. She wrote pamphlets and articles against slavery, and in print encouraged Abraham Lincoln to issue the Emancipation Proclamation as soon as possible. She continued to write books and wrote several after *Uncle Tom's Cabin*.

She told the story, and the whole world wept
At wrongs and cruelties it had not known
But for this fearless woman's voice alone.
She spoke to consciences that long had slept.
Her message, Freedom's clear reveille, swept
From heedless hovel to complacent throne.
Command and prophecy were in the tone,
And from its sheath the sword of justice leapt.

—Paul Laurence Dunbar, 1898
Excerpt from the poem
"Harriet Beecher Stowe"

HARRIET TUBMAN
1820–1913

RIGHTEOUSNESS

A nobler, higher spirit, or a truer, seldom dwells in human form.

—William H. Seward, President Lincoln's secretary of state and a friend of Harriet Tubman

arriet Tubman was a former slave who became known as the "Moses of her people." As a young woman in the mid-1800s, Tubman made a dangerous and momentous decision: She was going to escape the chains of slavery and be free—one way or another.

Tubman knew all too well the brutal life of slavery. The scars that crisscrossed her neck had been there since childhood, when her white owners whipped her. Once, in order to escape a beating from her mistress when she was a child, Tubman hid in a pigpen for days while fighting with the little pigs for food. Her respite was only temporary; upon emerging from the pen she received her whipping.

Tubman's rebellious nature was evident to all. A fifteen-year-old Tubman once blocked the path of an overseer who was in pursuit of a runaway slave. The overseer picked up a two-pound lead weight and threw it at the runaway slave, but it hit Tubman in the head and broke her skull. She lay unconscious as blood gushed from a wound that left a permanent dent on her forehead. She was in a coma for several weeks, and after recovering she suffered from blackouts for the rest of her life. Tubman's "masters," without bothering to consult a doctor, forced her to return to the hard manual labor of their fields. Many times under the strain of the labor she collapsed into unconsciousness.

While slavery was always cruel, slaves in Maryland, where Tubman lived, were treated somewhat better—by slave standards—than their brethren in the deep-South cotton states of Georgia, Mississippi, Alabama and Louisiana. In fact, the term "sold down the river" comes from slaves in the upper South being sold to plantations in the deep South. Tubman had nightmares about this happening to her. She imagined men on horseback swooping down and dragging screaming women and children off to the awful slavery of the deep South. Tubman was tormented by another dream as well—the dream of freedom.

"[Tubman] . . . used to dream of flying over fields and towns, and rivers and mountains, looking down upon them 'like a bird,' and reaching at last a great fence, or sometimes a river, over which she would try to fly," wrote Sarah Bradford in *Harriet Tubman: The Moses of Her People.*

"But," Tubman said, "It 'peared like I wouldn't hab de strength, and jes as I was sinkin' down, dere would be ladies all drest in white ober dere, and dey would put out dere arms and pull me 'cross."

Sarah Bradford was Tubman's friend. When quoting her, Bradford wrote phonetically, to provide readers the opportunity to hear Tubman as she really was, highly intelligent and eloquent in feeling. Like all slaves, Tubman had been denied an education and never learned "proper" English.

Tubman's worst fears came true in 1849. Some of the slaves on the plantation were going to be sold. One of her sisters had already been sold South and fitted with chains for her trip. Now the same fate awaited Tubman. She came to an important decision: She would run away. It meant leaving her husband, a free black named John Tubman, and not breathing

> *We had no more courage than Harriet Tubman or Marcus Garvey had in their times. We just had a more vulnerable enemy.*
> —Stokely Carmichael,
> CONTEMPORARY UNITED STATES
> CIVIL RIGHTS LEADER

a word about it to him. Harriet had previously discussed the subject with him, but John Tubman refused to join her and threatened to tell the plantation overseer of her plans.

Harriet and her three brothers escaped one evening and headed North to the free states. Her brothers were afraid, however, and turned back before anyone discovered them missing. There was much to fear. Runaway slaves had to elude posses of slave catchers with packs of barking dogs. Slaves who were captured were whipped, branded with a red-hot metal rod and had the tops of their ears cut off.

With her brothers gone, Tubman was completely alone in the night. Her destination was Philadelphia. One hundred thirty miles separated her from freedom. For direction, she followed the North star. For courage, she made a commitment to herself. "I had reasoned dis out in my mind," Tubman said. "[T]here was one of two things I had a right to, liberty or death; if I could not have one, I would have de oder; for no man should take me alive; I should fight for my liberty as long as my strength lasted, and when de time came for me to go, de Lord would let dem take me."

Tubman traveled by night and hid during the day. "Often her bed was only the cold ground, and her watchers the stars of night," Bradford wrote in *The Moses of Her People*. Tubman eventually made her way to the house of a white woman who she knew aided runaway slaves. The woman gave her two slips of paper and directed her to the next safe house. Tubman was now traveling on the Underground Railroad.

The Underground Railroad was the name given to a network of people who helped runaway slaves escape to the North. The Underground Railroad created routes for runaway slaves to follow by providing safe houses along the way. At a safe house a runaway could rest, eat, get some supplies and continue North. People who assisted runaway slaves were risking up to fifteen years in jail.

Tubman used the Underground Railroad, but she was on her own much of the time. "Without knowing whom to trust, or how near the pursuers might be, she carefully felt her way, and by her native cunning, or by God-given wisdom," Bradford wrote. "After many long and weary days of travel, she found that she had passed the magic line, which then divided the land of bondage from the land of freedom."

"I looked at my hands," Tubman said, "to see if I was de same person now I was free. Dere was such glory ober eberything, de sun came like gold trou de trees, and ober de fields, and I felt like I was in heaven."

She also felt alone without her family and made a promise to herself. "I had crossed de line of which I had so long been dreaming," Tubman said. "I was free; but dere was no one to welcome me to de land of freedom, I was a stranger in a strange land, and my home after all was down in de old cabin quarter, wid de ole folks, and my brudders and sisters. But to dis solemn resolution I came; I was free, and dey should be free also; I would make a home for dem in de North, and de Lord helping me, I would bring dem all dere. Oh, how I prayed den, lying all alone on de cold, damp ground; 'Oh, dear Lord,' I said, 'I haint got no friend but you. Come to my help, Lord, for I'm in trouble!'"

After arriving safely in Philadelphia, Tubman found employment as a cook. She also found a purpose to her life in the form of the Vigilance Committee. As the main eastern station for the Underground Railroad, the Vigilance Committee helped runaway slaves find clothing, food and jobs. Tubman met William Still, a black man in charge of the Vigilance Committee. From Still and the others there, she learned what she could do to contribute, and she chose the dangerous job of being a "conductor" for the Underground Railroad. A conductor went into slave states and helped lead slaves to safety in the North.

The first people Tubman brought out of the South were her sister Mary and Mary's children. They were being held in a slave pen in Maryland, where an auction was scheduled. The family was in danger of being sold into the deep South, but Tubman had a plan to save them.

Mary was married to a free black man, John Bowley. Tubman's plan called for Bowley to present himself as a representative of the people in charge of the auction. He went to the slave pen where Mary was being held and requested that he be allowed to take her to a hotel where a supposed buyer was waiting to inspect her. The auctioneers did not know that Mary and her children had been released to her husband. From there, Tubman had every detail of the escape meticulously worked out. First the family went to a safe house and waited until nightfall. Next Tubman arranged for a wagon, and everyone was hidden beneath blankets. The wagon headed for the river where a boat took them to Baltimore. From there the family—hidden under a load of vegetables—traveled to a new safe house. A week later Tubman took them the rest of the way to Philadelphia.

The escape was successfully completed, and it gave birth to the Underground Railroad. Tubman was given the nickname "Moses" because she led her people to safety.

In 1850, a stronger version of the Fugitive Slave Act became federal law. Before it, a slave still had to fear being recaptured by slave catchers and taken back to their masters. After it, slave catchers and federal officials were empowered with the legal right to capture escaped slaves and return them to their masters. Even free blacks were in danger, since the only "proof" needed that a black person was the escaped slave in question was the word of the slave catcher.

Tubman and the Underground Railroad were now forced to take escaped slaves across the border to safety in Canada. "I wouldn't trust Uncle Sam wid my people no longer, but I brought 'em all clar to Canada," Tubman said after the new Fugitive Slave Act was passed. "Farewell ole Marster, don't think hard of me, I'm going on to Canada, where all de slaves are free," went a hymn sung by runaways.

In order to succeed as a conductor, Tubman had to become a master of detail, planning, disguise, deception and most of all, resolve. Once Moses came in the shadow of night to whisk slaves away on their dangerous journey to freedom, there was no turning back for anyone. Tubman feared that a returning slave might be tortured into revealing information about the escaping party. For those slaves who tried to turn back, the five-foot Tubman stood in their path, with a drawn revolver: "Dead niggers tell no tales, you go on or die!" she'd say. Tubman later said of her methods, "If [a man] was weak enough to give out, he'd be weak enough to betray us all, and all who helped us; and do you think I'd let so many die just fer one coward man?"

Tubman was known to Maryland plantation owners only as the mysterious Moses, who was thought most likely to be a man. They eventually offered a $40,000 bounty for the capture of Moses. But, "No fear of the lash, the blood-hound, or the fiery stake, could divert her from her self-imposed task of leading as many as possible of her people [to freedom]," wrote Professor Hopkins of the Auburn (New York) Theology Seminary in March 1886.

Another chronicler of the time, William Still, wrote that "Great fears were entertained for her safety, but she seemed wholly devoid of personal fear. The idea of being captured by slave-hunters or slave holders, seemed never to enter her mind."

Tubman did have some narrow escapes. Once, on the verge of being discovered, she employed her gift for deception and evaded capture by boarding a train that was heading South. She knew a black woman heading North would be an object of suspicion. "Who would suspect a fugitive with such a price set upon her head, of rushing at railway speed into the jaws of destruction?" Bradford wrote.

As Tubman made her journeys into slave country, she would often disguise herself as an old, feeble woman. When she was spotted somewhere that might arouse suspicion, such as near a plantation as she awaited her runaways, Tubman bowed her head in false submission to the white onlookers and acted like a humble slave. She also often walked with strings attached to live chickens, so she could create a distraction, when necessary, by releasing the birds. This tactic once helped her avoid being recognized by a former master when she ventured into the town where he lived.

"[Tubman] went along the street with her sun-bonnet well over her face, and with the bent and decrepit air of an aged woman," wrote Bradford. "Suddenly, on turning a corner, she spied her old master coming towards her. She pulled the string, which tied the legs of the chickens; they began to flutter and scream, and as her master passed, she was stooping and busily engaged in attending to the fluttering fowls. And he went on his way, little thinking that he was brushing the very garments of the woman who had dared to steal herself, and others, of his belongings."

While leading runaways to freedom, Tubman made use of unlikely hiding places, such as drainage ditches, to evade pursuers. She once had her party hide in a manure pile and breathe through straws poking out of it.

Word about the work of Moses spread throughout Maryland's slave plantations and reached the ears of Josiah "Joe" Bailey. To his owner, Bailey was an extremely valuable "piece of property." Tall and strong, Bailey also doubled as an overseer. For many years, his master had rented him out to a planter, William Hughlett. Hughlett was pleased with Bailey's work and in 1856 bought him outright. "The purchase was made, and this chattel passed over into the hands of a new owner," Bradford wrote.

The morning after the sale, Bailey's new master called him out of his cabin. He was told to strip because he was about to be beaten. The following account was told to Sarah Bradford by Tubman, who heard it firsthand from Bailey.

"Mas'r, habn't I always been faithful to you?" Bailey said to Hughlett. "Habn't I worked through sun an' rain, early in de mornin' an' late at night, habn't I saved you an oberseer by doin' his work? Hab you anything to complain agin me?"

"No Joe, I have no complaint to make of you. You're a good nigger, an' you've always worked well. But you belong to me now; you're my nigger, and the first lesson my niggers have to learn is that I am master and they belong to me, and are never to resist anything I order them to do. So I always begin by giving them a good licking. Now strip and take it."

Bailey did, but as he put a shirt over his torn, bleeding back, he made a vow: "Dis is de first an' de last." As soon as he was physically able, under the cover of darkness, he made his way down river to the cabin of Tubman's father Ben. "Nex' time Moses comes," Bailey said, "let me know."

Joe went North with Tubman, but the journey was even more dangerous than usual. A $1,500 reward was placed on Bailey, and everyone was on the lookout for him. Tubman called on her vast network of contacts to get him out of Maryland. When she finally got Bailey safely to Canada, he broke his self-imposed silence. He had tears of joy in his eyes when he started singing, "Glory to God and Jesus too . . . Tank de Lord! Dere's only one more journey for me now, and dat's to Hebben!" Bailey lived out his years in Canada and remained friends with Tubman.

The next year, Tubman led her own parents Ben and Ritt Ross to freedom. The Rosses had not wanted to leave the only home they knew, and they remained slaves after Tubman first left. But at age seventy, Ben Ross faced legal charges for helping a slave escape. In 1857, he and his wife finally agreed to make their way to freedom, and Tubman led them to safety in the North.

On December 1, 1860, just five months before the Civil War began Tubman made her last trip as a conductor. That final one was especially significant to her, because she led to freedom her brother Stephen, his wife and their three children.

In all, Tubman had risked her life nineteen times to go back into the upper South, primarily Maryland, to help over 300 slaves escape. "I never ran my train off the track and I never lost a passenger," she said many times of her trips for the Underground Railroad.

William Still wrote that Tubman's success as a conductor was "attributable to her adventurous spirit and utter disregard of consequences. Her like it is probable was never known before or since." When Bradford was writing her book with Tubman, they asked another black freedom fighter, orator and free black Frederick Douglass, to write a few words about Tubman to be included in the book. Douglass wrote:

"You ask for what you do not need when you call upon me for a word of commendation. I need such words from you far more than you can need them from me. The difference between us is very marked. Most that I have done and suffered in the service of our cause has been in public . . . You, on the other hand, have labored in a private way.

"I have wrought in the day—you in the night. I have had the applause of the crowd and the satisfaction that comes of being approved by the multitude, while the most that you have done has been witnessed by a few trembling, scarred, and foot-sore bondmen and women, whom you have led out of the house of bondage, and whose heartfelt 'God bless you' has been your only reward.

"The midnight sky and the silent stars have been the witnesses of your devotion to freedom and of your heroism. Excepting John Brown—of sacred memory—I know of no one who has willingly encountered more perils and hardships to serve our enslaved people than you have."

During the Civil War, Tubman served as a nurse, spy and guide behind Confederate lines. As a nurse she helped soldiers who were "dying off like sheep," from dysentery and smallpox. She administered aid to captured Confederate soldiers with the same compassion she did to Union soldiers.

Either as a conductor or nurse, Tubman relied heavily on her faith. "The Lord will take care of me until my time comes," she said often, referring to her strong faith in God. "Brought up by parents possessed of strong faith in God, she had never known the time, I imagine, when she did not trust Him, and cling to Him, with an all-abiding confidence," Bradford wrote in her biography of Tubman. "[She] seemed ever to feel the Divine Presence near, and she talked with God [she said], 'as a man talketh with his friend.' Hers was not the religion of a morning and evening prayer at stated times, but when she felt a need, she simply told God of it, and trusted Him to set the matter right."

As a spy Tubman went behind enemy lines and gathered information from slaves. As a scout, she helped lead 300 black soldiers on a raid in South Carolina that brought the Union Army almost 800 new black soldiers who had been slaves, and thousands of dollars worth of property. "The cause of freedom owes her much; the country owes her much," said Tubman's friend, former Secretary of War Edwin Stanton.

Tubman's legend made it across the Atlantic, where Queen Victoria read Sarah Bradford's book. The Queen was so impressed that in 1897 she sent Tubman a silk shawl, a silver medal and an invitation to be honored at a London reception. Tubman, who at that time was close to eighty, declined the offer but treasured the Queen's letters, gifts and invitation. "She always told her tale with a modesty which showed how unconscious she was of having done anything more than her simple duty. No one who listened to her could doubt her perfect truthfulness and integrity," wrote Oliver Johnson, president of the New York Anti-Slavery Society.

The government never compensated Tubman for her wartime work, despite direct appeals to Congress on her behalf. Brigadier General Rufus Saxton was one of many who supported compensation for Tubman. He wrote a letter on her behalf and lauded her "remarkable courage, zeal, and fidelity," for her work behind enemy lines.

"Harriet Tubman was exemplar par excellence of that humanitarian spirit. What better evidence of this does one need than the absence of bitterness over the government's persistent refusal to reward her for four years of service," wrote Butler A. Jones, Ph.D., in a contemporary introduction to Bradford's book. The country that didn't compensate Tubman for her wartime contributions did see fit to give her a military funeral upon her death in 1913.

Bradford wrote of Tubman: "[No woman] has shown more courage, and power of endurance, in facing danger and death to relieve human suffering."

Tubman never stopped caring about people. In 1903, she donated land that she owned in Auburn, New York, to the African Methodist Episcopal Zion Church. In 1908, the Church fulfilled what had been Tubman's wish for the land: They built the Harriet Tubman Home for Aged and Indigent Colored People.

How to Be Like
Harriet Tubman

1. Be committed to your cause.

Tubman was going to be free. She said: "I had reasoned dis out in my mind; there was one of two things I had a right to, liberty or death; if I could not have one, I would have de oder."

2. Give back to society.

Tubman was free when she successfully completed her escape, but her social conscience made it impossible for her to forget those still in bondage.

3. Pay attention to details.

Tubman had every detail of an escape meticulously planned out.

4. Strategize.

Tubman had a flare for deception and the unexpected. When she ventured back into slave country to lead runaways to freedom she disguised herself as an old and feeble woman. She utilized live chickens for diversions, and once boarded a train headed South because she knew her pursuers would be looking for a black woman heading North.

5. Look for new ways to make a difference.

During the Civil War it was too difficult to lead runaway slaves to freedom, so Tubman helped the Union by serving as a nurse, spy and scout behind enemy lines. The United States government never compensated her for her wartime contributions, but she was never bitter about it.

6. **Develop a strong faith; courage will follow.**

Tubman, whether slave, runaway, conductor or spy, refused to be afraid. Faith gave her the courage to live boldly. She found her courage in her faith. "The Lord will take care of me until my time comes," she often said.

7. **Be modest.**

Tubman was known as the "Moses of her people," but she never changed as a person. "She always told her tale with a modesty which showed how unconscious she was of having done anything more than her simple duty," Oliver Johnson wrote about her.

SOJOURNER TRUTH
ca. 1797(?)–1883

FAITH

Sojourner has known what it is to drink to the dregs the bitterest cup of human degradation. That one thus placed on a level with cattle and swine, and for so many years subjected to the most demoralizing influences, should have retained her moral integrity to such an extent, and cherished so successfully the religious sentiment of her soul, shows a mind of no common order.

—*William Lloyd Garrison, abolitionist*

**F**or thirty years, starting in the late 1840s, former slave Sojourner Truth was an itinerant preacher who spoke out against the evils of slavery. She is remembered as the first prominent black woman orator in the United States who expanded her causes to civil rights, women's rights, suffrage and temperance. Sojourner Truth made the journey from slave to legend because she never lost the greatest resource she had: her faith in God.

Sojourner Truth was born Isabella Baumfree, into the brutal world of slavery in Hurley, New York, around 1797. Her mother Mau-mau Bett could only offer her daughter love and her religious beliefs. Mau-mau Bett had other children who were cruelly sold away from her. The deep sadness that Sojourner Truth often saw in her mother and father was related to losing those children. Her parents were deeply concerned about their two remaining children, Isabella and her younger brother Peter.

One night, when Isabella was around nine years old, her mother took her and Peter outside. "My children, there is a God who hears and sees you," Sojourner Truth remembered her mother saying. The children asked where God lived. "He lives in the sky," Mau-mau Bett answered, "and when you are beaten, or cruelly treated, or fall into any trouble, you must ask help of him, and he will always hear and help you."

Truth's belief in God gave her something the slave owners couldn't take from her or beat out of her. She was never taught to read or write, but she began to study the principles of the Bible by having others read it to her. She memorized Bible passages and was able to quote from them her entire life.

Because of her faith, Sojourner Truth was also able to endure sadistic beatings with hot metal rods when she was just a girl. One of her "transgressions," according to one of her mistresses, was that the Dutch-speaking girl wasn't learning English fast enough. Sojourner Truth endured living with thirteen other slaves in one filthy cellar room, being sold four times and having some of her children sold away from her. Emotional and physical pain was a condition of slave life.

When New York State passed a law in 1824 that all slaves born before July 4, 1799 were to be freed on that day in 1827, Sojourner Truth saw the hope of freedom for the first time. When emancipation day arrived, however, John Dumont, her fourth owner, refused to free her. Since the exact date of her birth was unknown Dumont didn't feel bound to the law or to the promise he made to her to set her free. He said that because of a hand injury she hadn't been able to work enough the past year and would have to stay on another year.

Sojourner Truth recalled Dumont's hypocrisy many years later in the book she dictated called the *Narrative of Sojourner Truth*. It was written to help people understand the evils of slavery. "The slaveholders are TERRIBLE for promising to give you this or that, or such and such a privilege, if you will do thus and so," she said, "and when the time of fulfillment comes, and one claims the promise, they, forsooth, recollect nothing of the kind; and you are, like as not, taunted with being a LIAR; or, at best, the slave is accused of not having performed his part or condition of the contract."

Bolstered by her faith and freed from a fear of consequences, Truth granted herself freedom. She simply left the Dumont farm, taking her infant daughter Sophia with her. She found refuge nearby with Mr. and Mrs. Isaac Van Wagener, a kindly Quaker couple. When John Dumont caught up with her, he said, "Well, Bell, so you've run away from me." She answered: "No, I did not run away; I walked away by day-light."

When Truth made it clear she wasn't coming back, Dumont allowed Mr. Van Wagener to buy her freedom for $20 and her daughter's for $5. Having done so, Mr. Van Wagener spoke loud enough for Dumont to hear and told her not to address him as her new master. "There is but one master," he declared, "and he who is your master is my master."

Truth had given birth to five children, some of whom were sold away. She remained a devoted mother and visited her children regularly at their different homes. New York had laws that slaves couldn't be sold out of state and must be freed upon turning twenty-one (if they were born after July 4, 1799). She vowed to provide a home one day for her whole family, but until that day, she did her best to stay close to her children.

Truth's uncompromising determination helped her reclaim her son Peter. In 1827, Dumont had sold five-year-old Peter to a New York doctor named Solomon Gedney. Then, unknown to Dumont, Gedney gave Peter to his brother-in-law, a man named Fowler, who owned a plantation in Alabama. There were no emancipation laws in the heart of slave country, and Peter was now a slave for life in an even more brutal place, the deep South.

Dumont had sold Peter to Gedney with the understanding he would eventually be freed. When Truth went to see Dumont, she received some sympathy from him but none from his wife. She recalled Mrs. Dumont's awful words in her *Narrative:* "Ugh! A fine fuss to make about a little nigger! Why, haven't you as many of 'em left as you can see to . . . Making such a halloo-balloo about the neighborhood; all for a paltry nigger!"

"I'll have my child again," Truth said to her. Mrs. Dumont scoffed, then asked her if she had any money to support Peter even if she could free him. "No, I have no money," Truth replied, "but God has enough, or what's better! And I'll have my child again."

New York allowed blacks to file lawsuits. With the financial backing of a Quaker group, Truth filed to have Peter returned. After months of delays, the hearing went in Truth's favor. She was one of the first black women in the United States to win a court case. After Peter was returned, Truth found his entire body covered with scars from repeated beatings that Fowler had given him. Fowler would later beat his wife to death.

Eventually Truth moved to New York City and found work as a domestic. She was active in several different religious communities, including one that helped reform prostitutes. In 1843, when Truth was around forty-six years old, she was certain God wanted her to become a traveling itinerant preacher and speak out against the evils of slavery. She dropped her old name, Isabella Baumfree, and took a new one—Sojourner Truth.

"Without doubt, it was Truth's religious faith that transformed her from Isabella, a domestic servant, into Sojourner

Truth, a hero for three centuries—at least," wrote Nell Irvin Painter (a leading contemporary biographer of Truth's) in *Sojourner Truth:A Life, A Symbol.*

Truth left New York City with twenty-five cents to her name to travel America and speak God's truth against slavery. She was the first black woman to do so. Her travels took her to northern states such as Connecticut and Massachusetts, and midwestern states such as Ohio, Indiana and Kansas. "From the late 1840s through the late 1870s, [Truth] traveled the American land, denouncing slavery and slavers, advocating freedom, women's rights, women's suffrage, and temperance," Irvin Painter wrote.

Truth's message was a peaceful one of nonviolent resistance. She wanted people to come to understand that slavery was immoral. She had developed a formidable intelligence and had a sincere yet dramatic manner of preaching on abolition. When she condemned the elitists who were trying to tie voting rights to education and ownership of property, she said, "I cannot read a book, but I can read people . . . What a narrow idea a reading qualification is for a voter! I know and do what is right better than many big men who read. And what's that property qualification! Just as bad! As if men and women themselves, who made money, were not of more value than the thing they made. If I were a delegate to the New York constitutional convention I could make suffrage as clear as daylight."

Biographer Painter wrote: "Throughout her life, Truth combined pleas for the abolition of slavery, [for] black voting, and women's suffrage into a commitment to human rights. . . . when the women's movement split between those who favored black male voting over universal suffrage for all adults, Truth made clear that women, black and white, needed the ballot."

Truth's detractors in the North and South despised her for being black, but she embraced her heritage and offered a bit of wisdom to

> *After the slaves were emancipated, Truth said, "If colored men get their rights, and not colored women theirs, you see the colored men will be masters over the women, and it will be just as bad as it was before."*

them that they hadn't considered: "I am coloured thank God for that; I have not the curse of God upon me for enslaving human beings." Women's rights leader Susan B. Anthony remarked that "Sojourner combined in herself the two most hated elements of humanity. She was black and she was a woman, and all the insults that could be cast upon color and sex were together hurled at her."

During the Women's Rights Convention of 1851 in Akron, Ohio, Frances Gage, a leader in the movement, invited Truth to speak. Not all in attendance supported that invitation. Gage recalled one woman saying to her: "Don't let her speak, Mrs. Gage, it will ruin us: Every newspaper in the land will have our cause mixed up with abolition and niggers, and we shall be utterly denounced." Truth spoke as scheduled and, in her natural dialect, stated: "Wall, chilern, whar dar is so much racket dar must be somethin' out o' kilter. I tink dat 'twixt de niggers of de souf and de womin at de norf, all talkin' bout rihts, de white men will be in a fix pretty soon."

She then turned her attention to a man in the audience. "Den dat little man in black dar, he say women can't have as much rights as men, 'cause Christ wan't a woman! Whar did your Christ come from?" Truth asked. Gage wrote: "Rolling thunder couldn't have stilled that crowd, as did those deep, wonderful tones, as she stood there with outstretched arms and eyes of fire. Raising her voice still louder, she repeated, 'Whar did your Christ come from? From God and a woman! Man had nothin' to do wid Him.' Oh, what a rebuke that was to that little man."

Truth had turned around her audience of doubters. "I have never in my life seen anything like the magical influence that subdued the mobbish spirit of the day, and turned the sneers and jeers of an excited crowd into notes of respect and admiration," Gage wrote. "Hundreds rushed up to shake hands with her, and congratulate the glorious old mother, and bid her God-speed on her mission of 'testifyin' agin concerning the wickedness of this 'ere people.'"

It was the great abolitionist William Lloyd Garrison who encouraged Truth to dictate the *Narrative of Sojourner Truth* to educate people on the cruelty of slavery. Selling the book also helped Truth support herself. "I sell the shadow to support the substance," Truth said often.

Her *Narrative* was powerful because with exceptional feeling, it captured the inhumanity of slavery. Truth recalled that as a teenager she was in a budding romance with a slave, Robert, who was from a nearby farm. Robert was ordered by his master, Catlin, to stop seeing her. He refused, and the next time he went to see her, Catlin and another man were there also. "They both fell upon him like tigers, beating him with the heavy ends of their canes, bruising and mangling his head and face in the most awful manner, and causing the blood, which streamed from his wounds, to cover him like a slaughtered beast," Truth told Olive Gilbert, who wrote down the narrative that Truth dictated to her.

Gilbert herself wrote, "If there can be any thing more

diametrically opposed to the religion of Jesus, than the working of this soul-killing system—which is truly sanctioned by the religion of America as are her ministers and churches—we wish to be shown where it can be found." Truth added: "Religion without humanity is very poor human stuff."

Former slave Frederick Douglass was a highly educated and eloquent orator, and at first looked down on the six-foot Truth. However, she had too much self-confidence to feel inferior to anyone, white or black. "Douglass was both put off and enchanted by this uneducated woman who considered herself his equal in discourse and intelligence, if not in literacy and posturing," wrote Margaret Washington in a 1993 release of the *Narrative of Sojourner Truth.*

Douglass wrote that he found Truth to be "a strange compound of wit and wisdom, of wild enthusiasm, and flint-like common sense." In one famous exchange between the two that took place before an audience, Douglass advocated ending slavery through armed conflict. Truth, a lifelong pacifist, stood up and admonished him to have faith, saying, "Be careful Frederick . . . is God Almighty dead?"

Truth lived her life by taking action and letting the consequences fall where they might. She presented the spirit of her ideals while addressing a women's rights convention in 1850: "Sisters, I ain't clear what you'd be after. If women want any rights more than they's got, why don't they just take them, and not be talking about it?"

Truth accepted that the Civil War was necessary to end slavery. "They don't know God, nor God don't know them," Truth said in reference to the white men who had perpetuated slavery. In order to garner support for the Union cause, Truth risked her life in Indiana. The state had a law forbidding blacks from crossing state lines, and had strong antiwar and antiblack sentiments, but Truth went anyway, sometimes facing angry mobs. She was arrested on numerous occasions and subsequently released. Her supporters there shouted, "Sojourner, Free Speech, and the Union."

In 1862, President Abraham Lincoln signed a law outlawing slavery in Washington, D.C. As a result, freed slaves lived in terrible conditions at refugee camps and in constant fear of slave traders. These men kidnapped blacks at random and sold them back into slavery. The kidnappers would kill anyone who reported them to federal marshals. As usual, Truth wasn't afraid or intimidated. She gave strength to the free slaves by going through the camps and encouraging them to demand that the federal government protect them under the laws they had passed.

Truth's reputation brought her to the attention of many influential people. She met with Harriet Beecher Stowe, author of *Uncle Tom's Cabin,* who wrote an article about her and called her the "African Sibyl." (Sibyl was a prophet during biblical times.) Truth also met Presidents Abraham Lincoln, Andrew Johnson and Ulysses S. Grant. She was a strong supporter of President Lincoln at a time when some abolitionists criticized him for not moving fast enough on emancipation. Truth urged her followers to be patient with the president.

When she met Lincoln during a White House visit Truth said that she'd never heard of him until he became president. He smilingly replied, "I had heard of you many times before that," Truth recalled. Lincoln signed Truth's *Book of Life:* "For Auntie Sojourner Truth, October 29, 1864, A. Lincoln."

Truth was asked by the federal government to work with the National Freedmen's Relief Association. Her job was to help former slaves make a smooth transition to being free. She also encouraged former slaves to pursue the American dream, because it was their unpaid, dawn-to-dusk labor that helped build the country.

Truth's legacy and legend continues unabated. The small, six-wheeled robot probe the United States deployed on the surface of Mars in 1995 was named "Sojourner" in her honor.

"Because we are apt to assume that the mere experience of enslavement endowed [Truth] with the power to voice its evils," Nell Irvin Painter wrote, "we may forget a shocking fact: No other woman who had been through the ordeal of slavery managed to survive with sufficient strength, poise, and self-confidence to become a public presence over the long term. Only [Truth] had the ability to go on speaking, year after year for thirty years, to make herself into a force in several American reform movements. . . . [Truth] was first and last an itinerant preacher."

Truth's last words before she died, appropriately enough, were "Be a follower of the Lord Jesus."

How to Be Like
Sojourner Truth

1. **Develop a deep faith.**

   With faith, anything is possible. Truth went from a penniless former slave with no influential contacts to a legendary figure who still endures. "Without doubt, it was [her] religious faith that transformed her from Isabella, a domestic servant, into Sojourner Truth, a hero for three centuries—at least," Nell Irvin Painter wrote.

2. **Act boldly and decisively.**

   Truth was a woman of action. Rather than wait for John Dumont to grant her freedom she took the initiative and left on her own. When she decided God wanted her to be an itinerant preacher she stopped one life and began another. She once said to a group of women regarding women's suffrage, "Sisters, I ain't clear what you'd be after. If women want any rights more than they's got, why don't they just take them, and not be talking about it?"

3. **Develop courage.**

   Truth's courage was rooted in her faith. As a black woman speaking out against the white male power establishment, she saw her share of unfriendly crowds and mobs, and put her life in jeopardy many times. To support the Union war effort Truth also risked her life in Indiana. The state had a law forbidding blacks from entering the state, and had strong antiwar and anti-black sentiments. Truth went anyway to garner support for the Union cause, sometimes facing angry mobs.

4. Know your strengths.

As a product of a slave system that forbade teaching the enslaved to read or write, Truth was illiterate. However, that didn't stop her from being a woman of influence. "I cannot read a book," she said, "but I can read people."

5. Speak from your heart.

Truth never put on airs and was always herself. During the Women's Rights Convention in Akron in 1851, the crowd was skeptical but ended up embracing her. That scenario took place many times during her career. Frances Gage, a leader in the movement, wrote of Truth: "I have never in my life seen anything like the magical influence that subdued the mobbish spirit of the day, and turned the sneers and jeers of an excited crowd into notes of respect and admiration."

6. Live each day with passion and enthusiasm.

Frederick Douglass wrote of Truth that he found her "a strange compound of wit and wisdom, of wild enthusiasm, and flint-like common sense."

I am pleading for my people,
A poor and downtrodden race,
Who dwell in freedom's boasted land
With no abiding place.
I am pleading that my people
May have their rights restored;
For they have long been toiling,
And yet have no reward.
They are forced the crops to culture,
But not for them they yield,
Although both late and early,
They labor in the field.
Whilst I bear upon my body
the scars of many a gash,
I am pleading for my people
Who groan beneath the lash.

—A favorite poem of Sojourner Truth's,
which she sometimes recited before
she began speaking

CLARA BARTON
1821–1912

DETERMINATION

Dare to do.

—*Clara Barton*

**C**lara Barton distinguished herself during the Civil War by personally bringing supplies to battlefield hospitals, and as the founder of the American Red Cross. To Clara Barton, the Civil War was a call to duty that she had been waiting for her entire life.

On April 19, 1861, the thirty-nine-year-old Barton was working at the United States patent office in Washington, D.C. Seven days earlier, Confederate forces had opened fire on Fort Sumter, South Carolina, to launch the Civil War.

Some of the 75,000 volunteer soldiers that President Abraham Lincoln had called to duty were traveling to the nation's capital. When the Sixth Massachusetts Regiment tried to change trains in tension-filled Baltimore, an angry mob who favored southern secession began harassing the soldiers. A skirmish ensued. When it was over four soldiers and twelve civilians were dead, and many soldiers were injured.

Barton had always had the desire to help people. When she was eleven, her older brother David was injured in a fall and Barton volunteered to become his full-time nurse. At seventeen, she started teaching and eventually helped start the first free public school in Bordentown, New Jersey, for all, including poor children. Her teaching career lasted fifteen years.

When the Sixth Massachusetts limped into Washington, D.C., they found Barton waiting to help them. She and her sister Sally cared for the wounded and provided them with supplies and shelter. After discovering that the regiment's supplies were nonexistent, Barton also used her own money to buy food and clothing. When she ran out of bandages she tore up sheets and used them instead. Once all of her resources were exhausted, she began writing to families of the soldiers and different charitable organizations asking for supplies. Three months later, Barton's efforts had been so successful she had three warehouses filled with food, clothing and medical supplies.

The more Barton learned about the soldiers' needs, the more she realized they were not receiving adequate care. Medical supplies weren't available at the front lines when needed, and the wounded soldiers were suffering and dying needlessly while waiting. In fact, the Union and Confederate Armies lost twice as many soldiers to disease and uncleaned wounds as they lost in actual battle. This carnage had a profound impact on Barton.

"I only wish I could work to some purpose," Barton wrote to a friend. "I have no right to these easy comfortable days and our poor men suffering and dying thirsting in this hot sun and I so quiet here in want of nothing. It is not rightly distributed; my lot is too easy and I am sorry for it."

Barton wanted to help the wounded soldiers, but didn't want to join any relief agencies because she viewed them as authoritarian and restrictive. "[Barton] was an ambitious loner, with a powerful need to get things done by herself," wrote Civil War historian Stephen B. Oates in *A Woman of Valor: Clara Barton and the Civil War.*

Barton decided she could provide the greatest assistance by bringing supplies to the battlefields and helping the wounded soldiers on the spot. However, her obstacles were formidable because it wasn't considered decent or proper for a woman to be on the front lines. But Barton had little patience for the status quo. "I have an almost complete disregard of precedent," she said. "It irritates me to be told how things always have been done. . . . I defy the tyranny of precedent. I cannot afford the luxury of a closed mind. I go for anything new that might improve the past."

In February 1862, Barton went home to be with her dying eighty-eight-year-old father Captain Stephen Barton, who encouraged her to help the wounded soldiers. Barton's father, whose military career included many Indian wars, was the biggest influence in her life, and it was on his knee that young Barton learned about patriotism and how soldiers lived.

> *When there is no longer a soldier's arm to raise the Stars and Stripes above our Capitol, may God give strength to mine.*
> —Clara Barton

"I early learned that next to Heaven our highest duty was to love and serve our country," Clara Barton said. "The patriot blood of my father was warm in my veins," she wrote in recalling her feelings about the Civil War. Barton even wanted to sign up as a soldier, but with that option unavailable to her, she felt bringing supplies to the front lines was the most useful service she could provide. "While our soldiers stand and fight . . . I can stand and feed and nurse them," she said.

In July 1862, Barton presented her idea to Colonel Daniel H. Rucker, head of the Quartermaster Depot in Washington. Rucker told Barton firmly that the battlefield was "no place for a lady." When a tearful Barton told Rucker she had three warehouses of supplies, he provided her with an army wagon, driver and written authorization to go where she needed to help wounded soldiers. This was the first step in the journey that led Barton to be forever remembered as the "Angel of the Battlefield." She did much of her work, usually with a couple of assistants, at the field hospitals of such battles as Cedar Mountain, Second Bull Run, Fredericksburg, Antietam and the Wilderness.

She developed a system that allowed supplies to arrive at the front in usable condition, and kept her supply network intact to supplement the army's medical supplies.

At the second battle of Bull Run, Barton helped 3,000 suffering men stretched out on beds of hay. "All night we made compresses and slings—and bound up and wet wounds, when we could get water, fed what we could, traveled miles in that dark over these poor helpless [men], in terror lest someone's candle fall into the hay and consume them all," Barton said.

> *My work was, and chiefly has been, to get timely supplies to those needing. It has taught me the value of "things."*
> —Clara Barton

Her only concern was the wounded men who needed help, and she risked her life on the front lines to care for them. At one battle, an exploding shell tore off a portion of her dress. At Antietam, a bullet pierced her sleeve before killing the wounded man she was treating. Antietam had produced the bloodiest day of the war. Barton wrote "I had to wring the blood from the bottom of my clothing before I could step, for the weight about my feet," she wrote.

During that battle, wrote Geoffrey C. Ward in *The Civil War: An Illustrated History,* "When rebel artillery seemed

sure to hit the field hospital and all the male surgical assistants scurried for cover, she stood her ground, holding the
rolling operating table steady so the surgeon could complete
his work." That surgeon wrote in admiration to his wife about
Barton's courage: "In my feeble estimation, General
McClellan, with all his laurels, sinks into insignificance beside
the true heroine of the age, the angel of the battlefield."

Barton found the simple kindness of offering a sip of water
or a bite of food made a difference in the life of a wounded
soldier. "I never realized until that day how little a human
being could be grateful for," Barton recalled after helping the
wounded at the second battle of Bull Run in late August 1862.

Barton expected no special treatment and lived in conditions like the soldiers did when encamped. Although petite,
Barton combined a soldiers bravery with a saint's compassion. When the Confederate wounded fell, they received the
same care as the Union soldiers. "I have taken the dying message and delivered it—and closed the eyes of many a dead
[Confederate] ... forgiveness is noble—it is divine—and poor
weak erring humanity can at least strive to attain it," Barton
said when lecturing in the years immediately after the war.

Barton cooked for the wounded soldiers, wrote letters for
them and held the hands of those awaiting death. A strong
Unionist at heart, the devastation of war was not lost on
Barton. "Victory, yes! But oh, the cost," she wrote. "Three hundred thousand dead in one year! Dead everywhere. On every
battlefield they lie! ... there in the strange beds they sleep, till
the morning of the great reveille!"

To assure that the supplies she garnered made it to the
front lines in usable condition, Barton became "the most scientific little box packer in the country." She kept supply

boxes small and tightly packed to prevent the contents from breaking during the rough trips. Fragile items were intentionally packed in usable staples like cornmeal or bran. "People talk like children," Barton wrote, "about 'transporting supplies,' as if it were the easiest thing imaginable to transport supplies by wagon thirty miles across a country scouted by guerrilla bands." Barton also clearly labeled each box to prevent any confusion at the front lines. On the battlefield, seconds could mean the difference between life and death. "Knowledge is time you know," she said. "It used to be said that it was money, but it is a great deal more than that."

Barton spoke up when necessary. On Morris Island, South Carolina, in 1863, she observed for eight months that the soldiers' primary nourishment was warm water, stale beef and crackers filled with worms. Medical supplies were also dangerously low. She complained constantly to army officials, but they were more concerned with their own needs and troubled by Barton's brash manner. They "punished" her by taking away her tent, and eventually General Quincy Gilmore said her services were no longer needed.

"I feel that my guns are effectually silenced—my sympathy is not destroyed, by any means, but my confidence in my ability to accomplish anything of any alleviating character in this department is completely annihilated," Barton wrote about the situation. Fortunately her work didn't go unappreciated. In the spring of 1864, Secretary of War Edwin Stanton requested Barton go back out to the battlefields, because the Union needed her help.

Barton never received any government pay for her wartime contributions. During the war she lived mostly off her savings until they ran out. After the war ended in 1865,

Barton wanted to remain useful. She tracked down missing soldiers and identified their final resting place. Union Army officials estimated as many as 180,000 soldiers were dead and unidentified. In March 1866, Congress granted her $15,000 to fund her work.

Barton faced her fear of public speaking and began lecturing about her wartime experiences. Between 1866 and 1868, she gave about 300 lectures and raised enough money to support herself. By 1869, Barton had finished interviewing soldiers and placing ads in newspapers requesting information about the missing in action. She managed to identify the final resting place of approximately 22,000 men who had died in battle and in prisoner-of-war camps.

With her Civil War work completed Barton traveled abroad. When she visited Geneva, Switzerland, her vacation turned into her next cause. She met men who worked for the International Red Cross. The International Red Cross was one of the results of the 1864 International Treaty of Geneva, an agreement the United States had not signed. The organization administered to wounded soldiers on the battlefield under the flag of neutrality, and it was well supplied and funded. The Red Cross motto is "In time of peace and prosperity, prepare for war and calamity."

In July 1870, France declared war on Prussia (Germany), and Barton joined the International Red Cross and worked to aid civilians. In Basel, Switzerland, she saw well-loaded warehouses of supplies and was impressed with the efficiency of the organization. "I . . . saw the work of these Red Cross societies in the field," Barton said in a lecture, "accomplishing in four months under this systematic organization what we failed to accomplish in four years of war without it—no mistakes, no needless suffering, no starving, no lack of care, no waste, no confusion, but order, plenty, cleanliness, and comfort . . . whenever that little Red Cross flag made its way, a whole continent marshalled under the banner of the Red Cross."

Barton's new mission was to begin a United States society of the Red Cross to be recognized by the government. That couldn't happen, however, unless the United States first signed the Treaty of Geneva. Barton lobbied President Rutherford B. Hayes to accept the treaty. She published an information pamphlet, "The Red Cross of the Geneva Convention: What It Is," and proposed that the American Red Cross would not only be a wartime agency, but provide aid during natural disasters. This idea was eventually adopted by the International Red Cross and is called the "American amendment."

Barton established the American Red Cross in 1881 and was elected president, a position she held until 1904. In March 1882, Congress ratified the Treaty of Geneva. Although she wasn't an official ambassador, Barton is considered by some the United States' first female ambassador, for representing the U.S. at the inaugural international conference of the Red Cross in 1884.

The Red Cross responded to forest fires, tornadoes and severe floods. The Johnstown Flood of 1889 is listed as the worst natural disaster of the nineteenth century, and the sixty-seven-year-old Barton was on the scene: "I shall never lose the memory of my first walk on the day of our arrival— the wading in mud, the climbing over broken engines, cars, heaps of iron rollers, broken timbers, wrecks of houses; bent railway tracks tangled with piles of iron wire . . . the smoldering fires and drizzling rain . . . to announce that the Red Cross had arrived."

When Barton was sixty-three she spent a few months helping flood victims in Mississippi and Ohio. She was still willing to risk her life to help others. She wrote that she had "run all manner of risks and dangers, but had lost no life nor property, sunk no boat, and only that I was by this time too weak to walk without help—all are well."

Throughout her ninety years, Barton strongly supported the abolition of slavery and the establishment of women's rights. She encouraged women to be educated and tackle life's problems with boldness. Barton made her first mark in war, but never lost sight of the sacrifice made by so many brave soldiers. "If I were to speak of war," she said, "it would not be to show you the glories of conquering armies but the mischief and misery they strew in their tracks; and how, while they march on with tread of iron and plumes proudly tossing in the breeze, some one must follow closely in their steps, crouching to the earth, toiling in the rain and darkness, shelterless like themselves, with no thought of pride or glory, fame or praise, or reward; hearts breaking with pity, faces bathed in tears and hands in blood. This is the side which history never shows."

Women particularly distinguished themselves during the Civil War. "The war had given Barton and her entire generation of women a new sense of worth," historian Stephen B. Oates wrote. Barton acknowledged that in a speech: "Only an opportunity was wanting for woman to prove to man that she could be in earnest. . . . that she had character, and firmness of purpose."

How to Be Like Clara Barton

1. Be useful and serve society.

Barton wrote at the start of the Civil War that "I only wish I could work to some purpose. . . . I have no right to these easy comfortable days and our poor men suffering and dying thirsting in this hot sun and I so quiet here in want of nothing." Barton's place in history was born from that sense of purpose.

2. Challenge the status quo.

Question the dictum, "It's always been done this or that way." Barton said: "I have an almost complete disregard of precedent. . . . It irritates me to be told how things always have been done. . . . I defy the tyranny of precedent. I cannot afford the luxury of a closed mind. I go for anything new that might improve the past."

3. Take the initiative.

Barton saw that the Union Army needed supplies and put her own plan into action to provide them. She made her way to the battlefield, although it wasn't considered proper for a woman to be there.

4. Be courageous.

Barton willingly risked her life around the hail of gunfire because helping wounded soldiers was more important than her own safety. Historian Geoffrey C. Ward wrote, "When rebel artillery seemed sure to hit the field hospital and all the male surgical assistants scurried for cover, she stood her ground, holding the rolling operating table steady so the surgeon could complete his work."

5. **Be compassionate.**

"I have taken the dying message and delivered it," Barton said, "and closed the eyes of many a dead [Confederate] . . . forgiveness is noble—it is divine—and poor weak erring humanity can at least strive to attain it."

6. **Pay attention to details.**

Barton made sure each supply box destined for the front lines was tightly packed to prevent the contents from breaking. Fragile items were packed inside staple items such as cornmeal or bran. Each box was also clearly labeled to avoid confusion for the doctors for whom time was of the essence when treating the wounded.

7. **Rise early.**

Barton was an early riser her entire life, usually beginning her day around 4:00 A.M.

8. **Go the second mile.**

In addition to bringing supplies to the wounded soldiers, Barton cooked, wrote letters for them and held the hands of those who could only wait for death.

9. **Don't rest on your laurels.**

Never stop looking for ways to make a difference. After the Civil War, the "angel of the battlefield" worked to identify the final resting place of around 22,000 soldiers killed in action or who died in prison camps. Then Barton founded the American Red Cross.

10. **Face your fears.**

Barton overcame her fear of speaking in public and lectured about her wartime experiences in order to raise money. Between 1866 and 1868 she gave about 300 lectures.

RELENTLESSNESS

Remember that the only fear you need have is the fear of not standing by the things you believe to be right. Take your stand and hold it: then let come what will, and receive the blows like a good soldier.

—*Susan B. Anthony*

Susan B. Anthony was one of the primary leaders in the women's suffrage movement of the nineteenth and twentieth centuries. She was its most visible symbol and voice. Her efforts and those of her associates resulted in women gaining the right to vote. In a United States that denied the rights of women, Susan B. Anthony stood out as the leading, dynamic voice for change. She fought the battle with rhetoric, editorials and reason. What drove Anthony could never be taken from her by men or outlaws—namely, her unwavering commitment to the cause.

A vivid example of her commitment took place on election day, November 5, 1872. Anthony, a resident of Rochester, New York, cast her vote for President Ulysses S. Grant and two congressmen. By today's standards there was nothing unusual about that. At that time in the United States, however, women didn't have the right to vote. It was a crime for a woman to do so, and a few weeks later, on Thanksgiving Day, a U.S. marshal arrested Anthony. She would stand trial for her "crime."

During that period women were relegated to the status of second-class citizens. Women had less educational and employment opportunities than men and earned only about one-fourth as much as men for the same work. Upon marriage, a woman took her vows and in return gave up even more rights: A married woman couldn't own property, initiate a divorce or be granted custody of her children. A husband could specify in his will that his children were to be raised by someone other than their mother. Married women who worked had their wages paid directly to their husbands.

To Anthony, the only way to change such sexist, draconian laws was for women to secure the right to vote. The history of the United States up to that time had shown that legislators—who were never accountable to a female constituency—were not going to make changes out of the goodness of their hearts. They did, however, offer ridiculous, dark age reasoning for maintaining the status quo. "We oppose woman suffrage (the right to vote) as tending to destroy the home and family, the true basis of political safety," read an 1894 resolution by the Democratic Party. "[We] express the hope that the [helpmate] and guardian of the family sanctuary may not be dragged from the modest purity of self-imposed seclusion to be thrown unwillingly into the unfeminine places of political strife." The Republican party was no more supportive.

"Women," Anthony said, "we might as well be great Newfoundland dogs out baying to the moon as to be petitioning for the passage of bills without the power to vote."

Anthony had four other women with her who also voted on that day in November 1872, but she was the only one arrested. Anthony was being made an example since she already had a national reputation as a women's rights leader. Across the United States in 1872, 150 women had voted. All of these women were testing whether the fourteenth and fifteenth amendments to the constitution, passed in the aftermath of the Civil War to guarantee the rights of black men to vote, were a basis to give women the right to vote also.

After Anthony's bail was posted she went out on a well-organized publicity campaign to do what she advised others in the women's suffrage movement to do: "All we can do is to agitate, agitate, agitate," she said often. In a speech in 1873 before her trial, she said: "I stand before you tonight under indictment for the alleged crime of having voted illegally at the last Presidential election. . . . It is downright mockery to talk to women of their enjoyment of the blessings of liberty while they are denied the use of the only means of securing them provided by this democratic republican government—the ballot."

Anthony's trial took place in June 1873. The case did not serve as a test for the interpretations of the fourteenth and fifteenth amendments, but it did bring national attention to the injustice that women were subjected to. Judge Ward Hunt declared her guilty and then imposed a fine of $100. Anthony told the judge she'd never pay "a dollar of your unjust penalty." She added, "Resistance to tyranny is obedience to God."

Throughout her career Anthony exhibited no fear when it came to taking bold, dynamic actions to bring publicity to her cause and to effect change. "Cautious, careful people, always casting about to preserve their reputation and social standing, never can bring about a reform," she said. "Those who are really in earnest must be willing to be anything or nothing in the world's estimation, and publicly and privately, in season and out, avow their sympathy with despised and persecuted ideas and their advocates, and bear the consequences."

In addition to showing the "audacity" to exercise her right to vote, Anthony made use of a celebration of the nation's centennial to stage another symbolic act. "The women of this nation in 1876, have greater cause for discontent, rebellion and revolution than the men of 1776," she said. At the Centennial Celebration in Philadelphia, Pennsylvania, on July 4, 1876, Anthony and four associates approached the speaker's platform after a reading of the Declaration of Independence. They had copies of their own declaration, the Declaration of Rights for Women, which they handed out to the vice president of the United States, Thomas Ferry, other officials, and to the crowd.

After that they headed to their own women's celebration at Independence Hall. Anthony spoke to the crowd: "We ask justice, we ask equality, we ask that all the civil and political rights that belong to citizens of the United States, be guaranteed to us and our daughters forever."

> *In disposition Miss Anthony is very lovable. She is always good-natured and sunny tempered. . . . she keeps an audience laughing during an entire evening. Miss Anthony enjoys a good joke and can tell one. She never fails to see the funny side of things though it be at her own expense.*
> — Nellie Bly
> JOURNALIST

Anthony wasn't the only reformer fighting for women's rights in the nineteenth and twentieth centuries, but her passion and total immersion in the cause has made her arguably the best known. Geoffrey C. Ward and Ken Burns, in their book *Not For Ourselves Alone,* wrote: "Though [Anthony] never held public office . . . she was the nation's first great female politician."

While she was also a lightning rod for issues such as abolition, temperance (the campaign to abolish alcohol), and equal pay for equal work, it was Anthony's relentless pursuit of a woman's right to vote that she is remembered for. "It is my life, all that I live for," she said in 1895 to a reporter about the women's suffrage movement.

"What distinguished Susan B. Anthony from so many others working for women's rights was her uncompromising insistence that no other right was more central, no other need more pressing," wrote Lynn Sherr in *Failure Is Impossible: Susan B. Anthony in Her Own Words.* "Despite her passionate concern for just marriage laws, for equal pay, for coeducation, she lectured time and time again that the key was suffrage, that without the vote, none of the others would last, that with the vote, all others would flow."

> *I do not demand equal pay for any woman save those who do equal work in value. Scorn to be coddled by your employers; make them understand that you are in their service as workers, not as women.*
> —Susan B. Anthony

In 1860 Anthony and Elizabeth Cady Stanton helped push the New York State legislature to pass the Married Women's Property Law. It protected the rights of women to keep their own earnings and share guardianship of their children. The law was struck down two years later in the midst of the Civil War. It was another painful lesson to Anthony that without the right to vote any advances were subject to change at the whim of male politicians.

To help advance the cause first, while supporting herself second, Anthony was willing to travel the United States for over forty-five years to make seventy-five to one hundred speeches per year on behalf of the women's suffrage movement. In addition, she made an annual speech on the subject before the U.S. Congress for more than thirty years, although talking in front of an audience was a great fear of hers. Because of her passion, however, Anthony had worked hard to overcome qualms about speaking and actually became a very effective communicator. "It always requires a painful effort to enable me to face an audience. I never once felt at perfect ease on the platform," she said. "I haven't gotten over it. . . . I have no natural gift for speaking."

Regardless of her modesty Anthony received high marks as an effective speaker. She delivered a straightforward message from the heart. "Miss Anthony's oratory is in keeping with all her belongings, her voice well modulated and musical, her enunciation distinct, her style earnest and impressive, her language pure and unexaggerated," wrote the *Roundout Courier* newspaper.

> There is scarce a town, however small, from New York to San Francisco, that has not heard [Susan B. Anthony's] ringing voice.
> —Elizabeth Cady Stanton

Anthony communicated with words, actions, humor and a wisdom that made the logic of her positions resonate with clarity. When famed newspaper editor Horace Greeley stated that voting privileges should be linked with eligibility for military service, and then asked Anthony if granted the former would she and other women accept the latter, she answered that she would fight a war the same way Greeley had fought in the Civil War—with a pen.

Abolitionist Reverend A. D. Mayo challenged the never-married Anthony to stop lecturing for divorce reform. "You are not married, you have no business to be discussing marriage," he told her. Anthony responded: "Well, Mr. Mayo, you are not a slave, suppose you quit lecturing on slavery?"

Another minister told Anthony she should stop devoting

her energies to women's rights and reforms, and instead marry and have children. She said: "I think it a much wiser thing to secure for the thousands of mothers in this [country] the legal control of the children they now have, than to bring others into the world who would not belong to me after they were born."

Anthony wasn't against marriage; she was for equality. As Lynn Sherr notes Anthony copied down words said by Lucretia Mott (another women's rights activist and a mentor of Anthony) which read: "In the true marriage relation, the independence of the husband and wife is equal, their dependence mutual and their obligation reciprocal."

Born in Adams, Massachusetts, Susan was the daughter of a reasonably progressive father Daniel and an encouraging mother Lucy. Daniel Anthony was a Quaker, and Quakers believed men and women should be treated as equals. Susan was the second of six siblings. Daniel Anthony believed so strongly in education that he hired a teacher and started a school for his children, rather than send them to the local school, which he felt was inadequate.

Daniel Anthony was a successful businessman who owned, among other things, a cotton mill. During the economic depression of 1837, however, he was swept up in the hard times when his mill went bankrupt and he lost everything. The family was forced to seek shelter in an abandoned tavern. To help support them Susan became a teacher. She taught from the time she was fifteen until she was twenty-eight, all the while earning only around one-fourth of what male teachers made. After seven years of classroom teaching, Anthony became the headmistress of students at a coed school in Canajoharie, New York.

While suffrage was Anthony's primary focus, she was also a staunch abolitionist. She and Elizabeth Cady Stanton helped secure passage of the thirteenth amendment to the Constitution in 1865, which abolished slavery in the United States. "Go and do all the good you can," Anthony's mother told her about her causes. Anthony also recalled her father's pride in her, as quoted in Lynn Sherr's book: "I remember once a man who had just met my father asked him if he was the father of Susan B. 'There was a time, Susan,' said my father, 'when a daughter might shine by reflected light from her father, but things seem to have changed considerably.'"

As a Quaker, Daniel Anthony also believed in abstinence from alcohol. Anthony followed her father's lead and joined women's temperance movements in the different cities where she lived. Speaking out against the evils of alcohol gave Anthony her first experience as a speaker and a reformer.

After attending a lecture on abolition in 1851 in Seneca Falls, New York, Anthony was first introduced to Elizabeth Cady Stanton by Amelia Bloomer. (Bloomer was the liberator of women's fashion with her comfortable "bloomers," which began female dress reform.) Elizabeth Cady Stanton had organized the first women's rights convention in the United States a few years earlier and, along with Lucretia Mott, was a leading voice in the movement.

Stanton was instantly impressed with Anthony. She wrote of that first meeting: "There [Anthony] stood, with her good, earnest face and genial smile . . . the perfection of neatness and sobriety. I liked her thoroughly." A friendship and eventually a partnership grew between the two that would forever link their names together in history. Stanton summed up her partnership with Anthony this way: "In thought and sympathy we were one, and in the division of labor we exactly complemented each other. In writing we did better work than either could alone. . . . I am the better writer, she the better critic. She supplied the facts and statistics, I the philosophy and rhetoric. . . . Our speeches may be considered the united product of our two brains."

Stanton's husband Henry described their partnership this way: "Susan stirred the pud-dings, Elizabeth stirred up Susan, and then Susan stirs up the world!"

> *I dedicate this volume to Susan B. Anthony, my stead-fast friend for half a century.*
> —Elizabeth Cady Stanton,
> IN HER BOOK
> *EIGHTY YEARS AND MORE*

When Anthony was denied the opportunity to speak at a Sons of Temperance meeting in 1852 because she was a woman, she walked out of the hall. She then began organiz-ing the Woman's State Temperance Society of New York (one of the first female organizations of its kind), and a convention to take place a few months later. Elizabeth Cady Stanton delivered the main speech, and the convention was a suc-cess. Anthony attended her first National Women's Rights Convention in Syracuse, New York, in 1852. Anthony and Stanton founded the National Women's Suffrage Association in 1869. They also published (from 1868 to 1870) a weekly women's newspaper called *The Revolution,* with a masthead that read: "PRINCIPLE, NOT POLICY; JUSTICE, NOT FAVORS. MEN, THEIR RIGHTS AND NOTHING MORE; WOMEN, THEIR RIGHTS AND NOTHING LESS."

In 1852 Anthony was elected secretary in a women's suf-frage society. She would hold some type of official office in the women's suffrage movement for the next forty-eight years and become the voice of the movement. She followed her own advice not only to "agitate!" but also to "organize!" and especially to "educate!" women to fight for their rights. The latter was necessary because there was actually a sizeable female antisuffrage movement that had the support of some prominent women.

"The women of this nation must be awakened to a sense of their degradation—political—or at least we who are awake must make an effort to awaken those who are dead asleep," Anthony said during a lecture.

Part of Anthony's formula was to organize large rallies, then flood Congress and/or state legislatures with petitions. She asked Congress for a constitutional amendment giving women the right to vote, and asked state legislatures to grant women the right in their state. She called upon presidents and their wives from Ulysses S. Grant to Theodore Roosevelt. "[Anthony] knew everyone who was anyone in public life," Lynn Sherr wrote, "or figured out a way to meet them if she thought they could help The Cause." The suffrage movement succeeded in getting three states to grant women the right to vote by 1897.

Anthony stood up not only for the cause and ideals, but for women with problems who needed help. The story of Phoebe Harris Phelps in Lynn Sherr's book not only illustrates Anthony's compassion, but also serves as another example of the appalling lack of rights women suffered during that era. Phoebe was the abused wife of a Massachusetts state senator, Charles Abner Phelps. When Phoebe confronted her husband about an affair he was having he threw her down the stairs. More abuse followed. To keep her from making good on her threat to go to the police he had her put in an insane asylum, which Sherr wrote was actually a very easy thing for a husband to do to his wife in those days.

"For eighteen months," Sherr wrote. "Phoebe Phelps lan-guished in confinement, protesting her innocence while barred from any contact with her friends or family, including her three children. Finally released and allowed brief visits with her children, she begged for more time with her daugh-ter. Her own brother (U.S. Senator Ira Harris) refused to help, telling her, 'The child belongs by law to the father and it is your place to submit.'"

Phoebe managed to run away with her thirteen-year-old daughter. She met Anthony, who was able to place them in the care of a friend. The Civil War was still raging and Anthony was pressured by her abolitionist friends to give up Phoebe Phelps and her daughter. They were afraid Anthony's involvement in the matter would distract from their cause and reflect poorly on them. "Trust me," Anthony said, "that as I ignore all law to help the slave, so will I ignore it all to pro-tect the enslaved woman." Even the great abolitionist William Lloyd Garrison advised her to give up Phoebe, citing Massachusetts law as giving guardianship to the father. Anthony pointed out that Garrison ignored the Fugitive Slave law when helping runaway slaves escape to Canada.

"You would die before you would deliver a slave to his mas-ter, and I will die before I will give up that child to its father," Anthony said. Senator Phelps eventually did find his wife and child by using a detective, and took his daughter away from her mother. Sherr says the two were never reunited.

While many women turned away from the plight of pros-titutes Anthony turned toward them and welcomed them into the suffrage movement. She saw them as victims of exploitation by a male-dominated society. She said if all men protected and cared for all women as they do for their own wives and daughters, there would be no prostitution. "I will take by the hand every prostitute I can find who seeks to escape the inequalities of that law which places all woman-hood at the mercy of manhood," she said in a speech to a suffrage convention.

Anthony refused to allow her advancing years to slow her down, working essentially up to the time of her death at age eighty-six. Elizabeth Cady Stanton wrote that Anthony was always working, an example of "perpetual motion." In 1888, at the age of sixty-eight, Anthony founded the International Council of Women. At age seventy-two, in 1892, she assumed the presidency of the National-American Woman Suffrage Association, and served in the position for eight years. "How do I keep so energetic? By always being busy, by never having time to think of myself, and never indulging in any form of self-absorption," Anthony said in an interview at age seventy-five.

"Susan B. Anthony asked nothing of her colleagues that she would not do her-self," Sherr wrote. "As her presence guaranteed a good turnout and larger contributions, she rarely declined a speaking invitation—even after she turned seventy and suffered a bout of ill health."

Her last public words were spoken just a few days before her death on March 13, 1906. She offered praise, prophecy

> *I believe that man has benefited by [Susan B. Anthony's] work as much as woman. For ages he has been trying to carry the burden of life's responsibilities alone and when he has the efficient help of woman he will be grateful. Just now it is new and strange and men cannot comprehend what it would mean but the change is not far away. The nation is soon to have woman suffrage.*
> —Clara Barton, 1906

and a recipe for success: "There have been other(s) also just as true and devoted to the cause—I wish I could name every one—but with such women consecrating their lives, failure is impossible!"

Anthony didn't live long enough to see passage of the nineteenth amendment to the Constitution in 1920, which gave women the right to vote, but she had helped lay the groundwork that made it not only possible but also inevitable.

Her work was of monumental importance. In the history of the United States, what rights weren't secured by war were won when the oppressors, first white males and then the white population as a whole, voluntarily acquiesced. It was the Frederick Douglasses, the Sojourner Truths, the Susan B. Anthonys, the Rosa Parks and the Martin Luther Kings of the United States who, through their tireless, peaceful efforts, changed public opinion. They made it possible and necessary for predominantly white male politicians to give black people citizenship, black men voting rights, women the right to vote, and civil rights to minorities.

> *Upon receiving best wishes from President Theodore Roosevelt on her eighty-sixth birthday, Anthony said: "I wish the men would do something besides extend congratulations. I have asked President Roosevelt to push the matter of a constitutional amendment allowing suffrage to women by a recommendation to Congress. I would rather have him say a word to Congress for the cause than to praise me endlessly."*

The nineteenth amendment was officially added to the Constitution on the one hundredth anniversary of Anthony's birth, August 20, 1920. In 1979, the United States Mint issued the Susan B. Anthony dollar in the form of a coin with her likeness on it. She was the first woman so honored. A statue of Anthony, her mentor, Lucretia Mott, and her friend and partner, Elizabeth Cady Stanton, sits at the United States Capitol.

"The secret of all my work is that when there is something to do, I do it," Anthony said in 1896.

How to Be Like
Susan B. Anthony

1. Be bold.

When Anthony registered and voted in the 1872 election she risked incarceration. Her powerful symbolism at the Centennial Celebration in Philadelphia garnered more publicity. "Remember," she said, "that the only fear you need have is the fear of not standing by the things you believe to be right. Take your stand and hold it: then let come what will, and receive the blows like a good soldier." She also said: "Cautious, careful people, always casting about to preserve their reputation and social standing, never can bring about a reform."

2. Decide what you are fighting for.

Anthony's primary objective was clear in her own mind: She was fighting to give women the right to vote and, therefore, have a say in their own self-determination. "What distinguished Susan B. Anthony from so many others working for women's rights," Lynn Sherr wrote, "was her uncompromising insistence that no other right was more central, no other need more pressing.... She lectured time and time again that the key was suffrage, that without the vote, none of the others would last, that with the vote, all others would flow."

3. Confront your fears to advance your cause.

Anthony's name might not be remembered today had she not had the courage to conquer her fear of speaking in public. "It always requires a painful effort to enable me to face an audience. I never once felt at perfect ease on the platform," she said.

4. **Attack hypocrisy.**

A great evil in our society is the reverence some people are given, due sometimes to their station in life, who ask others to accept situations and act by rules to which they themselves would never submit. Worse, nobody ever challenges them. Anthony didn't shy away from doing that. There is a difference between being arrogant and simply pointing out the inherent contradictions of a person's point of view, and thus asking for an explanation. Famed newspaper editor Horace Greeley linked voting privileges with eligibility for military service. He asked Anthony, if granted the former, would she and other women accept the latter. Anthony answered she'd fight a war the same way he did in the Civil War, with a pen.

5. **Choose a partner who complements your strengths and weaknesses.**

The success of the political partnership of Susan B. Anthony and Elizabeth Cady Stanton has forever linked them in history. Their secret was that their talents complemented each other, and they were honest enough with themselves to acknowledge their own weaknesses and recognize what each needed from the other. Elizabeth described their partnership this way: "In thought and sympathy we were one, and in the division of labor we exactly complemented each other."

6. **Stand up for the less fortunate.**

Anthony stood up for women such as Phoebe Harris

Phelps, and for prostitutes who wanted to escape that way of life. She received pressure from fellow abolitionists for her defense of Phoebe, but ignored them. "Trust me that as I ignore all law to help the slave, so will I ignore it all to protect the enslaved woman," Anthony said. Of prostitutes she said: "I will take by the hand every prostitute I can find who seeks to escape the inequalities of that law which places all womanhood at the mercy of manhood."

7. **Keep working as long as you are able.**

Anthony refused to allow her advancing years to slow her down, working essentially up to the time of her death at age eighty-six. In 1888, at the age of sixty-eight, she founded the International Council of Women. At age seventy-two in 1892, she assumed the presidency of the National-American Woman Suffrage Association, and served in that position for eight years.

8. **Don't just talk; take action.**

"Susan B. Anthony asked nothing of her colleagues that she would not do herself. As her presence guaranteed a good turnout and larger contributions, she rarely declined a speaking invitation—even after she turned seventy and suffered a bout of ill health," Lynn Sherr wrote.

ELIZABETH CADY STANTON
1815–1902

FOCUS

Elizabeth Cady Stanton [is the greatest woman of our age]. She is a philosopher, statesman and a prophet. She is wonderfully gifted—more gifted than any person I ever knew, man or woman—and had she possessed the privileges of a man, her fame would have been worldwide, and she would have been the greatest person of her time.

—Susan B. Anthony

lizabeth Cady Stanton was the driving force behind the early women's rights movement in the United States. She was also one of the primary leaders in the women's suffrage movement in the nineteenth and twentieth centuries. In many ways she was its heart.

The root of what drove Elizabeth Cady Stanton to fight for women's rights was best expressed, she said, by a line from friend and poet Ralph Waldo Emerson: "A healthy discontent is the first step to progress."

The world Stanton was born into was one in which women were not only unequal to men in the eyes of the law, but often in the eyes of their own families. This inequality stemmed from one simple fact: Men had the right to vote and pass laws. Women did not. Men had all the legal and financial power in a marriage. What belonged to a woman, such as salary from a job or inheritance, legally became her husband's upon marriage. (Stanton's father's first wealth came after he married her mother.) Mothers didn't even have legal right to their children. All of that added up to a powerful statement: Men considered themselves superior to women and of greater value.

When Elizabeth was eleven, her brother Eleazer died from an illness at age twenty-one. As the only male in a family of six siblings, the loss of Eleazer hit Stanton's father Judge Daniel Cady especially hard. His death also defined a woman's worth as compared to a man's for the young Elizabeth. "A young man of great talent and promise, he was the pride of my father's heart. We early felt that this son filled a larger place in our father's affections and future plans than the five daughters together," Stanton wrote in *Eighty Years and More: Reminiscences 1815–1897*.

"I still recall, too, going into the large darkened parlor to see my brother, and finding the casket, mirrors, and pictures all draped in white, and my father seated by his side, pale and immovable. As he took no notice of me, after standing a long while, I climbed upon his knee, when he mechanically put his arm about me and, with my head resting against his beating heart, we both sat in silence, he thinking of the wreck of all his hopes in the loss of a dear son, and I wondering what could be said or done to fill the void in his breast. At length he heaved a deep sigh and said: 'Oh, my daughter, I wish you were a boy!' Throwing my arms about his neck, I replied: 'I will try to be all my brother was.'"

Young Elizabeth was already indoctrinated into the male-dominated society's mindset. In her quest to take her brother's place, Elizabeth, who equated being a male with education and courage, immersed herself in her studies and in the art of horsemanship. She excelled in both, but failed to catch her father's notice. "I taxed every power, hoping some day to hear my father say: 'Well, a girl is as good as a boy, after all.' But he never said it."

Since men denied women the opportunities to prove their equality, the perpetual myth of male superiority endured. Years later Stanton wrote prophetic words about what it would take to change it: "When we shall have freedom to find our own sphere, when we shall have had our colleges, our professions, our trades, for a century, a comparison then may be justly instituted."

> *They who have sympathy and imagination to make the sorrows of others their own can readily learn all the hard lessons of life from the experience of others.*
> —Elizabeth Cady Stanton

The stakes for equality were the highest. Without the resulting opportunities every woman's life was severely limited as to what she could accomplish for herself and contribute to society. "Nature never repeats herself, and the possibilities of one human soul will never be found in another," Stanton said in her famous 1892 speech titled the "Solitude of Self," which she delivered to the Judiciary Committee of the United States Congress.

Stanton fought not only to give women the right to vote, but also the means to be independent through access to higher education and equal pay for equal work. She worked to help women become independent so they wouldn't have to depend on a man or be at his mercy. As she posed to the Judiciary Committee, "Who, I ask you, can take, dare take, on himself the rights, the duties, the responsibilities of another human soul?"

Elizabeth Cady Stanton was born to a life of privilege, in Johnstown, New York, in a time when those who sacrificed for America's independence were still living symbols. Her maternal grandfather Colonel James Livingston fought against the British during the Revolutionary War and reported to General George Washington. Her surroundings nurtured the ideal of independence, and all her life she referred to herself as a "Daughter of the Revolution." Her association with her older cousin Gerrit Smith, who was a well-known abolitionist, further developed her social conscience.

Smith's home, like Stanton's, was a mansion. Located in Peterboro, New York, Gerrit Smith's home also served as a station on the Underground Railroad, which helped runaway slaves complete their escape to Canada. During a visit there, Elizabeth, her other sisters and her cousins, after being sworn to secrecy by Gerrit, were taken up to the mansion's third story to meet a special guest: a runaway slave named Harriet.

"Harriet," Stanton recalled Gerrit saying, "I have brought all my young cousins to see you. I want you to make good abolitionists of them by telling them the history of your life—what you have seen and suffered in slavery."

For two hours Elizabeth and the others were left to listen to Harriet, who was around eighteen years old. "We all wept together as she talked, and when Cousin Gerrit returned to summon us away we needed no further education to make us earnest abolitionists," Stanton later wrote. Learning from others was a lifelong discipline for Stanton. "I was ambitious to absorb all the wisdom I could," she said.

It was taking up the cause of abolition that led Stanton to also take up the fight for women's rights. She and other abolitionists pointed out that women and slaves shared some of the same injustices in that both were denied similar rights under common law.

Long before she was a national leader in the women's rights movement Elizabeth was a young bride at the altar ready to marry Henry Stanton, a fellow abolitionist. After convincing her clergyman that being married on a Friday wouldn't bring them bad luck, she further requested that he omit the word "obey" from the wedding vows. She wanted to stay true

> *Either sex, in isolation, is robbed of one-half its power for the accomplishment of any given work.*
> —Elizabeth Cady Stanton

to her convictions. "I obstinately refused to obey one with whom I supposed I was entering into an equal relation," she wrote.

Stanton didn't have to sell her husband on the rewording of the marriage vows, because he was an advocate of women's rights as well. Their marriage lasted for over forty-six years, until Henry's death in 1887. They spent their honeymoon sailing to England, where they were delegates to the World's Anti-Slavery Convention, which was held in London on June 12, 1840.

While women were generally given equal status at American anti-slavery conventions, in England the practice was not to recognize them as full delegates and thus refuse to allow them a voice, both literally and figuratively. The convention was split between those abolitionists who were against women having the right to speak and vote there, and those, led by William Lloyd Garrison, who were for it. Stanton believed it was a contradiction, and the height of hypocrisy, to be for abolition and against women's rights. "It struck me as very remarkable that abolitionists, who felt so keenly the wrongs of the slave, should be so oblivious to the equal wrongs of their own mothers, wives, and sisters, when, according to the common law, both classes occupied a similar legal status," she wrote.

The Garrison wing of the abolitionists lost out, and the women were only allowed to attend the convention rather than participate in it. Garrison himself sat quietly with the women in a show of support. "After battling so many long years," he said, "for the liberties of African slaves, I can take no part in a convention that strikes down the most sacred rights of all women."

At the convention, Stanton met Lucretia Mott, a leader in the abolitionist and temperance movements and the woman who would become her most important mentor. It was out of their shared experience of rejection that they planned to create a society in America to promote women's rights. "My experience at the World's Anti-Slavery Convention, all I had read of the legal status of women, and the oppression I saw everywhere, together swept across my soul, intensified now by many personal experiences," Stanton wrote. "It seemed as if all the elements had conspired to impel me to some onward step. I could not see what to do or where to begin—my only thought was a public meeting for protest and discussion."

The Women's Rights Convention that Stanton called for was eight years in the making, and the nation's first one. It took place in a church in Seneca Falls, New York, in July 1848. Among the organizers and speakers was Lucretia Mott. Many leading male abolitionists also spoke on behalf of women's rights.

Stanton led in the writing of a Declaration of Sentiments and then read it to stimulate discussion. It used language from the Declaration of Independence, with some long overdue modifications, such as: "All men and women are created equal," and the statement that both men and women were "endowed by their Creator with certain inalienable rights," such as "life, liberty, and the pursuit of happiness." The Declaration further stated that the history of mankind was a history of men asserting "absolute tyranny" over women. That statement was backed up with facts: Men had denied women the right to vote and thus forced women to live by laws "of which she had no voice." Men limited the educational and occupational opportunities of women, and created a society where they were paid only one-fourth of what a man made for the same job. Men had turned marriage into an institution where the man became more than a woman's husband; in the eyes of the law, he became her "master."

Lucretia Mott read the last of the eleven resolutions presented at the First Women's Rights Convention, which read in part, "that the speedy success of our cause depends upon the zealous and untiring efforts of both men and women."

Seneca Falls was a great success and began a trend of annual national women's conventions. It drew a crowd of enthusiastic supporters, and all of the resolutions were adopted. The national press, however, was less than supportive. The only papers that stood by the convention were the abolitionist papers, such as Garrison's *The Liberator* and Frederick Douglass's *The North Star.*

As the mother of seven children, Stanton's time was limited. Until her children were older she could rarely travel to other states for conventions and speaking engagements. She helped lead the women's rights movement by doing what she could, from where she was, with what she had. Stanton was a gifted writer and put that skill to good use. ". . . I began to write articles for the press, letters to conventions held in other States, and private letters to friends, to arouse them to thought on this question," Stanton wrote. "It is our duty to assert and reassert this right [to vote], to agitate, discuss and petition, until our political equality be fully recognized. Let us . . . spend all our time, strength and moral ammunition, year after year, with perseverance, courage and decision."

Her powerful writing notwithstanding, the single most important way Stanton advanced the argument for women's rights—while meeting her family responsibilities—was through her partnership with Susan B. Anthony, whom she met in 1851. Anthony could carry the message that both of them crafted. "We made it a matter of conscience to accept every invitation to speak on every question, in order to maintain woman's right to do so," Stanton wrote. And they created a partnership that complemented their strengths. "It is often said, by those who know Miss Anthony best, that she has been my good angel, always pushing and goading me to work, and that but for her pertinacity I should never have accomplished the little I have," Stanton later wrote. "On the other hand, it has been said that I forged the thunderbolts and she fired them. Perhaps all this is, in a measure, true."

"With the cares of a large family I might, in time, like too many women, have become wholly absorbed in [family life], had not my friend been continually exploring new fields for missionary labors. Her description of a body of men on any platform, complacently deciding questions in which woman had an equal interest, without an equal voice, readily roused me to a determination to throw a firebrand into the midst of their assembly."

Together Stanton and Anthony wrote articles and set policy. They used the sympathetic abolitionist newspapers to deliver their message to women in different states. They helped organize petition drives, then flooded state legislatures with them. Progress was slow, but some changes began that were the first steps eventually that would lead to full reform. By the early 1860s, the Ohio and New York legislatures had passed laws allowing married women to own property. Some state legislatures, such as those in Wisconsin and Nebraska, were at least talking about women's suffrage. Some colleges started admitting women.

In 1869, Stanton and Anthony founded the National Women's Suffrage Association. Its platform called for a constitutional amendment to grant women the right to vote. In addition, Stanton worked to try to reform the law so married women would have unquestioned property rights, divorce rights and child custody rights. She also spoke out in favor of the women's labor movement and birth control.

"[Stanton's] talents were aptly suited to the role of agitator," wrote Elisabeth Griffith in *In Her Own Right: The Life of Elizabeth Cady Stanton.* "Well educated and widely read, she had keen intelligence, a trained mind, and an ability to argue persuasively in writing and speaking. Her personality was magnetic. In conversation and correspondence, she was witty and opinionated; in person she was funny, feisty, [and] engaging. Her most remarkable trait was her self-confidence. It gave her the courage to take controversial stands without hesitation."

In fact, according to Griffith, those controversial stands cost Stanton her true place in the history of the women's rights movement. Suffragists were more comfortable with Susan B. Anthony as the face of their movement, because she was less controversial and primarily limited herself to just the suffrage issue. "As a result," Griffith wrote, "Elizabeth Cady Stanton ... is better known as Susan B. Anthony's sidekick than as the instigator and ideologue of the first women's movement."

Stanton and Anthony believed in universal suffrage, meaning that everyone, male or female, rich or poor, should have, with no qualifications, the right to vote. For those who wanted to tie voting rights to ownership of property or level of education, Stanton had an eloquent answer to their self-declared superiority: "Where does the aristocrat get his authority to forbid poor men, ignorant men, and black men, the exercise of their rights?" she said. "All this talk about education and property qualification is the narrow assumption of a rotten aristocracy. How can we grade wealth and education? Shall a man . . . be disenfranchised . . . because by the statute laws of his state he was forbidden to read and write, or amass property in his own name?"

Stanton and Anthony's partnership was one in which they could make constructive criticisms of each other in private and engage in spirited debate on a topic without damaging their friendship. They made it a practice, however, to always present a united front to the public. When the last of Stanton's children was grown, she spent the 1870s and 1880s traveling extensively with Anthony throughout the United States to promote women's rights and bring about change. She spent time in Europe as well, and attended the International Council of Women in England in 1883. She coauthored six volumes of *The History of Women's Suffrage* with Anthony, and she wrote *The Women's Bible.* "I am always busy," she remarked, "which is perhaps the chief reason why I am always well."

In 1870, Stanton and Anthony saw the Wyoming and Utah territories grant women the right to vote. While Utah rescinded the right in 1887, Wyoming retained women's voting rights, and they were in place when it became a state in 1890. Utah again gave women the right to vote in 1896. At the time of Stanton's death in 1902, those two states, along with Colorado (in 1893) and Idaho (in 1896) had given women the right to vote.

Many states granted women voting rights after 1906. In 1920, because of the groundwork Stanton and Anthony had laid, the nineteenth amendment to the Constitution was officially passed, giving all women the right to vote.

Stanton, Anthony and Lucretia Mott are honored by our country in the form of a statue that sits at the United States Capitol building. In the end, Stanton's perseverance and patience won out.

"If I were to draw up a set of rules for the guidance of reformers," Stanton wrote, "I should put at the head of the list: Do all you can to get people to think on your reform, and then, if the reform is good, it will come out in due season."

How to Be Like Elizabeth Cady Stanton

1. Develop a social conscience.

Stanton's road to becoming an activist began when she became an abolitionist. Her first exposure to the cruelty of slavery came when her cousin, abolitionist Gerrit Smith, introduced Elizabeth and her cousins to Harriet, a runaway slave he was helping escape to Canada. "We all wept together as [Harriet] talked, and, when Cousin Gerrit returned to summon us away, we needed no further education to make us earnest abolitionists," Stanton later wrote.

2. Learn from others.

Learning about the evils of slavery from Harriet was but one example of Stanton's lifelong discipline of learning from others. "I was ambitious to absorb all the wisdom I could," she said.

3. Practice what you preach.

Long before Stanton was a national figure whose actions made people pay attention, she was an everyday bride, marrying the man she loved. But even on her wedding day, she stayed true to her beliefs, asking the clergyman to omit the word "obey" from the wedding vows. "I obstinately refused to obey one with whom I supposed I was entering into an equal relation," Stanton wrote.

4. When inspired, act.

Stanton was frustrated by the lack of rights women had. The first Women's Rights Convention came out of that, and thus the start of the women's rights movement. Stanton wrote: "My experience at the World's Anti-Slavery Convention, all I had read of the legal status of women, and the oppression I saw everywhere, together swept across my soul. . . . I could not see what to do or where to begin—my only thought was a public meeting for protest and discussion."

5. **Be persistent and work hard.**

   With persistence and hard work, even the seemingly impossible is attainable. What Stanton wrote about women's right to vote is true for all great goals: "It is our duty to assert and reassert this right, to agitate, discuss and petition, until our political equality be fully recognized. Let us . . . spend all our time, strength and moral ammunition, year after year, with perseverance, courage and decision."

6. **Accept no limitations.**

   Even if you can't do everything you want to do because of family or work, do what you can. Stanton was the mother of seven children. She couldn't travel on behalf of women's rights extensively until the 1870s, when all her children were grown. She still found a way, however, to contribute to the movement—while taking care of her children—and, together with Susan B. Anthony, become the movement's leader. "I began to write articles for the press, letters to conventions held in other States, and private letters to friends," she wrote, "to arouse them to thought on this question."

7. Take advantage of every opportunity.

Whether you're fighting for a national issue, or just trying to improve your life, be aware of the opportunities that come your way and take advantage of them. Stanton said of Susan B. Anthony and herself: "We made it a matter of conscience to accept every invitation to speak on every question, in order to maintain woman's right to do so."

8. Do everything you can to get your message out.

Stanton wrote articles, penned letters to women's rights conventions, sent private letters to people on the subject of women's rights and helped organize petition drives, among other things. "If I were to draw up a set of rules for the guidance of reformers," she wrote late in her life, "I should put at the head of the list: Do all you can to get people to think on your reform, and then, if the reform is good, it will come out in due season."

9. Choose the right partner.

The partnership of Stanton and Anthony was so successful it has forever linked them in history. "It is often said," Stanton wrote, "by those who know Miss Anthony best, that she has been my good angel, always pushing and goading me to work, and that but for her pertinacity I should never have accomplished the little I have. On the other hand, it has been said that I forged the thunderbolts and she fired them. Perhaps all this is, in a measure, true." It was also an open and honest partnership. Both understood that they could say what they needed to each other for the good of the cause without fear of ruining their friendship.

10. **Speak out about what you believe in.**

Stanton certainly wasn't always politically correct. She took many controversial stands and was criticized for them. But she stayed true to herself. "Her most remarkable trait was her self-confidence," wrote Elisabeth Griffith. "It gave her the courage to take controversial stands without hesitation."

11. **Stay active your entire life.**

Stanton said: "I am always busy, which is perhaps the chief reason why I am always well."

MARY KAY ASH
1918–2001

INTEGRITY

I put a lot of emphasis on how to treat people. The reason for this is simple. The real success of our personal lives and careers can best be measured by the relationships we have with the people most dear to us—our family, friends, and coworkers. If we fail in this aspect of our lives, no matter how vast our worldly possessions or how high on the corporate ladder we climb, we will have achieved very little.

—Mary Kay Ash

**M**ary Kay Ash was the founder of Mary Kay Inc., a $1.6 billion-dollar-a-year company ($3.2 billion at retail) in the field of women's cosmetics. Millions of women have sold Mary Kay's products and had their lives changed as a result. In addition to being named a Horatio Alger Distinguished American, Ash was named Lifetime Television's most influential businesswoman of the twentieth century in 1999. Mary Kay Ash, who planned to write a book about the way the perfect company should be run, instead created one herself. No company has so wholeheartedly embodied the values of its founder as has Mary Kay Cosmetics, now known as Mary Kay Inc.

When she began her company in September 1963, in Dallas, Texas, the devoutly religious Ash chose the Golden Rule as the company's founding principle. "Do unto others as you would have them do unto you" was first taught to her by her mother. Ash never wavered from that commitment with her employees and customers. "Before our doors opened for business, I vowed that no one associated with my company would ever be subjected to unfair treatment or unjust management," wrote Ash in her book, *Mary Kay: You Can Have It All.* "I can say unequivocally that every decision we make at Mary Kay Cosmetics is based on the Golden Rule."

Ash's guiding principle not only enriched her people's lives, which was most important to her, but it also made Mary Kay Inc. an incredible financial success. She characterized her life as a rags-to-riches story, but there was also an element of boldness involved. Against the advice of her accountant and lawyer, who predicted failure, Ash risked her life savings of $5,000 to start her company, and turned it into a thriving business that today

> *A person who lacks compassion is not an admirable leader.... It is a mistake to view benevolence as a weakness in business. Real strength entails being considerate and supportive of people's feelings.*
> —Mary Kay Ash

generates annual retail sales of nearly $3.2 billion. Mary Kay Inc., still headquartered in Dallas, has some 3,500 employees, manufacturing facilities in Dallas and China that produce over 200 different products, and one million independent beauty consultants worldwide.

Prior to starting her company, Ash, a single mother of three children, rose to the position of national training director at World Gift, a direct sales company. For eleven years she traveled the United States, working with the company's 1,500 salespeople in forty-three states. Eventually the company president hired a man to assist Ash with her workload. Within that first year, the owner of the company decided to create the position of national sales manager, and he had a candidate in mind: Ash's assistant! At twice her salary!

"That night, I went home and cried my heart out," Ash wrote. The next day she resigned. Unemployed after flourishing for twenty-five years in the direct sales industry, Ash decided to write a book about running the perfect company. Then something occurred to her: She had gold in her hands.

"After making a long list of the qualities of the dream company I would have wanted to work for," she wrote, "I thought,
'Instead of writing a book about how a good company
should [be] run, wouldn't it be great if somebody ran one?'
And so the idea of Mary Kay Cosmetics was born."

> *My prime motivation for going into business was to help women. I wanted to provide opportunities for them to create better lives.*
> —Mary Kay Ash

Ash went forward despite
the gloomy predictions of her
lawyer and accountant,
because she believed her
business plan was fundamen-
tally sound. "Had I listened to
their advice," she said, "Mary
Kay Cosmetics would never have opened its doors."

With the rights to a skin-care formula she had purchased,
Ash felt she had three key advantages: First, there wasn't a
strong competitor in the skin-care market. Second, experience taught her that women sell best when they believe in
the product. Third, the product line would generate repeat
business, provided the customer was satisfied and treated
well by the sales force.

While many companies create a work environment that
neglects to consider employees' need for a personal life, Ash
combined the Golden Rule with her priorities of "God first,
family second, career third," which also serves as the company's motto. "What value is professional success if family and
personal happiness must be sacrificed?" Ash said. "It's important that we keep sight of what really matters in life. If we
lose our families and our faith in the process of developing
our careers, then we have failed."

Ash's motivation was pure, but greater productivity was
also the by-product of such altruism. "From day one, how

people were treated at Mary
Kay Cosmetics was more
important to me than profits
and losses," she wrote. "That's
why I say, 'P & L means people

> *Never forget, your family
> should always have priority
> over your work.*
> —Mary Kay Ash

and love.' Of course I'm concerned about profits and losses. I
just don't give them top priority. If you treat people right, they
will work more efficiently and the profits will come in."

Ash scorned the selective application of fairness. "Many
people draw the line on where and when to practice the
Golden Rule," she wrote. "They may apply it at home, with
neighbors, and at church or synagogue, but they leave it at
the door when they go to work on Monday morning. Free
enterprise's dog-eat-dog doctrine is their Holy Grail."

Mary Kay Inc.'s sales volume through the years wasn't due
to having products that nobody else had; it was due to the way
its salespeople performed under Ash's leadership. "People are
definitely a company's greatest asset. It doesn't make any difference whether the product is cars or cosmetics. A company
is only as good as the people it keeps," she said.

One of those people is Anne Newbury. She was a school-
teacher who wanted to be a stay-at-home mom when she
decided to give Mary Kay Inc. a try in 1969. Newbury, who
credits Ash's influence on her for her success, is Mary Kay
Inc.'s Independent Executive National Sales Director, and has
earned commissions in excess of $7 million. "Mary Kay taught
us more about leadership, about mentoring and coaching
than anything else," Newbury said. "I would have done anything that she ever asked me to do. Not only because I
admired her and loved her, but because when I look back
over what my life could have been if I hadn't been drawn to

her influence, I shudder. Not just financially, but emotionally and spiritually. She helped me to believe that I could be anything in the world that I could ever dream of becoming."

God played an important part in giving Ash direction in her life and shaping her values. "I can affirm that the growth and success of Mary Kay Cosmetics is a direct result of having taken God as our guide," Ash said. She believed that "faith is a twenty-four hour a day commitment," and that, "no circumstance is so unusual that it demands a double standard or separates us from our faith."

> *If you are an entrepreneur planning to start your own company, I can't think of a better place to begin than by operating your business by the Golden Rule. Make this a high priority; never make a decision that contradicts the Golden Rule.*
> —Mary Kay Ash

Ash constantly worked to improve herself. "A laurel rested upon becomes wilted," she'd say. She was a voracious reader and studied business and self-help books, then incorporated them into her life and company. "There is a difference between being well read and being able to transfer what you read into action," said Yvonne Pendleton, director of Corporate Communications at Mary Kay Inc.

One book in particular that helped Ash during her tough times as a struggling single mother was Napoleon Hill's classic *Think and Grow Rich*. She embraced the book's concept:

> *Every achievement, big or small, begins in your mind.*
> —Mary Kay Ash

"Whatever the mind of man can conceive and believe, it can achieve."

Mary Kay was inspired by quotations from great thinkers such as Mahatma Gandhi, and read the books of leading business minds, such as General

Motors president Alfred Sloan. Her favorite quotation was from Benjamin Disraeli, who served as prime minister of Great Britain in the late nineteenth century. "The secret to success is constancy of purpose," Disraeli said. Ash felt that lack of focus and discipline was a primary cause of failure.

She also learned success lessons from her colleagues. When she was a new salesperson for Stanley Home Products, Ash attended a sales convention where she heard a vice president of the company deliver a formula for success. He advised the sales force to first set a goal, then learn from experts how to achieve it, and then tell someone what you're going to do, to reinforce the commitment. That advice, Ash said, "made a lasting impression" on her, and she took immediate action.

Ash set her sights on being the top salesperson in the company in one year. In order to achieve that, she asked that year's top salesperson, a woman, to throw her what was called a "Stanley product party." As the woman demonstrated how best to sell Stanley products, Ash diligently took nineteen pages of notes. The next morning Ash announced to the company president that next year she would be the top salesperson, a goal that came to fruition. "People are happiest when they have goals, small and large, because they can look forward to attaining them," Ash said. "Think about it. Don't our biggest thrills in life come from realizing goals?"

The efficient use of time, the one commodity we can never get back, was a particular area of self-improvement that Ash emphasized. One favorite time-management technique she

> *A person cannot do right in one department whilst attempting to do wrong in another department. Life is one indivisible whole.*
> —Mahatma Gandhi
> (A FAVORITE QUOTE OF MARY KAY ASH)

read about and used came from a story that took place at the turn of the nineteenth century, concerning Bethlehem Steel president Charles Schwab and respected efficiency expert Ivy Lee. Lee offered Schwab a proposition: He wanted to work with each one of Schwab's executives one time, for fifteen minutes. Three months down the road, Schwab could determine the value of the advice and pay him what he felt it was worth.

Lee asked Schwab's executives to promise that for the next three months they would put in writing daily the six most important things they had to do for that day, in order of importance. They were to scratch off each item upon completion, and if anything wasn't done, it was to go on the next day's list.

After three months, Schwab was so impressed he sent Lee a check for $35,000, a fortune at the turn of the century and not bad pay for one day's work in any era. Ash said she figured if Schwab found so much value in that advice, she too would incorporate it into her life. Doing that, she said, was "one of the smartest things I ever learned to do. I believe in it, heart and soul." She then passed it down to her employees and sales force by providing them with note pads that already had the words "Six Most Important Things" preprinted on them.

Ash maximized her time by giving herself deadlines to complete a task. She cited the 1958 work of British professor Cyril Northcote Parkinson, who wrote in his seminal work *Parkinson's Law*, that "work expands so as to fill the time available for its completion." Ash believed that and gave the example of getting ready for work in the morning. She said, "People usually give themselves a certain amount of time in the morning for the day, but if they get up late, they can still get ready in much less time because of their sense of urgency."

"Over the years, I've observed that nearly all high achievers know how to make good use of those 1,440 minutes in each day," Ash said. "In contrast, other people seem to do things in slow motion."

> *Mary Kay didn't believe in fear motivation. She believed in attitude motivation.*
> —Anne Newbury,
> INDEPENDENT EXECUTIVE NATIONAL SALES DIRECTOR, MARY KAY INC.

To help keep Mary Kay Inc. growing, Ash never became complacent with her company's success. "She was extremely open to change," Yvonne Pendleton said. "She knew, especially in the beauty industry, change is a matter of fact. And while your principles never change, your products need to and your business needs to."

Pendleton continued: "For instance, in the early nineties when Mary Kay began reading more and more about the Internet, she was curious enough about it to want to understand how it and technology in general might affect the life and work of her sales force. She had almost a sixth sense that these new communication tools were the wave of the future. She requested a member of the company's IST division come by and give her a personal lesson on using the Internet and the how-to of sending and receiving e-mails. Mary Kay knew that she probably wouldn't use the Internet, but her attitude was, 'If it will help our Independent Beauty Consultants do their business, we will definitely embrace it.' And there she was, in the twilight of her career, a woman who knew this was a coming thing, and she didn't want to be left behind. She had that thirst for knowledge and willingness to accept change, and I think that's part of her genius." As it turned out, new technologies have greatly enhanced Mary Kay Inc.'s business.

Ash empowered her people by helping them realize they really were important. "I have learned to imagine an invisible sign around each person's neck that says 'Make me feel important,'" Ash wrote. "I never cease to be amazed at how positively people react when they're made to feel important." Her sincerity made them believe it for themselves. Ash's logic was flawless: "God didn't have time to create a nobody—just a somebody. I believe that each of us has God-given talents within us waiting to be brought into fruition. Each person is unique and special."

> *When television's* 60 Minutes *came to interview Ash, Morley Safer asked if she was just "using God." She looked at him squarely in the eye and said, "I sincerely hope not. I hope instead that God is using me."*
> —Jim Underwood,
> AUTHOR

Enthusiasm is contagious, and Ash tried to spread it as often as possible, beginning with her warm "Hi! How are you?" when she greeted people. She elaborated on this approach in her book: "When a new employee answers, 'Uh, pretty good. How are you, Mary Kay?' I'll say, 'You're not just good, you're great!' This generally gets a faint smile, and the next time I see him or her and ask, 'How are you?' He or she will say, 'I'm great.' Each time afterward, the response is, 'I'm great!' and the smile gets bigger and bigger. If you act enthusiastic, you become enthusiastic."

Ash learned this lesson through her own struggles as a single mother of three children, who had to make ends meet while keeping up her family's spirits.

"We all learned from Mary Kay Ash herself that there is no other acceptable answer. . . . stop any [Mary Kay] employee and ask her how she is. I guarantee it, she'll be great," wrote Richard C. Bartlett, vice chairman of Mary Kay Inc., in the preface to *More Than a Pink Cadillac: Mary Kay Inc.'s 9 Leadership Keys to Success,* by Jim Underwood. "[Ash] often said . . . 'Nothing great was ever accomplished without enthusiasm.'"

Ash greeted groups of new employees at their company orientations to "personally welcome them into our family." Once, while in Washington, D.C., Ash declined a White House invitation from President Ronald Reagan because she had already made a commitment to return to Dallas to greet the company's new employees. "She honestly believed that her commitment to the new hires was far more important than socializing with the president of the United States," wrote Jim Underwood in his book.

To prevent what she called the "I'm boss, you peon" mentality from infecting her company, Ash insisted on being addressed by her first name. She was completely unpretentious and made it clear to everyone that she was approachable and receptive to helping them with company matters or personal problems.

During the company's annual sales convention, one night is reserved for "Awards Night." Ash compared the lavish event to a Cecil B. DeMille production. Top sales producers are recognized on stage and awarded prizes such as cars, diamonds and dream vacations. Ash's commitment to empowering her independent sales force led to Ash's most visible symbol of appreciation, the pink Cadillac. These cars, along with other makes totaling over 80,000 cars, have been awarded to the top sales producers in the company for over thirty years. (The cars are leased by the company for use by its top sales producers.)

"[The] Mary Kay Seminar is the ultimate expression of a simple concept in which we believe with all our hearts," Ash wrote. "We can praise people to success! We keep people aware of how we appreciate them and their performance. And how do they respond? They respond by doing even better!"

Ash was very generous with her charitable gifts as well. In 1996, she established the Mary Kay Ash Charitable Foundation, a nonprofit organization that funds women's cancer research. In 2000, her foundation added its support to the issue of domestic violence.

"My definition of success would include living a balanced life," she wrote. "Balance means advancing your career up to, but not past, the point where it interferes with your happiness and relationships. Worthy advancement does not promote neglect of your husband and children. Nor should you work to the point where your health is endangered either physically or mentally."

> *My definition of happiness is having something to do that you love to do, someone to love, and something to look forward to.*
> —Mary Kay Ash

Ash ran a business in which everyone benefited. "Too many salespeople are thinking 'What's in it for me?' Instead of focusing on how closing the sale will benefit the customer, they're focusing on the commission they'll earn," Ash said. "You have to think in terms of what's good for the other person. Learn to think this way reflexively in all dealings with people, and success will seek you out. No matter what you do for a living, this approach always works when sincerely applied."

How to Be Like Mary Kay Ash

1. **Live by the Golden Rule.**

   Ash showed the power of the Golden Rule as she built a $3.2 billion-dollar-a-year company—and left a legacy of admiration. "I can say unequivocally that every decision we make at Mary Kay Cosmetics is based on the Golden Rule," Ash said.

2. **Define your priorities.**

   Ash's priorities were "God first, family second, career third," which also serves as Mary Kay Inc.'s company motto.

3. **Trust your instincts.**

   Ash launched Mary Kay Cosmetics against the advice of her lawyer and accountant, who predicted she'd lose her life savings of $5,000. She trusted her instincts, basing her analysis on what her new business would have in its favor (no market leader in skin care, a product women would enjoy selling and the potential for repeat business).

4. **Continue to learn and improve.**

   "A laurel rested upon becomes wilted," Ash liked to say. She studied business and self-help books before and after she achieved great wealth. And she incorporated what she learned into her life and company. She also learned from her everyday colleagues.

5. **Practice disciplined time management.**

   Time is the one commodity we can never get back, so Ash practiced the "Six Most Important Things" to do each day, and gave herself deadlines to finish a task or project. "Over the years," she said, "I've observed that nearly all high achievers know how to make good use of those 1,440 minutes in each day."

6. **Be open to change.**

Yvonne Pendleton said of Ash: "She was extremely open to change. She knew, especially in the beauty industry, change is a matter of fact. And while your principles never change, your products need to and your business needs to."

7. **Make everyone feel important.**

"I have learned to imagine an invisible sign around each person's neck that says 'Make me feel important,'" Ash said. "I never cease to be amazed at how positively people react when they're made to feel important."

8. **Be enthusiastic.**

"If you act enthusiastic, you become enthusiastic," Ash said. She believed "Nothing great was ever accomplished without enthusiasm."

9. **Remain humble.**

Ash never fell prey to an unchecked ego because she had her priorities in order. Her belief in God and Christian teachings kept her grounded, for nowhere in the Bible does it say the accumulation of money makes one better than anyone else. "God didn't have time to create a nobody—just a somebody. . . . Each person is unique and special," Ash said.

10. **Be generous in praising people.**

People are motivated by pride, not fear. "Mary Kay Cosmetics is known for 'praising people to success.' We think this is so important, we base our entire marketing plan on it," Ash said.

EPILOGUE

So—how can we all become women of influence? What do the twenty women you've read about in this book have in common? Here is how they lived:

1. Each one figured out what the prime motivation in her life would be and then pursued it with passion. They had a mission and every decision in their life was driven by this purpose.

2. Each woman set specific goals related to her passion and then worked toward accomplishing those goals. They didn't just dream; they made things happen.

3. They made things happen because they were willing to work hard. Each woman inherently knew that she could never achieve her purpose without diligence and dedication.

4. Each of these women had a strong core belief in what she was doing and thus, never gave up on her dreams. They persevered in good and bad times with their eyes focused solidly on their mission.

5. Each one of these women had an "I can do" attitude. In their minds there were no limits to what they could achieve. They simply kept focused on their passion,

never letting "that's impossible" become part of their vocabulary.

6. These women of influence, in many cases, had to overcome seemingly insurmountable obstacles, but their dogged determination kept them on track. They did not let anything get in their way.

7. In every single case these women were individuals. They defined who they were and refused to let anyone change that. They were true to themselves, even when the going got tough.

8. There is great diversity among these women, but they all had great faith in God. They all realized there was someone or something greater than themselves and they practiced their faith.

9. Not only did each of these women worship in the faith of her choice, they all served others. They all felt the need to give back to the world. They had an abundance mentality that enabled them to go beyond themselves and help others who were less fortunate.

10. They were very courageous women. They each ventured into unknown fields and were willing to take the risks necessary to achieve their dreams.

11. To go beyond the limits of their time, these individuals were women of strong character. They lived their lives with honesty and integrity. They were not perfect by any means. They had faults. They failed from time to time. Despite their fame and prestige they retained a humble spirit and never lost sight of their lifelong mission.

12. These influential women took responsibility for their own lives. They didn't wait for someone else to make changes in society. When they saw a need, they took control despite what family, friends or society might think or say. When hard times came, they didn't blame

others or circumstances. They took what life gave them and marched head on into the battle with unwavering courage and determination.

13. Each of these women of influence was a lifelong learner and contributor to society. They understood the value of education and were curious about life.

14. By and large, most of these women had a parent, guardian, mentor or teacher who believed in them and encouraged them to reach their full potential. Because of this early support in their lives, you're reading about them today.

What a contribution each of the women made to the world! Because of their fierce determination and intense belief in something beyond themselves, they made the world a better place for all of us for generations to come. Because of their example, hopefully, we will all learn to search deep within ourselves to find the special contribution we can make. Because of them, we know we are each endowed with special gifts and all we have to do is reach out and use them to the fullest. It is our hope that the essence of these women will infiltrate throughout the world and, as Gandhi said, "We will become the change we seek in the world."

BOOK CLUB QUESTIONS FOR DISCUSSION

1) **Eleanor Roosevelt:**
   What can you do to make a difference in the world?

2) **Margaret Thatcher:**
   How do you evaluate when to see something through, or when you must cut your losses?
   At your core, do you know what you stand for?

3) **Anne Frank:**
   How do you carry on in the face of great adversity?

4) **Mother Teresa:**
   Is there anything holding you back from doing the work you want to do?

5) **Sandra Day O'Connor:**
   How would you deal with being told you can't do something that you are in fact qualified to do?

6) **Oprah Winfrey:**
   Have you put the wrongs done to you in your life behind you, or in perspective, or are they still holding you back?

7) **Golda Meir:**

Do you ask things of others that you yourself won't do?

8) **Rosa Parks:**

How can you make a stand for what you believe in or feel strongly about?

9) **Helen Keller:**

What are your excuses for not pursuing what you want?

10) **Marie Curie:**

Do you have a plan to accomplish what you desire?

11) **Babe Didrikson Zaharias:**

In what ways can you be more competitive in those areas that are meaningful to you? Why is it important to welcome competition in your life and career?

12) **Amelia Earhart:**

Are there any areas of your life in where you are coasting, when deep down you know you can do better?

Are you satisfied with praise from others, or are you willing to pay the price to achieve the satisfaction that comes from within?

13) **Florence Nightingale:**

How well do you persevere when family, friends and society are telling you to give up?

14) **Harriet Beecher Stowe:**

Can we learn from tragedies? How can we use those lessons to positively affect our lives and the lives of others?

15) **Harriet Tubman:**

How willing are you to correct what is wrong in your life?

16) **Sojourner Truth:**
Do you ever listen to your inner voice? When you have, what have the results been? Is there anything right now you want to do, that your inner voice is telling you to do, but that you're not?

17) **Clara Barton:**
Are you waiting for someone else's permission to get started in things that are important to you?

18) **Susan B. Anthony:**
Do you have a fear of something that is holding you back from pursuing your goals? When do you overcome such fears?

19) **Elizabeth Cady Stanton:**
Regardless of how busy you are, in what ways can you contribute to what is important to you?

20) **Mary Kay Ash:**
Have you ever been told you can't do something, or that you'll fail? What did you do? What would you do today? How do you determine when you're on solid footing, or when you should listen to the counsel of others?

BIBLIOGRAPHY

Eleanor Roosevelt

Gerber, Robin. *Leadership the Eleanor Roosevelt Way*. New York: Prentice Hall, 2002.

Lash, Joseph P. *Eleanor and Franklin*. New York: W.W. Norton, 1971.

Morey, Eileen. *The Importance of Eleanor Roosevelt*. San Diego: Lucent Books, 1998.

Roosevelt, David B., with Manuela Dunn-Mascetti. *Grandmere: A Personal History of Eleanor Roosevelt*. New York: Warner Books, 2002.

Roosevelt, Eleanor. *You Learn by Living*. New York: Harper, 1960.

————. *The Autobiography of Eleanor Roosevelt*. New York: Harper, 1961.

Mother Teresa

Mother Teresa. *The Joy in Loving: A Guide to Daily Living*. Compiled by Jaya Chaliha and Edward Le Joly. New York: Penguin/Arkana, 2000.

Ruth, Amy. *Mother Teresa*. Minneapolis: Lerner Publications, 1999.

Tilton, Rafael. *The Importance of Mother Teresa*. San Diego: Lucent Books, 2000.

Anne Frank

Frank, Anne. *The Diary of a Young Girl: The Definitive Edition*. Edited by Otto H. Frank and Mirjam Pressler. Translated by Susan Massotty. New York: Bantam, 1997.

Hurwitz, Johanna. *Anne Frank: Life in Hiding*. Philadelphia: Jewish Publication Society, 1988.

Muller, Melissa. *Anne Frank: The Biography*. Translated by Rita Kimber and Robert Kimber. New York: Henry Holt, 1999.

Wukovits, John F. *The Importance of Anne Frank*. San Diego: Lucent Books, 1999.

Margaret Thatcher

Garfinkel, Bernard. *Margaret Thatcher*. New York: Chelsea House, 1990.

Thatcher, Margaret. *The Downing Street Years*. New York: Harper-Collins, 1993.

————. *The Path to Power*. New York: HarperCollins, 1995.

————. *Statecraft: Strategies for a Changing World*. New York: HarperCollins, 2002.

Sandra Day O'Connor

Huber, Peter W. *Sandra Day O'Connor*. New York: Chelsea House, 1990.

Kramer, Barbara. *Trailblazing American Women: First in Their Fields*. Berkeley Heights, N.J.: Enslow Publishers, 2000.

O'Connor, Sandra Day, and Alan H. Day. *Lazy B: Growing Up on a Cattle Ranch in the American Southwest*. New York: Random House, 2002.

O'Connor, Sandra Day. *The Majesty of the Law: Reflections of a Supreme Court Justice*. New York: Random House, 2003.

Oprah Winfrey

Friedrich, Belinda. *Oprah Winfrey*. Philadelphia: Chelsea House, 2001.

Lowe, Janet. *Oprah Winfrey Speaks: Insight from the World's Most Influential Voice*. New York: John Wiley, 1998.

Thomas, Marlo, et al. *The Right Words at the Right Time*. New York: Atria Books, 2002.

Wooten, Sara McIntosh. *Oprah Winfrey: Talk Show Legend*. Berkeley Heights, N.J.: Enslow Publishers, 1999.

Golda Meir

Hitzeroth, Deborah. *The Importance of Golda Meir*. San Diego: Lucent Books, 1998.

McAuley, Karen. *Golda Meir*. New York: Chelsea House, 1985.

Meir, Golda. *My Life*. New York: Dell, 1976.

Rosa Parks

Brinkley, Douglas. *Rosa Parks.* New York: Penguin Putnam, 2000.

Parks, Rosa, and Jim Haskins. *Rosa Parks: My Story.* New York: Penguin Putnam, 1992.

Helen Keller

Ford, Carin T. *Helen Keller: Lighting the Way for the Blind and Deaf.* Berkeley Heights, N.J.: Enslow Publishers, 2001.

Herrmann, Dorothy. *Helen Keller: A Life.* Chicago: University of Chicago Press, 1999.

Keller, Helen. *The Story of My Life.* New York: Bantam Books, 1990.

Marie Curie

Birch, Beverly. *Courageous Pioneer in the Study of Radioactivity.* Woodbridge, Conn.: Blackbirch Press, 2000.

Curie, Eve. *Madame Curie: A Biography.* Translated by Vincent Sheean. New York: Da Capo Press, 1986, 1937.

Grady, Sean. *The Importance of Marie Curie.* San Diego: Lucent Books, 1992.

Babe Didrikson Zaharias

Cayleff, Susan E. *Babe Didrikson: The Greatest All-Sport Athlete of All Time.* Berkeley, Calif.: Conari Press, 1995.

Cayleff, Susan E. *The Life and Legend of Babe Didrikson Zaharias.* Urbana, Ill.: University of Illinois Press, 1995.

Freedman, Russell. *Babe Didrikson Zaharias: The Making of a Champion.* New York: Clarion Books, 1999.

Zaharias, Babe Didrikson. *This Life I've Led: My Autobiography.* New York: Barnes, 1955.

Amelia Earhart

Butler, Susan. *The Life of Amelia Earhart.* Reading, Mass.: Addison-Wesley, 1997.

Earhart, Amelia. *The Fun of It: Random Records of My Own Flying and of Women in Aviation.* New York: Harcourt, 1932.

Earhart, Amelia. *Last Flight.* Arranged by George Palmer Putnam. New York: Crown, 1988.

Lovell, Mary S. *The Sound of Wings.* New York: St. Martin's Press, 1989.

Florence Nightingale

Gorell, Gena K. *Heart and Soul: The Story of Florence Nightingale.* Plattsburgh, NY: Tundra Books, 2000.

Nightingale, Florence. *Notes on Nursing: What It Is, What It Is Not.* New York: Dover Publications, 1969.

Small, Hugh. *Florence Nightingale: Avenging Angel.* New York: St. Martin's Press, 1969.

Woodham-Smith, Cecil. *Florence Nightingale.* New York: McGraw-Hill, 1951.

Harriet Beecher Stowe

Hedrick, Joan D. *Harriet Beecher Stowe: A Life.* New York: Oxford University Press, 1994.

Stowe, Harriet Beecher. *Uncle Tom's Cabin: Authoritative Text, Backgrounds and Contexts, Criticism.* Edited by Elizabeth Ammons. New York: W.W. Norton, 1994.

Tackach, James. *Uncle's Tom's Cabin: Indictment of Slavery.* San Diego: Lucent Books, 2000.

Harriet Tubman

Bradford, Sarah H. *Harriet Tubman: The Moses of Her People.* Gloucester, Mass.: Peter Smith, 1981.

McClard, Megan. *Harriet Tubman: Slavery and the Underground Railroad.* Englewood Cliffs, N.J.: Silver Burdett Press, 1991.

Schraff, Anne E. *Harriet Tubman: Moses of the Underground Railroad.* Berkeley Heights, N.J.: Enslow Publishers, 2001.

Sojourner Truth

Baker, Jean, ed. *Votes for Women: The Struggle for Suffrage Revisited.* New York: Oxford University Press, 2002.

Bernard, Catherine. *Sojourner Truth: Abolitionist and Women's Rights Activist.* Berkeley Heights, N.J.: Enslow, 2001.

Buhle, Mari Jo, and Paul Buhle, eds. *Concise History of Woman Suffrage: Selections from the Classic Work of Stanton, Anthony, Gage, and Harper.* Urbana, Ill.: University of Illinois Press, 1978.

Painter, Nell Irvin. *Sojourner Truth: A Life, A Symbol.* New York: W.W. Norton, 1977.

Clara Barton

Oates, Stephen B. *A Woman of Valor: Clara Barton and the Civil War.* New York: Free Press, 1994.

Tilton, Rafael. *Clara Barton.* San Diego: Lucent Books, 1995.

Ward, Geoffrey C., et al. *The Civil War: An Illustrated History.* New York: Knopf, 1994.

Whitelaw, Nancy. *Clara Barton: Civil War Nurse.* Springfield, N.J.: Enslow Publishers, 1997.

Susan B. Anthony

Kendall, Martha E. *Susan B. Anthony: Voice for Women's Voting Rights.* Springfield, N.J.: Enslow Publishers, 1997.

Sherr, Lynn. *Failure Is Impossible: Susan B. Anthony in Her Own Words.* New York: Times Books, 1995.

Ward, Geoffrey C., and Ken Burns. *Not For Ourselves Alone: The Story of Elizabeth Cady Stanton and Susan B. Anthony.* New York: Knopf, 1999.

Elizabeth Cady Stanton

Cullen-DuPont, Kathryn. *Elizabeth Cady Stanton and Women's Liberty.* New York: Facts on File, 1992.

Griffith, Elisabeth. *In Her Own Right: The Life of Elizabeth Cady Stanton.* New York: Oxford University Press, 1985.

Salisbury, Cynthia. *Elizabeth Cady Stanton: Leader of the Fight for Women's Rights.* Berkeley Heights, N.J.: Enslow, 2002.

Stanton, Elizabeth Cady. *Eighty Years and More: Reminiscences 1815-1897.* Boston, Mass: Northeastern University Press, 1993.

Ward, Geoffrey C., and Ken Burns. *Not For Ourselves Alone: The Story of Elizabeth Cady Stanton and Susan B. Anthony.* New York: Knopf, 1999.

Mary Kay Ash

Ash, Mary Kay. *Mary Kay—You Can Have It All: Lifetime Wisdom from America's Foremost Woman Entrepreneur.* Rocklin, Calif.: Prima Publishing, 1995.

Underwood, Jim. *More Than a Pink Cadillac: Mary Kay Inc.'s 9 Leadership Keys to Success.* New York: McGraw-Hill, 2003.